SECURITIES LTD.

£290 million

INSURANCE

£14 million

Blackburn & Pioneer Insurance Companies (established
130 and 80 years respectively)
in the field of Industrial Life
Assurance, and another
Insurance Company in the
fields of Life Assurance and
Pensions.

INDUSTRIAL

£7 million

Solicitors' Law Stationery
Society and its subsidiaries

MANAGEMENT

£1 million

4 Investment Management
Companies in the UK and
Channel Islands managing
funds of over £200 million
for private clients and unit
trusts.

South Africa
£14 million

Canada
£3 million

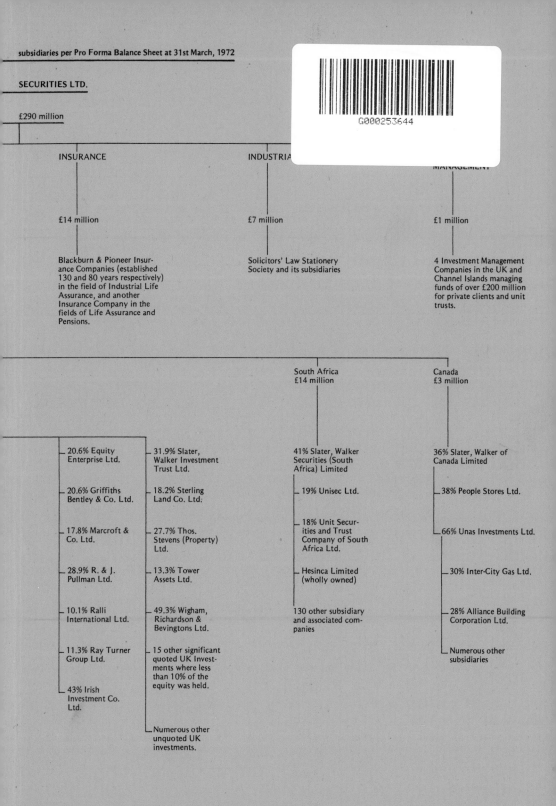

20.6% Equity
Enterprise Ltd.

20.6% Griffiths
Bentley & Co. Ltd.

17.8% Marcroft &
Co. Ltd.

28.9% R. & J.
Pullman Ltd.

10.1% Ralli
International Ltd.

11.3% Ray Turner
Group Ltd.

43% Irish
Investment Co.
Ltd.

31.9% Slater,
Walker Investment
Trust Ltd.

18.2% Sterling
Land Co. Ltd.

27.7% Thos.
Stevens (Property)
Ltd.

13.3% Tower
Assets Ltd.

49.3% Wigham,
Richardson &
Bevingtons Ltd.

15 other significant
quoted UK Invest-
ments where less
than 10% of the
equity was held.

Numerous other
unquoted UK
investments.

41% Slater, Walker
Securities (South
Africa) Limited

19% Unisec Ltd.

18% Unit Secur-
ities and Trust
Company of South
Africa Ltd.

Hesinca Limited
(wholly owned)

130 other subsidiary
and associated com-
panies

36% Slater, Walker of
Canada Limited

38% People Stores Ltd.

66% Unas Investments Ltd.

30% Inter-City Gas Ltd.

28% Alliance Building
Corporation Ltd.

Numerous other
subsidiaries

Return to Go

Jim Slater

Return to Go

My Autobiography

WEIDENFELD AND NICOLSON
London

First published in Great Britain by
Weidenfeld and Nicolson
11 St John's Hill London SW11

ISBN 0 297 77418 2

Printed and bound in Great Britain by
Morrison & Gibb Ltd, London and Edinburgh

To Helen

Contents

Illustrations

Introduction

I HAVE always had it in mind to write a book, but I used to see it as something to be kept for retirement or the last years of my life. In Slater Walker's heyday I had a number of approaches from publishers, but I was too busy and the idea did not really appeal. Since then I have had some traumatic experiences which have given me the motivation to tell my story.

There was a sharp contrast between the first seven and the last three years of my time with Slater Walker. In its early years Slater Walker made a very substantial number of acquisitions and became from very small beginnings, one of the largest companies in Britain. At its peak Slater Walker had a market capitalization of over £200m and for many years headed the *Management Today* Growth League tables. The company had a reputation for advanced management and investment techniques, and in 1971 I was invited to give my views on management at the Institute of Directors Conference at the Albert Hall together with Lord Goodman, Sir Christopher Soames, Lord Barber, Billy Graham and Lee Kuan Yew.

Since then, during the last few years, Slater Walker has been through the worst bear market of this century and I have resigned from the company; I have been the subject of very considerable criticism, and the Singapore authorities have made an attempt to extradite me; my personal fortune of some £8m has gone and my net financial position is now a very substantial minus figure.

I can, therefore, claim to have experienced in a very short time exceptional heights and depths in terms of both good fortune and reputation. Obviously, in the early days particularly, I must have done a large number of things right, and equally, because I am in my present position, I must have made a number of major mistakes. Certainly in recent years my philosophy has changed—looking back I can see much more clearly both

I

my own strengths and weaknesses and those of the company I was directing at the time.

Throughout the Slater Walker saga I always asked my secretaries to keep scrapbooks of the more important press cuttings, and I have also kept many of my old business appointment diaries covering the period. In addition I have a complete set of Annual Accounts together with the Chairman's Reports going back to the time when I first joined the company, and I also happen to be blessed with a good memory, so writing this book has not presented me with any undue difficulties. I had always imagined that it would be a very demanding task and take a great deal of planning; instead I found that I simply sat down at home and wrote incessantly. In the first week I had written 20,000 words and the first draft of the book took only three months to finish.

I decided to write the book in three parts. The first deals with my early childhood and education, followed by my accountancy training, army service and early industrial experience. The second and much larger part deals with Slater Walker, with a chapter for each year, and the third with the aftermath of my resignation and in particular with the Singapore Government's attempt to extradite me.

When I came to the Slater Walker part of the story I did have some difficulty in deciding how much detail I should go into, and this problem grew with the growth of the company. Eventually I decided that I would only write at length about matters of relative importance to me and to the company at the time they happened. For example, I have written at length about our first few contested bids. At that time we were learning the business and making the company's reputation in this field. In addition the early bids had a vital and major impact upon the company's financial strength and potential because the target companies were large in relation to the size of our company. As Slater Walker progressed, so each individual bid became of lesser relative importance, and for that reason I have written much more briefly about them in the later stages.

During the last eighteen months, which has been a time of stress, I have been very moved by the reaction of my family and friends, who have offered positive assistance and a great deal of encouragement.

I have enjoyed writing the story of my own career, and I hope that it will be of interest to businessmen and others who have been involved in the City and industry, particularly during the last fifteen years. More importantly, I hope it will also be of interest and help to younger men at the start of their careers.

PART ONE

· ONE ·

A Young Accountant

M Y childhood and early training in accountancy were not unusual in any way, and it was only when I took on my first industrial job that my experience became very different from the norm.

My father, whose name was Hubert, was the youngest of a family of six children. He had two sisters with whom he kept in close touch throughout his life, and three brothers with whom he had very little contact after his childhood. Both his parents died before he was ten years old, and he left school at the age of fourteen.

I am not quite sure what he did before enlisting in the army for the 1914–18 war. He served in France, and after a year in the ranks was promoted, eventually becoming a captain by the time he was ready for civilian life again. He was wounded in the leg at the Battle of the Somme, but made a full recovery. He stayed on in the army for a year or so after the war and spent some of the time in Egypt, which he very much enjoyed.

After he came out of the army the first I remember hearing about his business activity was when he was sales manager of Blackies, which specialized in children's books. After working in the provinces he eventually became their sales manager in London, but subsequently left them to become sales manager of a division of George Newnes.

My mother, Jessica Barton, was again the youngest child of a family of six children. She had one brother and four sisters, and she kept in close touch with them all. Both her parents died before she was eight years of age, after which she lived with her eldest sister, Dora, who married a retail chemist, and I understand they all lived over the shop. The chemist's name was Herbert Thatcher, and he subsequently built up a very successful chain of chemist shops in the Midlands in partnership with a man named Bannister. When he died Bannister & Thatcher had over fifty shops.

My father was thirty-four when he met my mother, who was only twenty-four, but already employed as manageress of a large restaurant. They were married in 1927, and moved first of all to Heswall in Cheshire where they lived for three years. I was born there on 13 March 1929 and I was their only child.

In 1931, when I was two years old, we moved from Heswall to South Kenton near Wembley, where we lived in a semi-detached house with three bedrooms and a quarter-acre garden until I was sixteen. Our life at 7 Windermere Avenue, South Kenton was a fairly typical suburban one. My father could not drive and we did not have a car. We used to go to the seaside most years, but we never went abroad; indeed, I cannot remember any of the families in Windermere Avenue having holidays abroad while I lived there. My mother and father were very fond of each other and our house was a happy one. My father worked a five-day week and loved to be at home at the weekends, when he would play a little golf but spend most of his time gardening. I am sorry to say that he put me off gardening for life by making me help him rather too often and, in particular, making me weed a long path of crazy paving which I learned to hate passionately.

When I was about eight years old I used to look forward to Saturday mornings when I would walk to Kenton, which was about a mile from our house. The local Odeon had formed a Mickey Mouse club to which most of the children in the neighbourhood belonged. On Saturday mornings they would show a few cartoon films and then a serial thriller, followed by a western which usually starred Tom Mix or Buck Jones. One of the serials, *The Clutching Hand*, remains vividly in my memory; at the end of each episode the hand would be reaching out from behind a curtain or some other hiding place about to throttle its unsuspecting victim. It gave me nightmares for months afterwards. I also remember the song we used to sing every Saturday:

> Every Saturday morning, where do we go?
> Getting into mischief, oh dear no!
> To the Mickey Mouse Club
> With our badges on,
> Every Saturday morning
> At the O-de-on!

Afterwards I usually had to go and do some shopping for my mother. Sometimes I would go to the greengrocer's and treat myself to a peach, which at that time used to cost one old penny. I have always seen this as

6

one of the more telling, if small-scale, examples of inflation as a good peach could now cost as much as 20p—an increase of 4,700 per cent over the last forty years.

We were not hard up, but on the other hand I was always made aware of the fact that money did not grow on trees. When I was about twelve I had only one pair of long trousers and I can well remember falling over and tearing them on one knee. They were 'invisibly' mended by a neighbour in a lighter cotton than the rest of the trousers, and I had to make do with them for a long time after that.

My mother has always been deeply religious, but my father, though he believed in God, was not a church-goer. I was encouraged to go to Sunday School regularly, and subsequently to Church of England services every Sunday at the local church until I was about eleven. Then I became a scout for a short while and used to attend their church parades. After that, like most other boys, I found that the weekends went by very quickly, and from about fourteen onwards I stopped going to church regularly.

I was educated first of all in a small preparatory school and then, from the age of five, at the local school, Preston Park, which was about a mile away. When I was ten years old the war started and as a result I did not have to sit for a scholarship at the age of eleven. During the war, exemptions based upon term work were granted in certain cases, and I was lucky enough to be given one. This meant that I could go to the local secondary school, Preston Manor, which was co-educational. I was fortunate in being able to go to Preston Manor because it was a school that was built just before the war and had very high standards. It was a show-piece for foreign visitors, the educational standards were high, and its amenities included a biology laboratory, chemistry and physics laboratories, extensive playing fields and an excellent gymnasium.

During my time at Preston Park I had usually been placed in the top quarter of the class, but the general standard of Preston Manor was much higher, and at first I wondered how I would keep pace. I had to have extra lessons in French and also at one stage a few extra lessons in maths. Once I had settled down my overall position in class was average, but I was only in the second set at maths.

As I have said, the war started when I was ten years old, and I can clearly remember the first time the air-raid siren sounded. I was playing on the nearby golf links with some other boys when several neighbours who were volunteer air-raid wardens came out into the streets and urged us to run home. I raced home to the deadly wail of the sirens, to find my mother and some friends of ours seated in the drawing room with the curtains drawn. We all got our gas masks ready and sat waiting for the end of the world, which we were sure was coming. After about half an hour the all-clear sounded—it had been a false alarm.

A large number of children from our area and others nearby were being evacuated to Edmonton in Canada, and my parents decided at one stage that I should join them. I was all ready to go when my mother had an instinctive feeling that it would be wrong, and she withdrew my name from the list at the last moment. The ship sailed and was sunk by a German submarine. Out of ninety children only thirteen survived, and one of my school friends was killed, as well as the daughter of a neighbour who lived opposite us. If we all have nine lives—I reckon that was one of mine.

It is surprising how we got used to the air-raids, which became a regular feature of our lives, especially at night. We had a shelter built in the garden, but soon gave up using it as it was very damp; instead we began sleeping downstairs, but over the years gradually crept upstairs again, only coming down when the air-raids were particularly violent. On one occasion I was woken by a bomb that dropped on a nearby house and caused the ceiling of my bedroom to collapse over my bed. My mother came into my room, brushed pieces of ceiling from my eiderdown, and simply wished me goodnight again. Many of the houses surrounding our own were bombed, the local golf links were peppered with bombs several times, and our school grounds were hit on one occasion.

My father was in the reserves and rejoined the army on the first day of the war. I think that he much preferred the army to the book business and was happy to enrol again as a second lieutenant in the RASC. Over the war years he was promoted to captain and then to major, and he ended the war as c.o. of Connaught Barracks in Woolwich.

I did not see a great deal of my father during the war years, and very much missed forming a close relationship with him. He was rarely home during my adolescence and I had to develop independent pursuits. I became particularly interested in chess, which I learnt at the age of eleven. A school friend of mine had a father who was very good at chess and had taught him to play. This boy, whose name was Peter Tomlin, soon taught me, after which we used to play together whenever we could. We bought pocket sets and played in school under our desks during some of the lessons and we also quite soon learned to play chess blindfold—in our heads without the use of boards and pieces. We often cycled to school together playing chess in this way, calling out the moves, but not infrequently we had an argument about the position when we arrived at school.

At a later stage a boy named John Fuller, who had been British Boys Champion, joined the school. He raised the standard of our chess very substantially, and by the age of sixteen I had become a very good player and could have gone on to greater things if I had decided to make it a career. John Fuller, Peter Tomlin and I were spending most of our pocket money on fares up to the West End, as we had joined the West London, one of the best London chess clubs. There I could play against masters such as Sir George Thomas, and I used to live for my Saturdays at the club. I also frequented the Gambit Chess Rooms at Mansion House, and used to play in their excellent Lightning Tournaments. My interest in chess has lasted to this day, and I think it is a wonderful pastime for young people, particularly as it helps them to concentrate, to plan and to think ahead. Chess bridges many gaps; people of all races, the young and the old, the blind and the deaf, can all find a shared enjoyment in it.

At weekends, and on week nights when I did not have much homework to do, I used to meet the other members of our gang of five boys from Windermere Avenue, to play cricket or football on the local golf links. In the hot summer months we would sometimes spend Saturday afternoons at the nearest public swimming baths in Sudbury, but I did not enjoy this much as I did not learn to swim until much later in life. Chess was always my main indoor interest at home, but I also had the usual schoolboy crazes on a variety of hobbies. At one time I became very keen on bird life and made quite a study of it. The highlights were the two occasions when my father took me out into the country for the whole day and showed me a large number of different birds' nests. He had lived in the country as a boy and it was all second nature to him, but very thrilling for me. At one time I had been keen on philately and built up quite a good stamp collection. I particularly enjoyed the swopping sessions, and quite frequently when I switched from one hobby to another, I would negotiate a major swop: for example, I exchanged my stamp collection for a collection of birds' eggs, and at a later stage I swopped the birds' eggs for a superb old microscope. I found great appeal in the idea of exchanging something in which I had lost interest for something in which I had just become interested, and the doing of the deal really excited me. In addition I used to enjoy playing Monopoly, draughts and other similar games with my friends. At one stage I played a lot of cards at school, but I was put off this pastime when I was caught and caned for playing Solo for money with some of the senior boys.

My mother always used to insist that I did my homework properly and both my parents gave me every encouragement to try to do well at school. I took it quite seriously at first but when I was about fourteen my attitude became more light-hearted, perhaps because I began to realize that girls were girls. In a sense that was the time when I should have made a real effort, but instead I started to get comments in my school report like 'Irresponsible and a bad influence upon others in the class'. I have a fond recollection of Mr Kernut, who was my English master at school and a particularly good teacher, but the other teachers did not really register with me, and the headmaster was a very remote figure. My best subjects were chemistry and physics, and I converted part of our garage at home into a laboratory. I remember once making some gunpowder and exploding it in a small thick glass bottle in our garden to the consternation of our neighbours. Looking back I regret not having worked harder when I was at school, but fortunately, just before I took the General Schools Certificate Examination at the age of sixteen, I worked really intensively for a few months. As a result, I obtained a credit in all the subjects I sat for, with Matriculation exemption and a distinction in mathematics.

My father by this time had left the army and taken four of his men with him to set up a small building business, which he had bought into, in Abingdon Road near Kensington High Street. His junior partner knew one of the partners in a medium-sized firm of Incorporated Accountants called Croydon & King, and offered to introduce me to them. I did not really know what I wanted to do in life, but I was good at maths, and accountancy seemed to be very flexible once one had qualified. I went for an interview with the senior partner, and I was taken on as a clerk, articled to a man named William Soper, at thirty shillings a week. In practice I did not have a great deal to do with Mr Soper, and I tended to work much more with the senior partner's nephew, John King, who had recently been demobbed from the Royal Artillery in which he had become a captain. He was still very military in his approach to life, frequently referring to me as a 'bloody man', and carrying his umbrella like a rifle.

Shortly after I was sixteen we moved to Stafford Terrace, just behind Kensington High Street, and near my father's business in Abingdon Road. It was a very large house on a short lease; we occupied two floors and sub-let two others to tenants. I found the move to Kensington much more convenient for Croydon & King, who had offices in Grosvenor Gardens, but on the other hand I had to move away from all the friends I had made in South Kenton.

My first two years in articles, from the age of sixteen to eighteen, were rather a shock to me. The work was hard and very dull, in addition to which in the evenings and at weekends I had to study through a correspondence course with H. Foulks Lynch & Co. Ltd. They prescribed numerous books to read and regular test papers to answer in a programme of work which led up to the Intermediate Examination.

Again I found the competition very formidable. There were two other articled clerks: Geoff Bowden, who had been captain of his school and had obtained six distinctions in Matriculation; and David Cowmeadow, who had also been awarded a large number of distinctions and had been Victor Ludorum at his school. Bearing in mind the high failure rate in the Intermediate, I felt that if they were typical of the competition there was not much hope for me.

We used to work at the bottom of the building in a room nicknamed the dungeon; it was dimly lit by a large circular light which for some reason that I cannot remember we called 'the bleeder'. We had a lot of hotel audits on the books of Croydon & King, and I became very familiar with the soul-destroying process of cross-checking and vouching hotel receipts and interminably adding up hotel receipt books. After a while I was allowed out on audit, usually under the supervision of John King, who was great fun to be with. He was a very unconventional man, and while I was still very young he made me the godfather of one of his children.

At weekends I used to travel back to Kenton to see my friends as I was only very gradually making new friends in London. My studies with Foulks Lynch were progressing badly, and in particular I found subjects such as executorship very difficult to understand. Eventually I decided that I had little chance of succeeding because of the formidable competition, and that in any case accountancy was merely a much duller extension of school life. I wanted a change, so I made up my mind not to apply for deferment of my National Service, as was my right, but instead to offer to go into the army early. At that stage I had no real intention of returning to accountancy, although I left my option open. I applied to join the Royal Artillery, inspired I think by John King's example, and his obvious delight in army life. My mother and father, who were at first horrified by my decision, eventually came round to the idea, but certainly in the hope that I would be returning to accountancy at the end of my National Service.

My two years in the army were not up to my expectations. I was sent first of all to a training unit in Hounslow. At an early stage it was found that I was underweight and also that I had high arches. I was then sent to a physical development centre in Chester. As soon as I arrived I was asked, together with everyone else, to run a mile, sprint a hundred yards, pull myself up on a beam as many times as I could and undergo a variety of similar physical tests. They also had a very careful look at my cavoid feet. After that I had a thirteen-week period of training involving a lot of physical exercise. At the end of the training programme I found that I had put on eight pounds in weight, all of which appeared to be muscle, and that I could run a mile a lot quicker, sprint a hundred yards much faster and pull myself up on a beam many more times than before. I felt altogether better, stronger and much fitter. They had another look at my high arches, and I was advised that they too had improved. I must admit they had never troubled me until that day and have never troubled me since, but I am very grateful to the army for putting them right, if that is what it did.

After the physical development course I was sent back to Hounslow and, following the initial training, I was selected to go to Larkhill as a trainee officer. Again I was worried by the competition. The majority of the men had been to public school and seemed much more confident and able than I was. Most of them found it relatively easy to make a speech or stand up in front of the class and give a lecture, whereas I was painfully shy in this respect, and would have gone a long way to avoid it. In addition the training at Larkhill was intensive and hard, and I felt as if I had leapt out of the frying pan of accountancy into the fire of the army. I wanted to escape from pressure and begin enjoying my life, so I decided to opt out by signing a non-desirability form, which meant that I stated that I did not want to obtain a commission in Her Majesty's Forces. This was a very unusual step and I was urged not to take it by my father who was particularly disappointed in me. Looking back I can see that I should not have signed that form and that it was the soft option to have done so. However, I can only say that at the time it seemed to me the logical course of action.

I was then posted to a barracks in Woolwich where I had the unusual job of looking after a recreation room, which included both a snooker and a table-tennis table. I became quite expert at both games and thoroughly enjoyed that brief interval. It was not long before I could pot all of the colours at snooker, and I remember that I was delighted at making a break of 37 on one occasion. I still play a lot of table-tennis, which is one of my favourite games. After this I was posted to Gosforth in Newcastle where I took a pay course and eventually became a lance-bombardier in charge of pay. As a result I was allowed to wear shoes instead of boots and gaiters, and there were a number of other benefits in kind of a similar nature.

Towards the end of my National Service I was beginning to wonder what I was going to do when I came out. I had all kinds of ideas, one of which was to buy an old ambulance and convert it into a mobile canteen to sell snacks at race courses. I also had the idea of starting a shoe repair shop, in which I would adopt the unusual marketing approach of cleaning people's shoes and putting in new laces before returning them. I was feeling much fitter and much freer mentally; the year or so I had had without pressure seemed to have done me good. Gradually I began to wrestle with the hard option, which was to return to accountancy and grapple with the horrors of executorship again. My parents maintained a wonderful calm during the period of my mad ideas, but were very relieved on the day I informed them that I was going to return to accountancy.

When I returned to Croydon & King in 1949 I was a little more mature, and after a brief refresher course I was sent out on audit. I always worked under a partner, but I would take the books to the trial balance stage, and later do virtually all of the work myself leaving only a few major points for discussion with the partner concerned. As a result I was finding my work far more interesting, and also I seemed to be making much better progress with my studies. One of the main discoveries I made in the army was that there were a large number of people in the world who had no ambition at all and were simply prepared to drift. Once I had made up my mind to go for accountancy again, I decided that I would try to master it quickly, so for three years I studied four evenings out of five and the whole of every Sunday. I remember that I used to study in my bedroom at night, and I was so tired after each day's work that I had to keep splashing my face with cold water to keep awake.

It paid off in the end, in that when I reached the difficult points in executorship which had always plagued me in the past I seemed to go through them this time like a knife through butter. I passed the Intermediate exam, and subsequently the Final Parts all at my first attempt. I finally qualified in 1953 when I was just twenty-four, which was quite soon considering the two years away from my studies on National Service. In spite of this hard work I found time to be a member of a social club near my old home in South Kenton, where I used to play a lot of tennis. I also had an attractive girlfriend who was a model at Rembrandts, a small fashion house, and life was fine until she married the dress designer.

I decided that I wanted a kind of finishing school in accountancy. Croydon & King was only medium-sized, with a staff of about twenty and no particularly large audits, so I joined Cooper Brothers for a year to see how big firms operated. I was taken on at £450 per annum which was a great improvement on the £7 per week I had gradually risen to at Croydon & King, but I found the work much more boring as in a big firm one tends to be confined to a small section of the overall audit as opposed to seeing everything in perspective. I much preferred medium-sized audits where I could do the whole job and see it right through to completion.

One of the Cooper audits I remember was Knights, the soap manufacturers, and I spent days simply looking at one section of their sales ledger. If things went well one might progress to the purchase ledger, but nothing much else could happen. It was here I met Peter Greaves, who has become a friend and now works with me in Wimbledon. We were on the same audit team, and he was the son of one of the partners.

The system adopted by Cooper Brothers was more detailed than that used by Croydon & King. They had an Audit Manual which had reduced auditing to a fine art, even down to spelling out the exact type of ticks to be used by their staff in different aspects of the work. Their whole approach was thoroughly professional and excellent for larger audits, but I would strongly recommend anyone going in for accountancy to start with a small firm and graduate upwards, rather than the other way around. It is essential to first grasp the whole picture on a small scale, so that when the scale is increased the part played by each feature in the complete pattern can be understood.

TWO

Lessons in Industry

I QUALIFIED as a chartered accountant in 1953 at the age of twenty-four. Shortly afterwards I decided that it was time for me to obtain industrial experience. I saw an advertisement in one of the papers which read as follows: '£700 per annum—accountant wanted to control expenditure of group of companies. Persons without keen sense of economy need not apply. Box No. . . .' I was very attracted by the £700, and it seemed the kind of job I was looking for so I applied. I was asked to go along to be interviewed by a man named Svend Dohm, who had built up a group of fourteen private companies, and also had other substantial investments. When I arrived for the interview we hit it off immediately. He was Danish, aged about fifty-five, with a rather plump, freshly complexioned face and greying hair. He told me that he wanted to employ someone who asked questions. As I was younger than he had expected he offered me only £650 per annum, but this was still a good salary as far as I was concerned, so I accepted the position.

When I arrived to start the job Dohm told me that he had changed his mind and that, instead of assisting the group chief accountant to control the expenditure of his group of companies, he wanted me to become chief accountant of one of his main subsidiaries, the Renu Plating Company, which was giving him a lot of trouble. He asked me to go down to their Blackfriars premises, introduce myself to one of the directors, and tell him that I was the new chief accountant. He also said that in addition to the £650 he would give me 2 per cent of the profits of the company. I thought that this was a wonderful gesture until I later learned that the firm was losing £40,000 per annum.

I went with some trepidation down a dingy road by the side of the river to the equally dingy premises of Renu Plating. I asked for the director who was expecting me, and I was shown to a small, sparsely furnished room with bare floor boards. It seemed to me that there was a strange smell in the room: this turned out to be because it was directly over an anodizing vat containing sulphuric acid in the factory below. The harshness of the smell during the course of a day was very difficult to take, and I wondered what I had let myself in for. Since I was the chief accountant I decided that I had better begin by having a look at the books. I found to my horror that they had not been written up properly for three years, and were of course unaudited. Dohm had only bought the company a year or so earlier, and since then only very broad management accounts had been supplied to him each month.

As I gradually got the books up to date I realized that Renu was running at a substantial loss, and also that it was desperately short of cash. An average creditor was owed for at least six months' materials, and even the PAYE deductions had not been accounted for to the Inland Revenue, and were many months behind. It was extraordinary how the suppliers had come to accept the position in which they were owed for supplies far beyond their normal credit terms. They had as a result become vitally concerned about the welfare of the company and had decided to continue to supply it with materials on extended credit as the idea of the company's bankruptcy would have been too painful for them to face. Staff morale in Renu was at a low ebb as the company struggled to survive.

Dohm became increasingly aware of all the difficulties and as a result his relationship with the executive directors deteriorated to such an extent that they decided to part company. This left the company devoid of top management and, to my surprise, Dohm decided to appoint me secretary and general manager, in spite of the fact that I had only been with the company a few months and had no previous industrial experience. It was a unique and very challenging opportunity for me as there was an enormous job to be done.

First of all overheads had to be considerably reduced, as a result of which I had the unenviable task of giving notice to a large number of the staff. In addition to this I had to institute an urgent drive for cash. Most of the customers' accounts owing to Renu were not being collected properly. Quite often a relatively small claim for goods damaged whilst being plated would hold up the payment of a large account. I authorized a generous settlement of these minor disputes and this brought in a substantial amount of cash due to Renu. I also instituted a system for the future, whereby damage to goods would only be paid for up to a certain multiple of the processing charge.

The sales side of Renu was a mess. There were about fourteen salesmen who were all employed on a commission basis and did not have specific areas. I removed more than half of them and allocated areas to the others, which had a most beneficial effect. We painted the premises, put up prices, increased sales and did a deal with creditors to give us time to pay. Within nine months the firm came round to a rate of profit of about £20,000 per annum and my 2 per cent began to mean something. I always argued with Dohm that I should have had 2 per cent of the losses saved as well as the profits made, but it was difficult to convince him of this.

I began to realize that Dohm was losing money in most of his companies because his real forte was stock exchange investments, and he tended to run his businesses as a hobby. There were two other plating companies which he soon agreed should come into the Renu group, and after a while he asked me to go up to another of his companies, National Colours, which was in Stockport. He said that he would give me a percentage of profits if I would put it right for him. He dictated a short note to the general manager, with a copy to me, saying that he had given me full power in his absence to reorganize the company; then he went off on a sea cruise for about six weeks and left me to it.

I went up to Stockport and stayed in an hotel while I investigated National Colours. I found that it was losing about £20,000 per annum. The company was mainly involved in the making of colours and the grinding of graphite and it had not occurred to anyone that these two processes were totally incompatible: the fine graphite got into the colours, and was particularly noticeable in the grey-flecked yellow. I decided to take Dohm at his word, and sold off the whole of the colour-making plant in his absence. We only received a few thousand pounds but it had been unprofitable anyway and the cash was badly needed elsewhere.

I then had a look at the graphite business, and found that our graphite was taking a long time to grind because the roof was leaking and it had got wet. I invested the proceeds of the sale of the colour plant in improving the roof of the graphite store. I also found that graphite was ground to mesh sizes, such as 200 to the inch or 300 to the inch. On studying our costings I found that, for example, to grind to 300 to the inch took several times longer than grinding to 200 to the inch. Our price structure did not reflect this, and therefore I cut out of our range some of the finest mesh sizes, and radically altered the prices of the others where necessary. We then did a deal with Risley, the atomic energy station, to handle a lot of their synthetic graphite. This, together with the other improvements, made a radical change to the fortunes of National Colours, which should perhaps have been renamed National Graphite or something more suitable. It was certainly a very different company when Dohm returned and, whilst I think he had a lingering feeling that he would rather be making colours, he was certainly pleased with the financial results.

I was fortunate, as a young man of twenty-five, to be given such full responsibility for the complete reorganization and management of companies such as National Colours and Renu. At first I could hardly believe that I had the authority to change things so drastically. However, money was critically short in the group and the problems were very pressing so I soon found that I was taking action quickly because decisions had to be made or the businesses would have foundered. As I continued to take decisions, and began to see things happen as a result, my confidence grew.

I learned a lot from Dohm, who was an amazing character. He was the first man who really taught me 'contrary thinking'. This was the principle on which he made his many stock exchange investments. For example, immediately after the war he bought German bonds, when most people would not have believed in the possibility of Germany recovering to the extent it did, and made a fortune on them. He also used to invest in small, out-of-the-way companies that were not doing very well. His main interest was in underlying assets as opposed to immediate earnings and he would buy when things looked bad. He was one of the very few investors who applied contrary thinking.

Dohm had two other maxims, which impressed me at the time and which I have endeavoured to follow ever since. The first was expressed in a motto across his mantelpiece which said, 'It can be done'. Whenever a problem arose, he always sought a positive solution, insisting that it could be found; the possibility that there was no answer simply did not occur to him. This approach is one which I consider invaluable. Dohm's second maxim was, 'Always try to turn a disadvantage to an advantage'. If a customer wrote to him complaining about some service or other, he would reply in such a way that he would make the man a customer for life; if one of his factories had a fire, he would immediately ask how the plant and machinery could be reorganized when it was replaced, to make the lay-out better than it had been before. Dohm was a difficult man to beat.

After two years with Dohm I was earning about £1,800 per annum, and I had a car. In 1955 this was not bad for a young man of twenty-six, and I had obviously gained invaluable experience. Once again, rather as with Croydon & King, I had the advantage of working with a small company first and seeing the whole ball-game. I had learned the importance of controlling overheads, making sure that selling prices were properly structured, and above all ensuring that cash flow was controlled and adequate. At one time at Renu we even had to send out salesmen to collect money from customers to pay into the bank the same day, so that the wages could be paid. This brought home to me in a very positive way the vital importance of cash flow, and it was something that would always concern me subsequently.

At about this time my father died. His building business was not doing too well, and I wanted to see what I could do to improve it. Dohm's son was entering his business so I felt that my chances of further promotion there would be limited and, in addition, a friend of mine named Ken Meyer, who also worked with Dohm, had decided to leave and set up on his own in a relatively new process known as shell moulding. I had got to know Ken quite well as we had been on a two-week holiday together, so when he asked me to join him I was tempted by his proposal, although, looking back, I took a big risk. I should really have simply moved on to another company, instead of having a break in my career pattern which could have been difficult to explain later. However, I took the plunge, and left Dohm on good terms, having decided to work from home with Ken. With £100 capital and high hopes we formed a little private company which was grandiosely called the Commercial and Industrial Development Corporation Ltd. My mother was very uncertain about it all and, when Ken arrived at my home at half past nine in the morning on the first day with his *Financial Times* tucked under his arm, she let us know her views in no uncertain manner.

Shell moulding is a technique in which moulds for foundry work are made from a mixture of sand and resin. Ken Meyer was the technical expert and was confident he fully understood this process. We went along to see British Resin Products which was a subsidiary of Distillers, and talked them into the idea that we might be able to help them. We also went to see General Refractories, which was one of the biggest firms of sand suppliers in Britain. We talked them into the idea that they needed our help as well. Then we went to see Herbert Morris in Loughborough, who produced machines for preparing foundry moulding sands and explained that with their machines, the resin of British Resin Products and the sand of General Refractories, there was the basis for an exceptional partnership in which we were to be the catalyst. We planned a demon-

stration for a Saturday morning, using free samples from British Resin
and General Refractories and borrowing a Herbert Morris machine free
of charge. Working it all out on an estimated future sales basis, we felt
that with the royalties we would receive our fortunes would be made. We
had a convivial dinner at a hotel in Loughborough the night before the
demonstration, and went to bed feeling very pleased with life.

The next day the demonstration took place at the works of Herbert
Morris. Ken Meyer wore a white coat and looked most professional. I
circulated amongst the guests, talking to them a little and generally trying
to ensure that they were happy. I first began to realize that the demonstration was not going too well when I saw Ken Meyer anxiously peering into
the glass panel at the front of the machine. I knew him intimately and
could recognize signs of trouble. It was a few minutes later that I noticed
that Ken Meyer's coat was no longer looking pure white. It was beginning
to be covered with brown specks, which I soon realized were globules of
resin and sand coming out of the top of the machine and spraying over
those who were near it. Ken explained to everyone that the sand was not
of the right quality and that he would try again with another sample.
Soon, however, our guests began to drift away, and we were left together
with the unhappy representative of Herbert Morris. For some reason I saw
the funny side of this at the time, which was a day or so before Ken, who
drove me back to London in high dudgeon.

I had already invested in a gold share called Amalgamated Banket Areas
and borrowed money to do this. This was my first stock exchange investment and it was not going well. In addition I had borrowed money from
some friends to finance my overheads for the shell-moulding venture. I
was out of pocket because I had spent three months without a salary and
there had, of course, been initial expenses. I had to cut my losses, and get a
job quickly. Ken Meyer and I wound up our partnership on amicable
terms, and he soon joined a company known as Feslente which was quite
successful subsequently in developing shell-moulding products.

I was now in debt to the tune of about £900, and without a job. In late
1955, when I was twenty-six, I applied for the position of Secretary of
Park Royal Vehicles Ltd, which was a wholly-owned subsidiary of
Associated Commercial Vehicles Ltd. The preference shares of Park Royal
were still quoted and it was therefore still a public company in its own
right, but only just. The salary offered was £1,400 per annum, and the
successful applicant would be responsible for the secretarial, accounting,
costing, wages and stores functions, with a staff of about a hundred. He

would be responsible to the director and general manager as a member of the management committee of four, the other members being the works manager, the sales manager and the chief engineer. I was asked to go for several interviews, and finally to one with the chairman who was then Sir Wavell Wakefield, now Lord Wakefield of Kendal, and the managing director, Mr W.R. Black, now Lord Black. This interview took place at Berkeley Square, which was the head office of ACV. I remember that Sir Wavell said to me, 'What do you know about the job?' I replied by spelling out to him in great detail all I knew about the management committee and the secretary's responsibilities; also, I had studied the accounts of the company at Bush House, so I was able to tell him a lot of the background. Mr Black then asked me, 'What do you know about costing?' and to my horror I heard myself say, 'That is rather like asking a chemist what he knows about chemistry!' I felt after a couple of rounds of this conversation that I had been much too forthright and would not stand a chance. I remember going home and telling my mother that I had overdone it. The other applicant was from within the group, and I was sure that he would get the job. In the event, however, it appeared that both of them had thought I might be a useful addition to the Park Royal team, and that it would be a good idea to have fresh blood from outside the group.

Because of my debts I had to sell my car. It was a small Standard 10 and I had grown used to it. I well remember the dealer coming to Park Royal shortly after I arrived there, buying the car from me, and then driving off in it. It was a terrible feeling to watch it gradually vanish from sight. I did not let everyone know that I was in debt and in fact invested part of the proceeds in two new suits to create the opposite effect. I took the line that I rather liked walking to and from the office and that the exercise would be good for me.

Park Royal Vehicles employed just over a thousand people. The main union was the National Union of Vehicle Builders, and several years before there had been a thirteen-week strike, which had left a bitter memory. The union was quite active, and there were often stoppages and strikes in individual shops within the factory, although during the time I was there we never had a general stoppage. Park Royal made cabs for AEC, but its main line of business was bus and coach bodies. These it made for both AEC and Leyland, although naturally as AEC was a member of the ACV group there were more bodies built on their chassis than on those of Leyland. The premises at Park Royal were next to the dog track, and occupied about twenty acres. The director and general manager was a man named Bill Shirley, who had previously worked for another large body-building firm. He in turn reported to Mr Black, who had been managing director of Park Royal and was now managing director of the ACV group, retaining, for auld lang syne, a special interest in the management of Park Royal. Mr Black used to come in to Park Royal every Monday morning, and quite often I would be called into Bill Shirley's office while he was there, for a general talk about outstanding problems. I used to look forward keenly to his visits, as I found him very stimulating.

Park Royal was run by Bill Shirley and directly under him there was a management committee consisting of the sales manager, the works manager, the chief engineer, and myself. The company was not trading particularly profitably. During the previous few years it had had a very substantial contract from London Transport, and once this ended it was left rather bereft of work. The overheads were considerable, and big contracts were difficult to find and highly competitive. In addition to this, labour costs were increasing through union pressure. The profits at the time were in the region of £25,000 per annum before tax.

My Dohm experience now proved invaluable. I had had a bird's-eye view of what made companies tick, and I rapidly got the feel of the whole of Park Royal's business. In particular I realized that there were two main areas which could be quickly improved. The first was overheads, which were on the high side, and the second was stock control. I made one of my first jobs the introduction of budgetary control, allocating all of the overheads between the four key members of the management committee, including myself. Thereafter each of these executives would be personally responsible for a specific part of the firm's expenditure, and would therefore control these costs more closely. As a result of this we gradually made economies and overheads were substantially reduced.

My second main area of attack was the stores, which were scattered throughout the works. There was no real central store: instead there tended to be an individual one for each of the main shops in the factory, such as bodywork, glazing, finishing, and so on. I soon found that in each of the stores there were hundreds of items left over from previous contracts, and if these were not readily suitable for new contracts they were simply left on the shelves to rot. These surplus materials included such expensive items as many tons of aluminium sections of various types. As a result of this policy considerable administrative time was spent looking after completely surplus stock, which continued to deteriorate in both condition and value. In addition to this capital was locked up, and obviously it made sense to have a radical review. I put this in hand, and approximately £100,000 worth of surplus stock was sold as a result. Although there was a book loss on this it was of course a non-recurring one and the money liberated, even in terms of interest alone, could be used to much better advantage. In selling off all this stock I became more familiar with the practice of selling surplus material, which I had to some extent already learned about at Renu Plating.

I got to know the ways of the scrap dealers, who are a law unto themselves. I knew that one of their tricks was to arrange for the driver to be on a lorry when it was weighed at the weighbridge on the way into a factory, and for him to absent himself from the lorry when it was weighed on the way out. This meant, of course, that there was a distortion of weights, and this was something that had to be watched very carefully. The man who was dealing with our scrap metal was a great character; at one stage he telephoned Bill Black and said that he did not get on at all well with me. Bill Black telephoned me to say that I should consider myself highly complimented and that I should carry on exactly as before. In the end I developed a happy *modus vivendi* with our scrap dealer, as a result of which we obtained good prices and there was very little friction. This sale of surplus stock did enable us to reduce the number of store keepers, and generally improved the overall efficiency of the Park Royal stores. It also meant that at a later stage, when it came to closing Crossley Motors and selling off surplus stock there, I was the natural man for the job.

Another interesting development at Park Royal occurred when I wanted to change the system of costing in the shops. There was a piece-work system, and at the end of each week the stewards, in conjunction with the management, used to value each individual job that was unfinished to assess the proportion of it to be used in calculating the amount due to the men that week. I had looked at the whole procedure and found that over a period, on average, it would be infinitely easier to take a simple fixed percentage and apply this to the overall total amount of unfinished work, rather than calculate it on an item-by-item basis. This would save all concerned a lot of time and work and, in the end, there would be no difference in the final result. The main difficulty in achieving this step forward was that I had to convince the shop stewards. I consulted the works manager, who suggested to me that I should start with a certain shop where the stewards were the most amenable. I had a meeting with them and they were soon convinced of the merits of my new scheme. They then went back to their shop to see the men, who unanimously rejected the idea. Rather than give up I asked the works manager to let me know which shop stewards were the most difficult. I then saw those shop stewards and after several much more difficult meetings convinced them that the idea was a good one and an improvement over the existing procedure. They had no difficulty with the men in their shop, who knew that their representatives were tough and that any idea that they had vetted would be all right. The idea then spread like wildfire through all the other shops, until the only outstanding one was the shop with the amenable shop stewards. It took a year or so for them to join in.

The London Transport contract was coming up again, as they wanted to buy a large number of Routemasters on a regular yearly basis. It was absolutely vital for Park Royal to get this contract, and it was in direct competition with its main competitor Metropolitan Cammell-Weyman. I reasoned that we should look on the Routemaster contract simply as a contribution to our total overheads and cost it on a marginal basis. This we did, and after a lot of heart-searching we put in a highly competitive tender, which was accepted. By the time the Routemaster contract was flowing through Park Royal I had already left, but I am sure that the basic policy of getting the work, albeit on a marginal basis, was the right one.

There was an excellent snooker table at Park Royal, and Ted Needs, the chief engineer, and I often used to have a game after work. Quite frequently I would go back with him to have supper at his house, and we developed a very happy relationship. He was about fifty-five, married, and had a daughter of about five years old who was the apple of his eye. Otherwise my social life at this time tended to be rather barren as I was very busy saving up to pay back my debts. I lived with my mother just behind High Street Kensington and most evenings I could only afford to go home and read a book or watch television. To give an idea of how keen I was to repay my creditors, I used to walk from High Street Kensington to Hammersmith Station night and morning, and frequently debated whether or not the bus fares saved were worth the extra shoe leather.

During my time at Park Royal its profits began to climb. The first year they were £42,000, the second year £108,000 and the following year they reached £180,000. This was at a time when the whole of the ACV group was only making £432,000, and yet Park Royal had less than 10 per cent of the group's total capital invested in it. Clearly there was a lot wrong with the rest of the group, and Bill Black was very worried about it. One of the more obvious decisions was for ACV to close Crossley Motors in Manchester. Crossley did not have a worthwhile range of vehicles and it was losing a lot of money each year, as well as having considerable group capital employed within it. The ACV board took the decision to close Crossley, and I was asked by Bill Black if I would go up there for as much time as I could spare each week to help them sell off their surplus stocks and machine tools. I should explain that Crossley, in addition to making chassis, had a body works, so that part of their stocks was very similar to those of Park Royal.

An ex-AEC executive had been brought back from retirement to help look after Crossley during its close-down period. In addition to this, the assistant works manager of AEC was seconded to Crossley to help on the works side. They had the very difficult job of finishing off production orders, arranging redundancies and generally closing down the works. My own first priority was to delegate my job at Park Royal to the maximum possible extent. I had an excellent assistant, and he took over from me, so that I could visit Crossley regularly each week. First of all, I arranged for a detailed schedule of all available stocks and all available machine tools to be prepared and then circulated within the ACV group. Each group company, including of course Park Royal, was given the opportunity to buy these stocks and machine tools if they had any use for them. Once reservations had been made from within the group, we had to deal with the balance, and as far as stocks were concerned I put in hand sales on a massive scale, in a rather similar way to that which I had used at Park Royal.

The residual machine tools were a very different problem and represented several hundred thousand pounds worth of surplus machinery, some of which was in excellent condition. We contacted a few other manufacturers directly, and I well remember selling a stretching machine to Jaguar. I was particularly struck by the fact that Sir William Lyons dealt with me personally over this sale; he clearly had a great grip on everything that was happening at Jaguar, which made quite an impression on me. I then decided to offer the rest of the surplus machinery to the secondhand dealers. I had a detailed list made and, thinking that I would take advantage of the fact that we had the use of the factory for about a year, I offered dealers the opportunity of buying all of the machinery and then selling it to their customers direct from the works. This would save them storage and transport, which would, I thought, be reflected in the prices we obtained. I had the detailed list prepared in such a way that they could offer for each machine individually as well as for the whole package. In the event the prices were very favourable, and we received the top offer from George Cohen, who bought the main batch of machinery for £95,000 which was a lot of money at that time. They did an excellent job in selling it off, and I think that it worked out as well for them as it did for Crossley.

Once the Crossley closure was finished I returned to Park Royal, to find that my much-delegated job did not really hold my interest any longer. At this particular time Prince Philip was about to visit the Park Royal works. Bill Shirley was away abroad, and the works manager was away with flu. Bill Black telephoned me one morning and said that he wanted to come down to Park Royal to have a look around the works and have lunch there to make sure that everything was in order for Prince Philip's visit. I welcomed this idea as I always enjoyed seeing Bill Black, but more particularly because on this occasion I wanted to sell him the idea that I should be given an executive position within AEC as opposed to Park Royal. I made careful preparations and asked my secretary to type out a job specification for me at AEC. I decided that they needed a commercial director, and I remember listing the various functions and responsibilities of the job as I envisaged it. Bill Black came down and had a look around the works; then we had a drink in Bill Shirley's room before lunch. I put my proposal to him, and I will always remember his words, which were, 'In the unlikely event of my ever giving this proposal serious consideration, you would of course have to report to the sales director.' After lunch he had to go back to London and the discussion finished on an inconclusive note, but the seed had been planted in his mind.

It was about three months later that Bill Black saw me one Monday morning on the way out from seeing Bill Shirley, and offered me the job as commercial director of ACV (Sales). By that time I was earning £1,800 per annum at Park Royal, and he offered me £2,250 per annum with a company car. I would be responsible to a man named Eric Hollands, who was then sales director but would be retiring within the next year or so. The prospects were obvious and I accepted the job with alacrity.

· THREE ·

Commercial Director

IN early 1959, when I was twenty-nine, the time came for me to join ACV (Sales) and say a sad good-bye to Park Royal. I remember they presented me with a briefcase during a farewell lunch. At that time I was not at all good at making speeches and I dreaded the lunch for some days in advance. As it happened, I only had to say a few words, but occasions of this kind were always a nightmare for me.

At this point I think I should say something about the general position of Associated Commercial Vehicles Ltd. It was a public company and not a particularly successful one. Though the second biggest commercial vehicle manufacturer in the country, it was only a pale shadow of Leyland Motors. The main companies in the ACV group were AEC, Maudsley, Crossley, Park Royal and Charles Roe. Each of the main manufacturing companies continued to work to a large extent independently until gradually a group selling company was formed, called ACV (Sales). This company sold for the group as a whole, except for the body building side, and its head office was in Berkeley Square. The idea did not work at all well; the AEC people used to refer to the distance between the factory and Berkeley Square as the 'nine mile gap'. In contrast, Leyland had been moving from strength to strength, especially on the export side. Donald Stokes, following in the footsteps of Sir Henry Spurrier, had done a wonderful job of building up Leyland's exports. They had wholly-owned subsidiaries in many parts of the world, and were making profits in the region of £6m per annum against ACV's £432,000.

Bill Black had started to reorganize ACV gradually, having come in through the smallest subsidiary, Park Royal Vehicles. I looked upon this as a favourable precedent. He had become chairman of ACV (Sales), and subsequently executive managing director of the ACV group. The rest of the board of ACV were non-executive, including the chairman, Lord

27

Brabazon of Tara, who was a great friend of Bill Black. The main members of the management were John Bowley, who was the director and general manager of AEC, responsible for the works, engineering and design side of the business, and Eric Hollands, who was the director and general manager of ACV (Sales). I was commercial director of ACV (Sales), and the three of us were the only members of the management who attended the monthly ACV board meeting.

By this time I had left home and taken a flat in Ealing, overlooking the common, while my mother had moved to Richmond. My flat was very near the Southall works of AEC, and with a car again and my debts fully repaid I was beginning to feel that things were on the up and up. When I first moved into AEC I identified a few young men within the company who I thought would be able to help me in the major job of reorganizing its commercial and sales side. First amongst these was John Ford, who was the secretary and chief accountant of AEC, and about two years older than myself. Underneath John Ford, several layers down, I found Dick Tarling, who was working on the costing side, and on the export side I took a liking to the European sales manager, Robert Bennett, who seemed to have a lot of promise. He was soon promoted to export manager, and helped me very considerably in developing AEC's exports.

One of the first things to get right was the marketing policy. In particular there was a lot of confusion about the ACV and AEC names. The name of AEC was a shortened version of the original name of the company, which was Associated Equipment Company Ltd. AEC's name was very well known and popular in the truck and bus world, and the idea of selling AEC chassis under the name of ACV (Sales) was a bad one. Little persuasion was needed to drop the name ACV (Sales) entirely, and as a result it was changed to AEC (Sales), which was soon effectively absorbed by AEC itself. At this time I also became a director of AEC, as did Eric Hollands.

In the home market AEC's main competitor was Leyland. The cheapest Leyland chassis was the Comet, and the cheapest AEC one was the Mercury. The Mercury, however, had a superior specification to the Comet and was considerably more expensive to make. I thought it was far better to stress the extra quality in our advertising and in our marketing generally and, if anything, to put our prices up rather than try to meet the competition head on. When we did this, we also gave our distributors an extra $2\frac{1}{2}$ per cent discount to use as they saw fit, and this had a dramatic effect in boosting sales. The key point is that distributors take old chassis from customers in part exchange, and the extra discount enabled them to offer better prices. Taking a simple example, if a new Mercury was £2,000 originally and the distributor was offering £900 for the old chassis, under the new system the new Mercury would cost £2,100, but the distributor would be offering £950 for the customer's old vehicle. Because the new vehicle had a list price of £2,100 and also had a superior specification to Leyland's comparable product, it was in the customer's view likely to be worth £2,100. The fact that our distributor was offering £950 against the £900 offered by Leyland in part exchange for the customer's old vehicle made AEC more likely to land the sale than Leyland. This idea may be easier to follow by relating it to two refrigerators, one of which is selling in a shop window for £140, while the other is selling in another shop window for £160. If the more expensive one had a better specification you could not help thinking that it was likely to be worth the extra £20. If, in addition, you were offering your old refrigerator in part exchange to each shop in turn, and the one displaying the more expensive model offered you £10 more for it, this would be very likely to attract you.

We also put up the price of spares. There is no doubt that if a customer wants a spare he wants it immediately, and is not unduly concerned about the price. It is rather like wanting a Rennie; I remember that there was a classic case in the marketing of Rennies when the price was dramatically increased, as was the budget on advertising. This had a fantastic effect upon profits, because when someone wants a Rennie, he wants a Rennie, and is not too bothered whether a packet costs 18p or 22p.

We also introduced a quality image into our coach-chassis marketing. In this case the comparable chassis to the Mercury was the Reliance. We decided to base our advertising policy on the theme 'Reserve Your Reliance Now'. We had plenty of Reliances, but the idea that they had to be reserved was a new one and again helped to uplift the image in terms of price.

However, the main job to be done was on the export side. This is where Leyland were light-years ahead of AEC. To give an example, Leyland were selling comparable vehicles to AEC in South Africa to the extent of 600 per annum, against AEC's sales of only 50. It was difficult to decide how to catch up, as a massive capital outlay was needed to build the necessary spares and repair depots throughout the country. In addition to this, it had to be appreciated that both distributors and manufacturers make very little money selling original equipment, as the real profits come from spares sales once there are a considerable number of vehicles on the

road. The profit margin on spares is many times that on original equipment, and this is the secret of successful heavy chassis marketing overseas.
The policy I worked out was to try to buy into the equity of large and
successful firms of general distributors overseas, persuade them to take on
the AEC distributorship, and subsidize their selling activity by price reductions until a substantial number of chassis were on the road in their
country, producing sufficient spares revenue to make the distributorship
profitable in its own right.

Our previous distributors in South Africa were a firm called Dowson &
Dobson, and the chief executive was a man named Firman. Bill Black had
been having some correspondence with him about the renewal of the
distributorship for a further three years, but concurrently he had been in
touch with a man named Jack Plane, who ran J.H. Plane (Africa) Ltd,
which distributed amongst other things Gardner Engines. At that time
Plane's company was making about £100,000 per annum. Although an
engineer by training, he had an exceptional grasp of the financial side of
his business. I liked the tone of his correspondence with Bill Black, so I
suggested that I should go out to South Africa to try and terminate the
Dowson & Dobson distributorship, buy into Plane (Africa) and switch
the AEC distributorship to them. This was to be my first business trip
overseas, and after I got the necessary authority from Bill Black I set off
to Johannesburg.

First of all I had some very difficult negotiations with Firman, but
eventually I managed to persuade him that one way or another he was
going to lose the AEC distributorship, and might as well do it on the
favourable terms that I was prepared to offer. I then went to see Jack Plane
at his house at Bryanston on the outskirts of Johannesburg. As Jack drove
me there he pointed out landmarks of interest; he always tells the story
better than I do, but the gist of it is that every time he would say something
like, 'That is a Jacaranda tree' my response would be, 'Yes, now about this
deal.' At that time I was extremely keen on business which to me was like
a game of chess. I was primarily interested in the pieces and the moves
as opposed to what the other player was wearing that day or had eaten for
breakfast that morning.

I stayed with Jack, and at the weekend he told me that he normally
played cricket on Saturday afternoons and asked if I would like to come
and watch. I said I would, and after lunch he went up to change into his
whites. To my surprise we then simply walked across the road to a nearby
neighbour, John Hodgson, with whom Jack apparently had his weekly

match. The pitch was a sunken tennis court around which stumps were placed at strategic intervals, and if the batsman placed the ball between certain of the stumps he obtained differing numbers of runs according to the exact position. On the other hand if the ball was hit out of the tennis court it was deemed to be caught by an outfielder. The only other participant was a very scared-looking African gardener fielding much too close to the batsman for his liking. The game went on for about two hours, at the end of which they were both exhausted. They kept a complicated cumulative weekly score and each year a small silver statue of a nude woman was the property of the winner and proudly displayed in his office.

Jack and I got on like a house on fire, and it was not long before we had agreed on a deal whereby ACV bought 25 per cent of J.H. Plane (Africa), and had an option on the balance of Jack Plane's shareholding in that company. We also negotiated a tapered form of subsidy linked to the number of chassis that were put on the road. Jack taught me a great deal about how a distributorship works financially from the distributor's point of view. He explained to me in detail how spares were marked up in price on landed cost, how the discount structure worked, and how secondhand vehicles were dealt with by distributors. In a very short space of time he gave me a bird's-eye view of these vital factors. In the years to come I was able to apply this new knowledge, not only in Great Britain but throughout the world, to excellent effect and to the great benefit of both AEC and its distributors. I would strongly recommend anyone on the sales or commercial side of any exporting or distributing business to get a full and detailed idea of how it all works, from the time the product leaves the factory right through to the final distribution to the customer. I am not referring to the actual process of manufacture—that has always been a mystery to me—but principally to the commercial structure of the business, and how the manufacturer and the distributor make their respective profits. In particular, it is vital to understand the main problems of the distributor, as it is only by solving those problems that sales can be increased on a long-term basis.

Very shortly after my trip to South Africa I went to Leyland's next biggest market, Australia. There we had a long-standing relationship with a distributor who performed reasonably well, had an embryo team of keen executives, but had never examined further marketing possibilities with the manufacturer really critically, as we did during my visit there. Although overall the AEC distributor's sales for the country compared moderately well with those of Leyland, we found on a state-by-state analysis that there were glaring deficiencies in their performance. In New

31

South Wales and Victoria AEC sales were roughly comparable with Leyland, but elsewhere they were very poor and in South Australia for example AEC was only selling three chassis per annum against Leyland's sixty. Our distributor had depots in each of the other states, but clearly a bigger sales effort was needed there to get things moving. We arranged subsidies for sales in the different states, and I also persuaded them to order well in advance a substantial number of additional chassis, as this in itself puts great pressure on a distributor. Even if credit is given for a reasonable period, at the end of that time it expires, and then either interest is ticking away or the bill has to be met.

During my first visit to Australia our distributors arranged for me to take a helicopter and fly over the Snowy Mountain project. Dams were being built and vast areas deliberately flooded with a view to irrigating large tracts of land that hitherto had been very short of water. AEC vehicles were in extensive use in the area, and the visit was for goodwill purposes with operators as well as for my interest and education. I remember that while we were on our way in the afternoon I felt in great need of a cup of tea, and as we were flying over a golf course the pilot obligingly took us down, landing near the club house. It was a ladies' afternoon, and the ladies were in the club house having something to eat and drink. We went in and to everyone's surprise asked for our cups of tea. Whilst it was being prepared I tried my luck on the fruit machines, which were at that time very popular in Australia and played at two shillings a time, as opposed to the more usual British sixpence. After two or three goes I won the jackpot—the machine made a loud stuttering noise as two-shilling pieces poured out of it. We drank our tea quickly when it came, and then flew off into the blue with our winnings. I have often wondered what those Australian lady golfers must have felt about the strange visitation from the skies, but in the circumstances I felt it best not to wait too long to find out.

Throughout the time I was with AEC I travelled at least 50,000 miles each year developing its export business. I visited South Africa two or three times a year, and there were many other trips to such places as Southern Rhodesia, Australia, New Zealand, Canada, Spain, Holland, France, Belgium and Portugal. The policy of equity participation was also applied in Holland, Belgium, Spain and France, and I became AEC's representative on the boards of most of the local companies. Also the policy of subsidizing distributors was successfully applied throughout the world. The effects were excellent, and AEC's previously miserable export performance began to improve rapidly, led in the main by South Africa. Jack Plane was making great inroads into the businesses of both Leyland and Mercedes there, and his activity became a model for other distributors to follow.

One of the other problems that was always present with vehicle manufacture was that in many countries severe import duties were imposed. This meant that local manufacture had to be considered. As a first step chassis would be sent 'PKD' (partially knocked down) and then eventually 'CKD' (completely knocked down). At later stages certain parts would be manufactured locally, until eventually only components would be sent and the rest made in local factories. As this meant a capital investment on the part of distributors, it was always vital to make sure that they could finance the whole operation. The inter-link between the sales and financial functions was well expressed in my title of commercial director. It was essential to have a thoroughly commercial and financial approach, as otherwise sales would have been impossible to maintain. The days of the 'gin and tonic' salesman had, with rare exceptions, gone and the financial side was in many ways more important than the purely sales aspect of the problem.

About a year after I joined AEC, Thorneycroft at Basingstoke came on the market. It had a good factory and moreover its range of vehicles supplemented to a small extent that of AEC. Thorneycroft had been losing a lot of money, and Bill Black knew that the company could be bought. John Bowley and I went up there to look it over, and prepared a joint report. Both of us thought it was worth well over £2m, but Bill Black managed to buy it for a lot less, arguing that a loss-making company is worth very little to its owner. This was another important lesson to me— one that I was not going to forget.

At a certain point in my career at AEC I was very unhappy about the outstanding account of Guy Motors, which was in the region of £50,000. I had the idea that we might be able to insure the debt, but I was told we could only do this if we insured all our debts. This was clearly impracticable as well as wrong, and therefore I made further inquiries and found that for a worthwhile premium one could in fact insure an individual debt. I cannot remember the premium exactly but it was something like two per cent, and very shortly afterwards Guy Motors was declared bankrupt.

During this time I contracted a virus illness on a visit to Spain. I was in Madrid for a few days, and one evening, on returning to my hotel, I began to feel rather ill. Next morning I felt much worse, and this lasted for about three months after I got home. It subsequently developed into colitis, as a result of which my weight came down from about thirteen to ten and a half stone. From the moment I had that illness my whole outlook changed. First of all I lost my physical energy, and secondly I realized that I might not be able to go on earning my living at AEC for the rest of my life. The AEC job was very demanding and involved a lot of travel. Since I was now feeling quite ill for long periods at a time, it was plain that I would have to rethink my career.

During a period of convalescence in Bournemouth I decided that I would have to try and make some capital. By then I had quite a good salary together with a car, but I had very little capital of my own. My mother had inherited about £7,000 from my father, and she gave me some of this money in return for a deed of covenant I made out in her favour. This suited both of us, and the sum that she gave to me, together with my own savings, formed the nucleus of my small capital base. I wanted to expand this, as I had grave doubts whether I would be able to continue to earn a high salary in a very active job. I had to think of something extra that I could do in my spare time, and in the end I decided to try to develop and perfect a system of investment on the Stock Exchange, in which I had always had a general interest.

I have always been a great believer in what I call the Zulu principle. By this I mean that if you take a relatively narrow subject and study it closely you can become expert in it compared with other people. This is of course a truism, but a very important one, and I use Zulus to illustrate the principle as they do it very well. If you picked up the *Reader's Digest* one month and in it there was an article of, say, four pages on Zulus, after reading that article you would be one of the few people in your town who knew anything about them. If this made you quite interested in the subject, and you noticed two books about Zulus in your local library and read them, you would probably by then be the leading authority in your county on Zulus. If you had now become so interested in the subject that you read all the other books you could find about it, and even visited South Africa to do some research on the spot, you might well find yourself recognized as one of the leading authorities on Zulus in Great Britain. The important point is that Zulus are a fairly narrow subject and you would be putting a relatively disproportionate amount of effort into it. It is the same principle as using a laser beam rather than a scatter gun, and is analogous to Montgomery's excellent strategy of concentrating the attack.

I applied the Zulu principle to the Stock Exchange. Instead of tackling asset situations, which were Dohm's forte, I decided to work on earnings situations, and in particular those of small to medium-sized companies as opposed to the very large ones. Here was a narrow area of the stock market upon which to concentrate my attack. At that time the *Stock Exchange Gazette* and the *Investors Chronicle* were separate magazines. I bought two years' back issue of both and then spent a remorseless fortnight in Bournemouth steadily reading through them. In particular I looked at early share recommendations and then traced them through to see how they had actually performed. I was looking for shares which, following a bad period, had a steadily rising earnings trend. Quite often after a period of losses it would take a long time for the stock market to forgive and forget, so the rating given to these companies was not high enough in relation to their recent earnings trend. Therefore, when they came out with another set of good figures which were up by, say, 30 per cent, the share price would rise not merely 30 per cent, but more, due to the company undergoing a status change and obtaining a correspondingly higher market rating.

Clearly it was necessary to try and eliminate the 'joker' factors. I soon found that if companies had very large overdrafts and were generally illiquid they might not stay the course. I also liked to see a substantial asset backing, and wanted the shares to be widely held, as these factors gave added hope of a takeover. In addition to this cyclical companies had to be avoided. Gradually I evolved a system that would have stood up well if it had been applied in practice during the two-year period covered by my *Stock Exchange Gazettes* and *Investors Chronicles*. I was able to test this system without any cost, simply by following the fortunes of my chosen shares through the back issues.

I remember that when I was studying costing I read a book which outlined the process of management thinking. It went like this—Investigation, Observation, Inductive Thought, Experiment, Conclusion, Action. I had gone through this process thoroughly, even to the stage of experiment, without cost. My conclusion was that the system was a winner, so the next step was to find out which shares to invest in for the future. I reasoned that there could only be one best share and that I would rather invest all of my money in it than spread for the sake of spreading. A friendly broker supplied me with Exchange Telegraph cards which gave the financial details of the companies I had selected, and eventually I homed in on Bernard Wardle. I telephoned the buyer of AEC to ask him excitedly what he knew about Bernard Wardle, as it was a supplier to the motor industry. He soon reported encouragingly that they were very busy and everything looked all right. The company had experienced losses, but these had then been followed by several years of dramatically rising profits. I telephoned the company secretary of Bernard Wardle and asked him how things were going. He was not indiscreet, but nevertheless made me feel that things were going rather well. When I returned from Bournemouth I ascertained from my bank manager that I could borrow quite substantially against quoted shares, and then invested my own £2,000, together with about £8,000 of the bank's money, in Bernard Wardle. Whilst I sold some of them on their way up I also retained a large number, and they eventually increased in value many times from my original buying price. This was in a period of about three years, and was mainly due not only to Wardle's rising profits but also to the colossal status change that the company underwent.

After I had been at AEC for about two years I suggested to Bill Black that I should take a look at the purchasing side. I had made substantial economies in that area at Renu and wanted to try my hand at AEC. As the purchasing function came under John Bowley, it was a little difficult to arrange for my intervention. Fortunately, however, John also thought it would be a good idea to try it out, though he quite rightly insisted that I should do it all in close conjunction with the chief buyer. I hit upon the idea of taking just six main items of expense, which accounted for probably as much as 50 per cent of the cost of a chassis. Tyres were an obvious example and also fuel pumps. The key point was that I was out to achieve big savings and had to examine big items of expenditure critically to do this. Whilst there may be something in the philosophy of looking after the pennies and letting the pounds look after themselves, it is obviously far more productive and worth-while to make sure that the pounds are being looked after and not worry unduly about the pennies. For example, there would have been little point in my bothering whether or not the ACV group used standardized paper clips—the obvious targets were a few items of major expenditure.

After these had been identified I sent a letter to the main suppliers in question, explaining to them that we at AEC were trying to build up our export volume, which was essential not only for our own survival but also for that of the country. I stressed to certain of the suppliers how in due course their spares volume would rise with our extra chassis sales, making the point that export markets were much more competitive, so that our own prices had to be much keener. I ended up by asking them all for a special export rebate which would be related to our overall volume of export sales. I then went along to see senior executives in the various firms in question, and managed to negotiate special rebates which totalled over £50,000 per annum. This was a very worth-while contribution to AEC's profits, which were at that time in the region of £800,000 per annum. The interesting point about purchases of raw materials in the case of chassis manufacture is that they form possibly as much as 70 per cent of total costs. Since the overall profit margin on chassis is negligible, a very small percentage off the cost of purchases has a dramatic effect upon it. This was another lesson I was to remember and apply elsewhere.

ACV's profit record did improve dramatically during the time I was with AEC. While I was at Park Royal and Crossley was being closed the group's profit was £432,000; the following year it was £966,000, the year after that £1,513,000, and then it rose to £1,920,000. Over the four-year period I spent with AEC we gradually and persistently increased the level of chassis production. This was always a big decision which could go very wrong, as material had to be ordered months in advance, and plans for labour availability also had to be made early. The decision to raise chassis production was usually taken ultimately by John Bowley, but gradually it became much more of a joint decision, as he was of course very dependent upon our sales estimates before taking the plunge. When I first joined AEC we were making 55 heavy chassis per week, and this total was gradually raised to about 110 two years later.

We were always plagued by technical problems. I did not understand them, but I came to recognize the word 'gasket' as being something which was an essential part of an engine and very unreliable. We always thought our problems were peculiar to AEC, and the sales side of the business had a low opinion of our technical ability. It was only when we subsequently merged with Leyland that we realized that they had virtually identical problems, some of which they had hoped to solve by merging with us.

John Bowley was himself fairly near to retirement, being in his early sixties. He was a very tall, imposing man, and when he walked around the works he always had a friendly word for everyone. He knew by name a large number of people out of a work-force of several thousand and was admired and respected by all. It was largely due to him that excellent labour relations existed during the time he was responsible for the AEC works. John used to hold a weekly management meeting attended by about ten people. Eric Hollands, John Ford and myself were always there, together with the works manager, chief designer, chief buyer and production control manager. I was very conscious of the fact that anyone going into a management meeting, or for that matter, a board meeting, is at a great advantage if he has positively identified something that he wants to achieve in that meeting. In a typical meeting one of the people would be thinking of something he did over the weekend, one would be waiting for coffee, one would be worried about a major personal problem and another would be a person who never speaks up anyway. Any opposition that arose would usually stem from one person only, and provided one had lobbied a little support in advance it was usually remarkably easy to get a major point generally accepted. I am not condemning the AEC management meeting as such, but simply trying to explain how things really happen at management and board meetings in many companies. I recall that Professor Parkinson goes into this in some detail.

I grew very fond of Bill Black, who became a kind of father-figure to me. He was affectionately regarded by everyone and was a very popular man in the motor industry. He had an excellent principle which has always stuck in my mind—it was that one should be 'firm in decision and considerate in execution'. A good illustration of this was his approach to difficult cases of redundancy. At this time the law relating to redundancy was not very advanced, and did not protect employees sufficiently. Bill Black's thinking was well ahead of his time. If he had to deal with the problem of an executive who drank too much, had family problems, and was simply not up to the job, Bill Black would be 'firm in decision', insisting that the man be removed from his position. He would, however, also be 'considerate in execution': the man would be allowed plenty of time to find another job within his existing one, and then, when he left, would be given compensation which was generous by any standards. Bill Black's view on redundancy made a great impression upon me and years later, when faced with difficult human problems of this nature, I always tried to approach them in his way.

He had another equally apt maxim which was to 'back or sack' his executives. In practice it was almost always a case of backing them, but his strength was that he did this full-bloodedly. You always felt that he was a hundred per cent behind you. On one occasion I went to see him to suggest a solution to a difficult problem. He replied, 'Are you asking me or telling me? If you are asking me, there are a number of people I will have to consult; if you are telling me—get on with it!' On another occasion I asked him about quite a knife-edged decision within my responsibilities, and after I had explained the background in detail, he said, 'Very interesting and very difficult—let me know what you decide to do.'

Bill Black had a lot of friends and he believed in making sure that there could be no misunderstanding when doing business with them. He told an amusing tale of how a coal merchant in Barrow gave him similar advice when he was about to leave his home town. The coal merchant illustrated his point by saying, 'Bill, because I am your friend I sell you your coal at nineteen shillings a ton, which is a shilling less than to anyone else. Also, because you are my friend, when we deliver to your house my man only gives you nineteen hundredweight to the ton.' When doing business with friends it clearly pays to have a firm, detailed, and preferably written, understanding, as otherwise it is only too easy to fall out over some relatively minor point and lose a friend as well as the deal.

During this time I also gradually got to know Lord Brabazon who was then in his late seventies. He was about six feet three inches tall, with an imposing, patrician face. He was a quite extraordinary man in many ways. He could make a brilliant speech, and had been successful in politics as well as business. During the war he had been Minister of Aviation and also Parliamentary Secretary to Churchill. His great belief was that everyone should have 'many outposts' in their life, by which he meant many different interests, so that if one particular 'outpost' collapsed there were others to fall back on. He had, for example, been the first Englishman to obtain a flying licence in this country, had become a scratch golfer within three months of taking up golf, and was a champion on the Cresta run. He was very keen on sailing and also had an elaborate 'O' gauge model railway, which took up the whole of the floor in one of the rooms of his flat. I used to see him mainly at the monthly ACV board meeting, which was followed by lunch at his flat. I found him fascinating company. He liked young people, had a very active mind and often used to ask me to sit next to him. I was reading a lot of biographies at the time, and was interested to talk to someone who knew such legendary figures as F.E. Smith and Winston Churchill. I remember asking what impressed him most about Winston Churchill: he thought for a while before replying that it was his power of rhetoric. He then went on to relate how on one occasion he had been in Churchill's room at the House of Commons after lunch, when Churchill was waxing eloquent on the subject of a storm at sea. He said that Churchill's great voice described the pitching and rolling of the ship and the enormous waves that were beating against it. Then, turning to me, he added disarmingly, 'Do you know, Slater, that within ten minutes I felt seasick!'

Lord Brabazon had a keen sense of humour and an excellent memory. I remember him once suddenly asking me, 'Slater, do you bath?' I replied, 'Frequently, my Lord.' Nothing more was said for a few months, but at Christmas he sent me a very large sponge as a present. On one occasion when we were visiting Thorneycroft with Bill Black and John Bowley, Lord Brabazon asked me to lunch to advise him on shares. I recommended Bernard Wardle to him. To my surprise he immediately said that he was going to buy a thousand pounds' worth, but added, 'If they go down—as much as a halfpenny—you are out!' As I have explained they went up, so I remained in.

· FOUR ·

The Leyland Years

THE success of AEC in developing its export sales, particularly in South Africa, together with its improved performance in home markets, was beginning to register with Leyland. It had recently taken over Standard Triumph, which was in a terrible mess. Sir Henry Spurrier had put his top production man, Stanley Markland, into the Standard works, which was a great loss for Leyland itself. In addition Donald Stokes, the sales director of Leyland, was now also responsible for Standard Triumph car sales, which was inevitably taking up a lot of his time and energy. At the same time AEC's improved performance across the board was really beginning to hurt them.

In many ways Bill Black had really done the job he set out to do and put ACV right. However, Lord Brabazon was in his seventies and Bill Black was in his late sixties, so there was a problem of continuity of top management at ACV. If the group had remained a separate entity I think that John Bowley would have been given the top job, and I would have become his deputy, with a strong possibility of succeeding him when he retired. But this was never to be, as Lord Brabazon and Bill Black, Sir Henry Spurrier and Donald Stokes got together for dinner one day in mid-1962, and rapidly arranged a merger. It was done on a very informal basis, and professional advisers were only brought in at the last moment. The idea was that Lord Brabazon, Bill Black and Lewis Whyte would join the Leyland Motors board, and Sir Henry Spurrier, Donald Stokes and Stanley Markland would all join the ACV board. ACV would become a wholly-owned subsidiary of Leyland Motors and be dominated by it, and the two main operating companies, AEC and Leyland, would gradually be integrated. I was offered from the beginning the job of commercial manager of the whole Leyland group, reporting to Donald Stokes, whom I had only met briefly once or twice before. We had a get-together at

AEC, and a few days later he took me out to lunch from Berkeley Square. I liked him and knew that I could work for him. I was to be responsible for the same sort of thing within the Leyland group as I had been at AEC, but in addition to this I would have special responsibility for liaison with AEC. In a sense I had left my colleagues at AEC behind me, as I was the only one who was being promoted into the new group.

Shortly afterwards, and quite unexpectedly, Sir Henry Spurrier had a bad heart attack. Bill Black had become deputy chairman as a result of the takeover, and to everyone's surprise, including, I think, his own, he then became chairman of the Leyland group. There had always been internal rivalry between Markland and Stokes, which was to some extent natural, as there is usually rivalry within a company between production and sales. Both men were very strong characters, and either would have welcomed the position of managing director of the group. In the event it was given to Donald Stokes, and as a result Stanley Markland left to join Guest Keen & Nettlefold. I had great admiration for Markland, and I think everyone in the company thought that his leaving would be a sad loss to the group as a whole. His position at Standard Triumph was taken over by George Turnbull, who after this reported to Donald Stokes.

I moved up to Leyland's offices at Berkeley Square, where I was given a pleasant, spacious office on the sixth floor, directly opposite to that of Donald Stokes. Adjoining my office there was another quite sizeable one with space for two secretaries, one of whom was to work for me and the other for Ron Ellis, who was sales manager of Leyland Motors. He had been a star apprentice at Leyland, and was a very able man, particularly on the technical side; he and I were to be rivals for the next few months.

One of the main problems I was first asked to deal with was that of South Africa. Leyland, as I have explained, had a vast organization there, with depots throughout the country. Jack Plane was on the *Windsor Castle* coming over by sea on his honeymoon, when he heard the news that Leyland had taken over AEC. I remember that when he arrived he said that he felt a great sense of loss as he had enjoyed hating Leyland and fighting them. Jack was the natural choice for the top man in South Africa, and the obvious man to supervise the complete integration of the group's activities there. In South Africa in particular, the need to manufacture to a greater extent locally was becoming more apparent, and to do this it would be both necessary and desirable to bring in local partners. After several meetings in London I went out to South Africa and helped to arrange for a merger of Jack Plane's company there with that of Leyland. J.H. Plane

(Africa) took over the whole of the assets, and the new quoted company was renamed the Leyland Motor Corporation of South Africa Ltd. This was a very big deal by any standards, and we had to work very closely with local professional advisers. It was invaluable experience for me, since it embraced stock exchange and corporate finance problems as well as the more mundane commercial ones. The whole thing went through smoothly and everyone was very pleased with the result.

I was subsequently sent by Donald Stokes to the Argentine. Both AEC and Leyland had distributors there, and the sons of the Leyland distributor were anxious to start up their own separate business. It was a complicated set-up, but I managed to work out a compromise with those concerned which seemed to work reasonably well. Unfortunately during this time my illness persisted. The virus which had originally caused it in Spain had long since gone, but it had left me with a weakness which, as I have said, developed into colitis. This in turn had really become psychosomatic, and I was becoming a hypochondriac. I was very underweight as a result of the colitis, and I had much less energy than I had been blessed with previously. This cut down my social life very considerably, and it was not a particularly happy period for me.

I was still fascinated by the Stock Exchange, and I had become interested in quite a number of shares besides Bernard Wardle; I had evolved a system of investment of which I was very proud. The market was in quite a bullish phase, and in retrospect this obviously helped. I was only too happy to share my good fortune with friends, so when Jack Plane asked me whether I would give him some investment advice I was pleased to do so. I formed a small investment club within Leyland for the executives there, and I was also giving advice to Donald Stokes, Lord Brabazon, and a number of other colleagues. At no time did I thrust my advice on people: they simply came to me knowing of my interest and success, and I freely and happily shared my ideas with them. It was like having a new toy; and it was for rather similar reasons that I wrote to Nigel Lawson, the city editor of the *Sunday Telegraph*.

I had noticed that a 'Mr Bearbull' was running a ghost portfolio in the *Stock Exchange Gazette*, and that it was not performing very well. I suggested to Nigel Lawson that the general idea of a ghost portfolio was a good one, but I argued that the performance could be dramatically better if a system of investment was used. Nigel Lawson liked my letter, and we arranged to meet to talk about it further. I made it clear from the beginning that I was an active investor, and that there would be very few shares that would fulfil the harsh criteria to comply with my system. I explained that I would therefore need to be free to invest in the same shares as the ghost portfolio, as otherwise the thirty pounds an article that they offered would be ludicrous compensation for me. He accepted this, chose for me the pseudonym of 'Capitalist', and arranged for the column to commence. He introduced the first article on 3 March 1963 with the words:

> Today we welcome a new contributor to the City Pages of the *Sunday Telegraph*—'Capitalist'. This is the pseudonym of a director of a number of well-known industrial companies in Britain and overseas who, in his spare time, has developed a highly successful new approach to investment. In this first article he explains his methods and selects the first three shares for his portfolio. In subsequent articles he will add further shares to the portfolio and review its progress to date.

I explained in the article that I was looking for shares with an above-average earnings yield (the equivalent today would be a below-average price-earnings ratio) coupled with above-average growth prospects, and I outlined nine important investment criteria. It is interesting to look back on them, and I quote directly from the article:

1. The dividend yield must be at least 4 per cent.
2. Equity earnings must have increased in at least four out of the last five years.
3. Equity earnings must have at least doubled over the last four years.
4. The latest Chairman's statement must be optimistic.
5. The company must be in a reasonable liquid position.
6. The company must not be vulnerable to exceptional factors.
7. The shares must have a reasonable asset value.
8. The company should not be family controlled.
9. The shares should have votes.

The column attracted a great following although I only wrote an article once a month. It ran for about two years, and I stopped doing it about a year after I left Leyland, by which time investment advice had become a business to me. The 'Capitalist' portfolio did appreciate in value by 68.9 per cent against a market average of only 3.6 per cent during the same period.

The standards observed by people giving investment advice to others, and by journalists writing about shares, have changed in recent years. This is a necessary and highly desirable process. Looking back on it, it is obvious

that there could be conflict of interest if anyone advises others on shares
and buys some of them himself. Similarly it is clear that there could be a
conflict of interest if someone buys some shares and recommends them in
a newspaper. But at that time Stock Exchange investment was relatively·
new to me, and I had evolved what I thought was a particularly attractive
and unique system, which I wanted to share with my friends, and others
who were interested. Looking at it with hindsight, and with consciousness
of today's different standards, I can see how it could be open to a different
interpretation.

My own investments were progressing exceptionally well, and I used to
work out my position every month. My original capital of £2,000 had
increased to about £50,000 before I left Leyland. It has to be realized that
for most of this three-year period there was no capital gains tax, which
changed the whole concept of investment. I also had the benefit of the loan
from my bank, which did of course improve the performance of my
portfolio.

At Leyland, meanwhile, I was beginning to help Donald Stokes on a
more general basis. Each morning he would give me different jobs to do,
which usually arose from his own voluminous post, and I was also responsible for liaison with AEC. There was definite rivalry between Ron Ellis
and myself, and a certain amount of overlap between his job and my own.
The logical answer was for Donald Stokes to select one of us to become
deputy sales director. Bill Black and I had discussed the problem over
lunch a month or so before Donald raised the subject with me. The discussion with Bill had been left on the note that if the opportunity arose he
would have a word with Donald about it, but that it would of course be
very much a personal decision for Donald to make one way or the other.
I was of course delighted when Donald Stokes said to me one day in early
1963 that he wanted to resolve the problem and to appoint me as his
deputy. Donald immediately said that he would go and get Bill Black's
agreement, and left Berkeley House a few minutes later to see Bill, who
was just across the road in ACV's old premises at 49 Berkeley Square. I suddenly had the horrible thought that before Donald could say anything,
Bill Black might remember the vague conversation we had had together
and suggest the idea to Donald. That would have been highly counter-
productive, so I quickly telephoned Bill to warn him that Donald Stokes
was coming over to see him, and was in favour of the idea that I had suggested during our lunch a month ago. He had always told me that I had a
habit of over-stressing a point, even when I had made it very thoroughly

and the other person had accepted my argument. At such times, he said, to save me going on he would simply hold the lobe of his ear between his fingers, and this signal would save both of us a lot of nervous energy. On this occasion, as I was about to put down the telephone, he said to me, 'Jim, I am holding my ear.'

When Donald Stokes returned he called me into his office and told me that I was to become deputy sales director. As he was managing director of the group, as well as sales director, my position as his deputy was rather stronger than if he had not had these extra responsibilities. When he was away abroad I would take his place as far as I could, and on some occasions this involved duties of a rather broader nature than sales alone. Donald Stokes was an amazingly energetic and dedicated man, whose entire business life had been concentrated on building up Leyland and in particular its sales. He had been an apprentice there, and had great admiration for Sir Henry Spurrier and everything that was Leyland. Donald had almost incandescent charm of manner, which he could switch on when necessary with important visitors; he was extremely hard-working, commercially astute, and also knowledgeable technically, knowing the business from A to z. If Leyland Motors had continued on its own simply as a commercial vehicle group, I think that it would still be a very powerful and profitable company today. It was the diversification into the motor industry, and in particular into BMC, that spread Donald too thinly, giving him a job that would have been beyond most people. In 1963, when I was made deputy to Donald Stokes, he was thought by the media to be Mr Industry: when there was to be a television programme with a prominent industrialist on it, he was the natural choice; when anyone was eulogized for export services, he was the man. Later on, after the BMC merger, he became much less popular with the media, who began to criticize him for not putting BMC right, and for the relatively poor performance of the Leyland group as a result. Here was a dedicated man working his heart out for a business he loved and knew. It was very sad to see how public opinion could be influenced so quickly to forget all his good qualities.

It was at about this time that I had an extraordinary experience. I had taken my mother down to a hotel in Hove for a few days, so that she could recuperate from an accident in which she had been knocked down by a motor-scooter. There was not much to do, so I decided one morning that I would investigate the fortune-telling business. I set off down the front towards Brighton, and came across my first fortune-teller. He did not impress me, and I cannot remember anything he said, except that near the end of the session he told me I should avoid games of chance because I was unlucky. His charge was ten shillings, and as I only had pound notes with me and he did not have sufficient change I suggested that we should test the strength of his powers and toss up double or nothing. He agreed and I won!

Feeling that there was very little in the fortune-telling business, I continued on my way down the sea-front. Soon I arrived at the Aquarium in Brighton, and noticed that just outside there was a small hut advertising the fortune-telling services of a Madame Holden. I decided to give it another try. Madame Holden first asked whether I wanted a full reading with the crystal, which would cost five pounds, or just a hand reading. I thought I would go the whole hog and opted for the full treatment.

I was immediately electrified when she began to talk to me. She held one hand and looked into the crystal. Her first words were: 'You are an accountant, but you do not work as an accountant.' She went on to say that my father was dead, but that she could see him clearly. She described him as a tall, dark-haired man smoking a pipe. He had indeed been tall, dark and rarely without a pipe. She said I had been unwell, but that there was nothing to worry about as it was all in my mind. I would leave my present position and as a result become very well known and make a great deal of money. When I asked how much money she said, 'Many, many notes.' Then came the most extraordinary part: she said that I was not married, but that I would meet 'a tall, slim girl on the secretarial side'. We would 'meet, and part, and come together again', and would be married within the next two years. She said that my mother had just had an accident and must be very careful when looking down. At that time my mother had double vision *only* when she looked down, and this lasted for three months after the accident. The only thing Madame Holden got wrong was when she told me about children, for she said we would have only one. We did in fact have four, but I shall always remember the chill of fear I felt when my wife fell over during her second pregnancy. As far as the 'many, many notes' were concerned Madame Holden could not have looked beyond the age of forty-five.

After this I felt that I had investigated the fortune-telling business sufficiently for that day, or indeed for any other day. I returned to the hotel and recounted the experience to my mother. When I told her that the fortune-teller's name was Madame Holden she was not surprised. She had had a very similar experience about eight years earlier in Eastbourne, when on holiday with my father. They became very friendly with another couple who were staying at the same hotel; the two men used to play golf each day, and my mother spent quite a lot of time with the woman, who was a sister in a hospital. One morning the two women went to have their fortunes told by Madame Holden, who was at that time in Eastbourne. The other woman went in first, and was surprised to be told among other things that she was a sister in a hospital but would never become a matron because there was too much jealousy. When my mother's turn came Madame Holden told her that she was surrounded by cancer. At that time my father was gradually dying of cancer and had, in his case wisely, not been told about it. Madame Holden told all this to my mother, and confirmed that it would be much better not to tell him. She then went on to say that he would die that winter. He did in fact die on 17 December that year.

I realize that a large number of readers will find it hard to credit this story. I have told how I won money from the first fortune-teller to make it clear that I was very sceptical myself when I went to see Madame Holden. Since then, however, I have experienced, and been directly concerned with others who have experienced, many extraordinary happenings of this kind. I now believe that there are a very few people who do have gifts of an extra-sensory nature, which add another dimension to their perception of the world.

It was about six months before I left Leyland that I took on a new secretary named Helen Goodwyn. There were quite a number of applicants, but as she came into the room for interview I realized that I had met just the type of girl I wanted to marry. I remember that when John Ford first saw her he came in to say that he thought she was a great addition to the outer office. I asked him to lay off as I had plans for her myself. She knew nothing of this, and we did not in fact go out with each other until I left Leyland.

By late 1963 I was worth in the region of £50,000 and my salary was £5,600 per annum, together with a car. While I was going out to South Africa on the *Windsor Castle* with Donald Stokes and his wife, I talked to Donald about the future. My illness was a major factor in my mind as it was very enervating, and I felt there must be easier ways of earning a living, especially as I was having such success on the Stock Exchange. Donald told me that if I remained with the company I would become financial director at a salary of £10,000 per annum together with a car, and that I would be eligible to join the directors' profit-sharing scheme. He also pointed out that Bill Black was nearing retirement, that he himself was fifty-five and that for me—at thirty-five by far the youngest man on the board—the prospects were obvious. It was a very exciting concept, and had it not been for my conviction that I was not well enough to tackle the job on a long-term basis I would undoubtedly have accepted it. In the event, however, I decided to resign and gave six months' notice from the end of October 1963.

I had been thinking that I would set up an investment advisory business. I had already bought my house at Esher, which I did very impulsively one day when I thought that it would be much nicer to have a house with a garden, lots of trees and a dog, instead of my flat at Ealing. I looked around on the outskirts of London, and found that Esher was quite near to comparatively unspoilt countryside, yet well placed for commuting to town. I telephoned an estate agent there, who showed me first one house which I did not like and then my present house, High Beeches, which I liked immediately. It was built in the mid-thirties, and has a three-acre garden with some beautiful beech trees. On one side is Claremont Gardens, which is owned by the National Trust, and on the other Esher Common. I asked my mother to come and look at it, and I remember being rather upset when, as she went round, she complimented the lady who was selling on each and every room, the condition of the house and the general attractiveness of it. Suffice it to say that I bought it very quickly afterwards, and I have never had cause to regret that decision.

In September 1963 I first met Peter Walker, who was at that time shadow Minister of Transport. We had both been featured in a series of articles in the *Evening News* entitled 'The Under Forties'. Peter had formed a dining club of those who were featured in the articles, and I met him as a result. He subsequently asked me to dine with him at his house at Walton-on-Thames, which was a few minutes away from my house in Esher. I well remember how during the dinner, when I complimented him upon the wine, he immediately turned to his personal assistant who was dining with us and said, 'Tim, make a note to send a case of this wine to Mr Slater in the morning!' I thought this was a wonderful gesture, but it was only when I received the invoice a week later that I realized that perhaps I had found a potential commercial partner.

PART TWO

FIVE

Choosing Partners

BEFORE I begin the Slater Walker story, it might be helpful to give my own assessment of the thirty-five-year-old accountant who was leaving such a good position at Leyland to try to set up on his own. It is worth making an evaluation at this point, because in the subsequent seven years an obscure £1.5m company named H. Lotery & Co. Ltd was developed and expanded by me to a stage when its market capitalization was in excess of £200m.

My illness, both imagined and real, continued to plague me and this meant that I did not have a great deal of surplus energy. In a sense my ambitions were limited by my physical problem. I was also still very shy as far as public meetings of any kind were concerned. I could definitely 'sell' when dealing with one person or a small group of people but the thought of speaking to a crowd of any kind terrified me.

I had gained invaluable industrial experience with the Dohm group and subsequently with Park Royal, Crossley, AEC and Leyland. In all cases I had obtained a bird's-eye view of the whole business and I was used to the buck stopping with me. I had little or no knowledge of the technical and manufacturing side of business, nor was I particularly interested in acquiring it. This has always been a blank spot of mine but it did not seem to impede me as I always tried to approach business problems from a common-sense point of view, backed up by my accountancy knowledge and growing financial, sales and commercial expertise.

Whilst I had little or no knowledge of stock exchange practice and procedures—nor for that matter of merchant banking—I had acquired a good knowledge of fundamental investment analysis and had built up a small capital stake of about £50,000 through stock exchange investment.

It was shortly after I decided to leave Leyland that an amazing thing happened to me, which began to change my whole outlook on life. I had been seeing various specialists, including on one occasion the late Lord Evans, all of whom were trying to help me deal with my colitis and allied problems. One of them referred me to a Miss Ilona Ghero, who described herself as a specialist in medical relaxation. I was advised that she specialized in illnesses that were mainly psychosomatic, and it was felt that I would have nothing to lose by seeing her and maybe something to gain. I went to see Miss Ghero, and within a few weeks I was as good as cured. She had also taught me some techniques for both sleeping and relaxing which I was to find invaluable in the years ahead.

Ilona Ghero, who unfortunately died in 1975, made such an impact on my life that I would like to tell you a little more about her teachings. Her basic philosophy was that all of us cannot help instinctively responding to our environment. If, for example, we are working in the vicinity of a road drill, it is much more upsetting than being near the sound of sweet music; the noise someone makes by scraping a saucepan with his fingernails is unpleasant in contrast to the gentle lapping of the sea on a calm day. These noises cause us to react automatically whether we want to or not. Equally, we cannot help reacting to the things we see or imagine. If we look at a man with a large, fat, happy, smiling face we find ourselves smiling with him. In contrast, if we look at a man with a narrow, pinched face and a nervous twitch, we almost pick up the twitch. The aim, therefore, is to control our thoughts and direct them towards things that inspire a positive and pleasant reaction in our own bodies. In my case, I was so conscious of my physical problems that I was 'watching myself' all the time, to see if there was any improvement or set-back. I was not giving myself a chance to relax and get well naturally.

Ilona Ghero gradually taught me how to control my thoughts when I wanted to relax completely. The technique is to lie on your back with a pillow under the legs and none under the head, and with arms at sides. The mind is then concentrated upon a series of imaginary patterns which induce a progressively more relaxing reaction in one's body. A state of complete relaxation can be induced in this way in as short a period as ten minutes. It is particularly beneficial just before going to sleep, and I am sure that the quality of the sleep is greatly enhanced by it. As a result, I began to manage regularly on at least two hours less sleep than in the past, and I now awake feeling much fresher in the morning.

Another good time to use Ilona Ghero's method of relaxing is after a hard day's work, before going out in the evening. Within ten minutes of deep relaxation I found that I could completely recharge. As far as my 'illness' was concerned, it began to disappear after I perfected the relaxation techniques, and within a year I was no longer troubled in any way. My energy came flooding back, I returned to my normal weight and in every way soon felt my old self. In retrospect, the twists and turns of fate are very interesting, because I would almost certainly have stayed at Leyland if I had met Ilona Ghero a year or so earlier.

Ilona Ghero was a wonderful woman and we became good friends over the years. I recommended her to several of my friends and almost without exception she was able to achieve major improvements or complete cures for them. It is a pity that her approach has not become a more accepted part of medical practice, as it is generally recognized that a very large proportion of illnesses are psychosomatic in nature.

At the beginning of 1964, three months before I left Leyland, I began to look for a very small public company in which control might be available. I was intending to put my lay investment advisory service on to a commercial basis. Together with share dealing profits, I estimated that I could have a very sizeable annual income, and I was naturally anxious to avoid paying most of it away in surtax. If I could buy control of a small public company, I planned to inject my investment business into it. By doing this I would 'lose' the income, but instead I would have a substantial shareholding in a company which would have the benefit of it. Provided the company was small enough to start with, the extra income would increase profits dramatically, and I would benefit in capital terms through my shareholding. In short, it was a way of converting excess income into capital.

I did not know how to go about buying control of a public company. The firm of stockbrokers who were dealing with my investment business used to issue a small monthly booklet containing details of the various companies quoted on the London Stock Exchange. I started searching through their booklet, identifying small and therefore promising companies, which I subsequently checked out in more detail with Exchange Telegraph cards. I eventually came across a tiny company named Productofoam Holdings Ltd which was in the textile laminating business. The chairman was a man named A.E. Cheshire, who had an office in nearby Mount Street, and must have been surprised to get my telephone call out of the blue. If I had realized at the time the problems he was having with Productofoam, I would have understood a little better the welcome I received.

Freddie Cheshire was a financier who had experienced many ups and downs. He was a slightly built, shortish man with greying dark hair, and he had a partner, Bertie Hardman, who shared his offices with him. Freddie was a dealer *par excellence* and had many imaginative ideas, one of which was a quoted loan stock with the interest rate geared to the cost of living index; I do not think he would have had the same enthusiasm for this particular concept if he had known what was going to happen to the cost of living in the years ahead. One of his better ideas was an investment trust which he called 'Assets at a Discount'. Like Dohm, he was keen on asset situations, and this helped to point me further in that direction.

Cheshire's companies had a substantial shareholding in Productofoam, and over the lunch we had together he was excited about the prospect of our doing a deal. My plans were to inject my investment advisory business into Productofoam, which would in turn form an investment dealing company, in the hope that these steps would help to increase dramatically its minuscule profits. The other half of the plan was for Productofoam to buy in the other half of Sebec Laminations, which was its main profit-earning subsidiary. If all of these plans materialized Productofoam would be completely transformed, to the great benefit of its shareholders—one of whom I planned to be.

I had been in touch again with Ken Meyer, who had moved from Feslente to a public company associated with it in Birmingham. He agreed to join me to look after the technical side. The idea was that when Productofoam bought in the other half of Sebec, Ken Meyer and I would buy a large proportion of the shares Productofoam issued to do this. This would provide us both with our initial stake in Productcfoam.

In early February 1964, about two months before I left Leyland, Productofoam announced that it was buying the other half of Sebec and issuing 500,000 shares as purchase consideration. A small merchant bank placed the 500,000 shares and I purchased 200,000 of them, and Ken Meyer together with his mother purchased a further 100,000. Freddie Cheshire introduced me to Eric Knight of Lombard Banking, who were prepared to lend me the finance to fund the purchase of my 200,000 Productofoam shares at five shillings each. This £50,000 outlay was big money to me, and meant that I was now highly motivated to ensure that Productofoam succeeded.

I left Leyland on 30 April 1964, leaving both Bill Black and Donald Stokes on the most amicable terms, and moved into offices consisting of two small rooms in Mount Street, which were part of the suite occupied by Freddie Cheshire. It was at this time that I began to attract publicity and, on 26 April, I received a telephone call from a reporter working for the *Daily Express* 'Under the Clock' column. He asked me about my plans, and I gave him some details of the proposed expansion of my investment advisory business. He then asked me amongst other things how tall I was, and I let him know I was 6ft 3in. The next day I was horrified to see the column headline, 'Big Jim Sets Up In The City', followed by the words: 'He is thirty-five years old. Jim Slater, known to his friends as "Big Jim"—attributed to his 6ft 3in height. . . .' The reporter had a vivid imagination, and as a result for many years afterwards I kept coming across articles referring to me as 'Big Jim'. This incident made me very careful in my future dealings with the press, particularly when there was a risk of being quoted in any way. The danger is well illustrated by the story of the archbishop who went to New York for the first time. He was asked by reporters the reason for his visit and said that he had come to discuss some theological problems with their clergy. He was then asked whether he would be visiting any nightclubs to which he replied, 'Are there any nightclubs?' He was surprised by the headline the next morning which read: 'Visiting Archbishop's First Question—Are There Any Nightclubs?'

In June 1964 there was a disastrous fire at Sebec, the main profit-earning subsidiary of Productofoam. I learned afterwards that laminating had a very high fire risk, and it subsequently became progressively more difficult to insure against it. There had been several other fires in the industry, and insurance premiums were escalating rapidly. At a later stage we had to syndicate the fire insurance on Productofoam over a very large number of insurance companies, as, quite rightly, no one company was prepared to take all the risk.

The fires were a major set-back, but we were fully insured for loss of profits as well as actual physical damage. I therefore sailed on, and on 1 July 1964 Ken Meyer and I joined the Productofoam board. Ron Brand, who was articled with me at Croydon & King, also joined the board, and was made responsible for Latex. I had by now, with the agreement of all concerned, abandoned my idea of injecting my investment advisory business into Productofoam. On reflection it was a very unsuitable vehicle for this purpose, and I began to look instead for a more purely financial public company.

By that time my relationship with Peter Walker had matured. I very much liked his sense of humour, quick mind and boundless energy, and we had become good friends. We had dined with each other on several occasions and had found that we had a common interest in the idea of setting up a financial services company, which might one day become a merchant bank. Peter's own insurance broking company was quite small at that stage but growing fast, and we thought that later on there might be scope for merging our business activities. It was agreed that if I did find a suitable vehicle Peter would join me as a non-executive director, and that we would change the name to Slater Walker.

Cheshire was on the board of several other public companies, one of which was called Hawkins Developments Ltd. This building company owned the key 48 per cent shareholding, and thereby had effective control of another public company, H. Lotery & Co. Ltd, which had in the past made uniforms. It had become a property company, and 95 per cent of its assets were in one main long-leasehold property called Beaufort House, which was let to P & O. In May 1964 I suggested to Cheshire that I should buy the key shareholding in H. Lotery, and that I would try and form a syndicate for this purpose. I would then inject my investment advisory business into it, and obtain a substantial mortgage on the Beaufort House property with a view to investing the proceeds in the stock market. The dealer in Freddie Cheshire responded immediately to this plan, and he went off to negotiate with the board of Hawkins Developments.

Hawkins Developments' shareholding in Lotery totalled 1,442,415 shares, and I planned to purchase as many as possible of them personally. I went along to see Lombard Banking again and this time met Iain Macleod who was a non-executive director. I found him a most interesting man. I have always admired his philosophy of the 'encouragement of excellence', and at home I still have the record of his speech on this subject. I remember that I was slightly disconcerted at our meeting, because he carried a small pocket radio and seemed to be rather more interested in the test match than in my proposals. However all was well as Lombard were prepared to lend me a further substantial sum, and they also came into the syndicate with a direct investment. Through Peter Walker's introduction Lazards also participated, together with a number of other friends and associates. When the deal was announced, on 16 July 1964, I purchased 700,000 shares personally at ten shillings each, Peter Walker and his close friends purchased 100,000 and the balance was taken up by Lombard, Lazards, Cheshire interests, and friends and associates. The announcement was reported in a small paragraph in the *Financial Times*, which attracted very little attention. It was on 27 July 1964 that I became chairman of Lotery, Peter Walker became deputy chairman, and Ken

Meyer became a director. We also confirmed that it was our intention to change the name of the company to Slater, Walker & Co. Ltd.

My investment advisory business was doing quite well, growing by recommendation and, to a lesser extent, through the publicity I had been given. I was still working from Cheshire's offices in Mount Street, and by now had a staff of three in addition to my secretary. The first man to join me was Bryan Quinton, a qualified thirty-year-old accountant, who had made a hobby of investment analysis, and had written for the *Investors Chronicle*. A few months afterwards he was joined by another young accountant, Simon Pendock, who had previously worked at Minster Trust. He in turn subsequently persuaded Eric Farrell, also from Minster, to join us. Together they brought a better knowledge and understanding of the administrative procedure necessary on the investment side. In particular Eric Farrell was very well versed in dealing with stockbrokers, and Stock Exchange practice and procedures. Later in the year I gave my investment advisory business to Slater Walker in accordance with my original plan.

I soon decided that the Mount Street premises were not large enough, and began to look for something bigger and better. Through Peter Walker's connection with Rodwell, I eventually found a delightful office at 8 Hertford Street, less than half a mile away and quite close to Berkeley Square. I gave Simon Pendock the job of ensuring that it would be ready for occupation by early January 1965. In the meantime we struggled on at Mount Street, which was beginning to get very overcrowded.

I mentioned earlier that while at Leyland I had a secretary named Helen Goodwyn. She was the 'tall, slim girl on the secretarial side' forecast by Madame Holden. After I left Leyland at the end of April I invited her out to dinner, and we went out together three or four times after that, but for some reason we did not seem to click at that time and in June gradually drifted apart again. She found a new job working for a quantity surveyor, and I had a new secretary who was a pleasant girl, but not quick enough at shorthand and typing. I have always been very fast at dictation, and ideally need someone who can comfortably take shorthand at 140 words a minute. That September I was walking from Mount Street to the Ritz Hotel when I met Helen unexpectedly. While we were exchanging news she told me that her work was boring, and in turn I told her that my present secretary was finding the job too much for her. The result was that we agreed to have lunch together a week or so later, when we arranged for Helen to rejoin me as my secretary on 1 January 1965.

In the meantime, in late August 1964, I obtained a mortgage on the Beaufort House property of £850,000 from the Prudential which had an interest rate of $6\frac{7}{8}$ per cent per annum. Those were the days! We announced that we would commence an investment programme with the proceeds, and at the same time a partner of Slaughter & May, and friend of Peter Walker's, named Tommy Walmsley joined our board as an additional director. Slater Walker bought further shares in Productofoam, and also bought effective control of George Wilson Gas Meters Ltd, a quoted engineering company with a factory in Coventry.

I had borrowed on two occasions from Lombard Banking, and as a result of the contact I had with its management I had become very interested in the company. I had invested clients' funds as well as Slater Walker's in Lombard, and our combined shareholding was then just over 10 per cent. There was also a further 10 per cent that might have been available from the Bernard Sunley Trust, and I was fascinated by the idea of buying it. Having worked at Leyland I had the great advantage of not being frightened by big numbers, and even at that early stage in our development my mind did not boggle at the thought of trying to obtain a very strong voice in the affairs of such a comparatively large company. My attitude was reinforced by Peter, who also thought conceptually on a bold scale, and was not easily intimidated. We both agreed that the idea was an excellent one, but we did not have the finance to tackle it completely on our own, and we needed a partner. On the introduction of Sebags, our stockbrokers, we went to see Basil Samuel, the chairman of Great Portland Estates, which was and still is a substantial property company. At the time they wanted to diversify out of property, which was an unpopular sector of the market, and had its problems. We talked about the Lombard idea with Basil Samuel, who seemed quite interested in it. After thinking it over for a week or so, however, he thought that taking over Lombard would be too big a move for us at that time and suggested that instead Great Portland Estates might take a stake directly in Slater Walker. In the meantime Eric Knight had been talking with Maxwell Joseph, who as a result made an offer for both Sunley's Lombard shares and our own at just over the market price. His offer gave Slater Walker and its clients a pleasant, if relatively small, profit on the quite substantial investment we had in Lombard, so we accepted.

The idea that Great Portland would buy directly into Slater Walker appealed to both Peter Walker and myself. A Labour Government had been elected in October 1964, and the stock market, fearing the worst, had begun to weaken significantly. My total borrowings were in the region of £400,000, which meant that my interest bill was at least £800 a week, and a relatively small percentage change in the price of Slater Walker shares could, on paper at least, wipe me out completely. This had been brought home to me by an incident a few weeks earlier, when Simon Pendock had telephoned me at my home late one Friday night. He said that Sebags, our stockbrokers, had just been in touch with him to say that the Quotations Committee of the Stock Exchange wanted to see me the following week, as they were considering suspending the quotation of Productofoam's shares. The Quotations Committee were concerned about Productofoam's share price, which had risen sharply from five shillings to over ten shillings during the previous few months, and such a rapid and substantial rise had made them feel uneasy about the position, which they felt needed explaining to shareholders. A suspension would have been a disaster for me because, even though it would have been possible to obtain a re-quotation in due course, it would in the meantime have created considerable uncertainty, not least at Lombard, with their loan to me secured against what would have been unquoted shares in Productofoam. I was in my bedroom when Simon telephoned, and I suddenly noticed that my teeth were chattering. I have always disliked central heating in a bedroom, and it was probably the cold, but this reaction was entirely in accordance with the way I felt. I knew that I had a major problem on hand.

After a worrying weekend, on Monday afternoon when the Stock Exchange had closed, I went to see the Quotations Committee, which was chaired by a very pleasant and able stockbroker named Jock Hunter. I was accompanied by Peter Walker and Tommy Walmsley, together with Sandy Gilmour and David Eastham of Sebags. There were five of us against six of them, but Tommy Walmsley was a very big man indeed, so we weighed in about even. Jock Hunter, whom I had not met before, asked me to explain the Productofoam position to him in detail. It was all very informal, and as I began to explain the Productofoam story I warmed to the theme. Within half an hour the meeting was over, and the following day we were advised by Sebags that the risk of suspension of Productofoam shares had been averted. It was, however, suggested that we should bring Productofoam shareholders up to date with a circular as soon as possible.

The fright I received from this incident impressed on me how vulnerable I was with such heavy borrowings and made me determined to reduce them as quickly as possible. In addition I felt that it would be highly

beneficial for Slater Walker to have the backing of a sizeable and prestigious property company such as Great Portland, and it would also help
to have a substantial number of Slater Walker shares held in absolutely
firm hands. I liked Basil Samuel from our first meeting and so did Peter
Walker. He is a precise, meticulous man; I felt that he would be a good
influence on the company, and that his advice would make a real contribution to our progress. We quickly struck a deal, and on 16 December 1964
it was announced that Basil would join the board of Slater Walker, and
that 400,000 existing shares in Slater Walker had been sold to Great
Portland out of the total of 3,000,000 shares in issue. A few weeks later
Great Portland bought a further 200,000 shares to bring their total
holding up to 20 per cent.

Around this time another fortunate event occurred. Much to my surprise P & O approached me, and suggested that they might buy our long
leasehold of Beaufort House. I was delighted by this prospect: we had
never really wanted the bulk of our assets locked up in one property, as
cash would be much more flexible and useful to us. The book value of
Beaufort House was £1,350,000, and I had always thought that it was
worth about that figure or at the most £1,500,000. However, P & O
were sitting tenants and would have the advantage over any other
buyer of being able to marry their lease with ours. Their first offer was
£1,750,000, to which I responded with a suggested £2,000,000; after a
few weeks we finally agreed on a price of £1,850,000, although £50,000
of this had to be paid to the Prudential in order to redeem the mortgage
granted by them only a few months earlier.

In anticipation of this sale I was already busy with a new idea, which
was to form an industrial group which Slater Walker would manage. The
total share capital would be £2.5m, of which Slater Walker would hold
£1m and the balance of £1.5m would be subscribed for by influential
city institutions. In the event the main subscribers to the share capital of the
Slater Walker Industrial Group (SWIG) were the Drayton group, Lazards,
Schroder Wagg, Lombard Banking and Great Portland Estates, together
with a number of smaller participants. I already had a relationship with
Great Portland, Lazards and Lombard, and had forged one with Schroder
Wagg and the Drayton group during the preceding months.

Schroder Wagg had been merchant banking advisers to Leyland, and I
had met one of their partners in this capacity. Through him I met others
and eventually Gordon Richardson who, as chief executive, wanted to
quiz me before they finally invested in SWIG. I remember being very im-

pressed with his mental grasp and the penetration of his questions, and I was very pleased when they finally agreed to participate. I became involved with the Drayton group through Angus Ogilvy, whom I met one morning in the suite of a mutual friend at the Savoy Hotel. The main object of the breakfast meeting was for us to be introduced to each other and, after we were, our host found it difficult to get a word in edgeways. We had similar views on investment and were on very much the same wavelength from the start. Angus was at that time one of the key executives in the Drayton group, directly responsible to Harley Drayton and Sir Robert Adeane. Harley Drayton had built up his very considerable investment empire by backing hunches and investing in a relatively small number of situations in a big way. One of their investment successes at that time was Lonrho, which they had backed from the earliest stages, and Angus represented their interests on its board. Angus and I met a few times afterwards and then I met Sir Robert Adeane. I understand that Harley Drayton subsequently checked me out with Bill Black, and after that they decided to participate in SWIG and also bought a stake in Slater Walker itself. I kept in touch with Angus afterwards and through him later met Tiny Rowland of Lonrho.

The formation of SWIG was finally announced on 3 February 1965, and was very well received by both press and market, as it was thought to be quite a coup to have obtained such strong financial backing. Two months earlier I had placed my Productofoam shares to further reduce my borrowings to a more comfortable level. After that I had no direct financial interest in Productofoam but only an interest in it through Slater Walker's shareholding in SWIG, and all my eggs were in the same Slater Walker basket. Following the sale of Slater Walker shares to Great Portland, I had also placed a further considerable number of shares with leading institutions. This left me with about 300,000 Slater Walker shares, and whilst it considerably reduced my borrowings and vulnerability it also reduced my prospects of making a great financial fortune.

The last two months of 1964 had transformed the company remarkably —firstly the participation and backing of Great Portland; secondly the substantial cash flow and asset boost arising from the unexpected sale of Beaufort House, and thirdly, and most importantly, the formation of SWIG with such prestigious and influential city backing.

SIX

First Takeover Battle

O N 1 January 1965 Helen had rejoined me as my secretary. Within three weeks we had moved from Mount Street to Hertford Street, which Simon Pendock had got ready for us in very attractive style. It was a Georgian building with a great deal of character; we occupied initially only two floors with relatively few rooms, but over the years we gradually expanded until we had taken over the whole building.

It was a very enjoyable period in a business sense. For quite a long time we had a total staff of under ten people, who felt rather like the 'Magnificent Seven' because so much seemed to be happening from their efforts alone. Everyone was very busy and the office atmosphere was informal but effective. At lunchtime Bryan Quinton and I often used to play Scrabble together over a bottle of wine and some sandwiches from a nearby pub. I shall always remember his howl of anguish as I linked the word 'quaffed' with another word and laid it down over a double-word score. I quickly followed with the word 'jorum', placing the 'j' on a triple-letter score. We continued in desultory fashion with a few more words, but it signified the end of that particular game. We had a delightful telephonist called Erica, and my sixty-five-year-old chauffeur, Sam Mooney, was on reception. He was a wonderful character who had come with me from AEC, and he made a big personal contribution to keeping everyone happy. If anything needed doing in the office it was always 'Ask Sam'.

In February Helen and I began to see each other outside the office, and we were engaged by the end of April. I had already met Helen's parents at their home in Angmering-on-Sea, but we agreed that I should now go and see them more formally, and I was invited down for Sunday lunch. Her father and I went out for a drink and I broached the subject, ending on the note that I thought I could keep Helen 'in the style to which she was rapidly becoming accustomed'. He seemed very pleased about it, replying that 'You never know what girls might do nowadays'. We planned to get married on 18 September that year, and in the meantime Helen stayed on as my secretary at Hertford Street until the end of June. Not everyone at the office knew that Helen and I had been going out with each other, although my interest in her must have been apparent. We decided to have an engagement party at lunchtime on the day of the announcement, so I rang Bryan Quinton on the internal telephone to tell him that Helen Goodwyn was getting engaged and that I wanted to give a party for her and her fiancé. I could tell from his voice that he assumed that this was a major set-back for me, and that I was putting on a brave face. At the party I was very touched by the relief in his voice when he said, 'I'm so glad it's you!'

Our investment advisory business, now named Investment Analysis Ltd, continued to grow, but it was having its teething troubles. In February I had retired as 'Capitalist', and my identity had been revealed by the *Sunday Telegraph*. This had brought an influx of letters, and many of the people writing in became investment clients. We were still tending to take on portfolios that were far too small, as a result of which it was very difficult to administer the business efficiently. When we first started we managed portfolios with a minimum value of only £5,000, which was quickly raised to £10,000, then to £50,000, and eventually to £100,000. At a later stage we formed a unit trust to take over the portfolios of the smaller clients. The market had turned sour and investment management was far from easy. There are always problems when trying to deal effectively with a large volume of individual clients' funds, and Simon Pendock and his team were beginning to experience them all. Many of the clients came, telling a tale of woe, from other merchant banks, investment counsellors or stockbrokers; in some cases they were people who were compulsive wanderers and were soon on their way again to yet another adviser. Some clients would complain about bad investments whilst giving no credit for good ones, whereas others were never happy unless they were fully invested and would say that they were not paying us a fee to look after their cash.

In these difficult conditions, and because there were inevitably a few bad investments, we lost a considerable number of clients, but their numbers were more than made up by new clients, and overall the business continued to grow. In the end a hard core began to emerge and we developed a really worth-while relationship with a nucleus of clients who stayed with us through thick and thin. Unfortunately at about this time we lost the business of the Standard Triumph Pension Fund, mainly because our kind of investments were not really suitable for a pension fund. We had tended to concentrate upon the smaller, more out-of-the-way companies rather than blue chips, and we had no experience then of fixed interest stocks. The parting was an amicable one, and the management was transferred to Schroder Wagg, who were much more experienced in the handling of pension funds.

I had kept in touch with John Ford, who had become a client of Investment Analysis. At one point, when the market was in a very bearish state and he had suffered from a particularly bad buy, he sent me a cartoon showing a man hiding as an envelope was being slipped under his front

door. There was no caption on the original cartoon and the reader was simply invited to draw his own conclusion. John had written in: 'Another letter from Investment Analysis!' I have always liked cartoons that leave you to draw your own conclusions and many of my favourites are by James Thurber, the American humourist who is perhaps best known for his book *Men, Women and Dogs*.

On 1 July 1965 Investment Analysis was granted a Principal's Licence to deal in securities by the Board of Trade. This put us in the position of being able to arrange new issues and to advise and act for clients in acquisitions, mergers and other financial problems. It was a big step forward, particularly the fact that we could now advise upon acquisitions. I had become very interested in a public company named Cork Manufacturing, and I was actively considering the idea of Productofoam making a cash bid for it. The decision to bid for Cork Manufacturing was not taken lightly: Productofoam was very short of assets and needed an asset boost. Our analysts had identified Cork as a takeover prospect, when it announced that its Chingford property had been revalued at £1m. At that time Cork shares were quoted at 13s 0d in the stock market, and at the revised property value the assets worked out at 40s 0d per share. It was a classic asset situation.

The Cork board and their families held about 30 per cent of the equity. We had been investing in Cork on behalf of clients, gradually stepping up our investment programme, and by the time we were ready to make a bid we had a 25 per cent shareholding. I concluded that this was probably about the same as the total shareholding of the directors and their families, as some of the family had been selling in the market. The critical balance of 50 per cent was held by the investing public and institutions and the winner of a contested bid would be the one who could persuade more than half of them around to his view.

Malcolm Horsman, who had just joined us, had been down to Chingford to have a good look at the Cork factory premises. Malcolm was an extraordinarily dynamic and active man physically. I remember that when I used to ask him on the internal telephone to come down to my office he would appear only a few seconds later, almost like a genie from a lamp. About two months before we were married Helen had come back to the office to help for a few days and the girl with whom she shared an office had warned her to stand away from the door, as there was 'a new chap in the office who bursts in unexpectedly'. Indeed, on one occasion, in his eagerness to get to another office quickly, Malcolm hit his head on a beam and had to have several stitches in it.

As a result of Malcolm's survey we had a very clear idea of the likely value of the Cork premises and we planned to do a sale and lease-back, which would have liberated sufficient cash to fund the entire purchase consideration. We also felt that we would be able to improve Cork's general business, which consisted mainly of the manufacture of cork gaskets, seals and bottle-closures.

Our newly acquired Principal's Licence meant that we could in theory handle the bid ourselves. It was, however, very much the exception rather than the rule for a licensed dealer to handle a takeover bid, and in 99 per cent of cases the normal course would have been to approach a merchant bank, which would have the necessary expertise. However, since we had aspirations to move into banking ourselves, this seemed as good a way as any of learning the ropes. We therefore took the big decision that we would handle the bid for Cork from within, using our own licensed dealer. There was only one problem, and that was that none of us knew how to do it!

The first thing I did was to get hold of a collection of offer documents, which had been sent out by merchant banks in other bids. I made a close study of them, and in conjunction with our solicitors we drafted a letter of offer and concurrent press release ready for me to take around to Colonel Coote, the chairman of Cork Manufacturing. I telephoned him early on 12 August 1965, and arranged to see him at the Chingford factory that afternoon. On arrival I was shown into Colonel Coote's office, and within a few minutes he arrived, accompanied by his managing director and his merchant banking adviser, who was also on the board. I introduced myself, explaining that Productofoam intended to make a cash bid of 24s 0d a share, and handed him the letter of offer, which was about the ninth draft and had been most carefully prepared by us. He looked at the first page very cursorily and then tossed it in the air in the general direction of the merchant banker, who did not bother to pick it up.

The Colonel told me that the bid was most unwelcome and suggested that as he was about to go on holiday for a fortnight it might all wait until his return. I said that I was getting married on 18 September and going on honeymoon for a fortnight afterwards. As it was already 12 August, and the offer had to be with shareholders for a minimum of three weeks, there could be no possibility of postponing our plans, but we would wait a few days before posting the offer to shareholders to allow time for discussions to take place in the hope of reaching agreement. 'You mean this whole bid is geared to your honeymoon, then?' asked the Colonel. 'Yes,' I replied, 'but surely a honeymoon is more important than a holiday?' It was obvious that we were not going to agree on anything. After a short silence he stood up, declaring that there was nothing more to be said. Within ten minutes I was speeding back to London, and our first takeover battle was under way.

I decided to write a personal letter to the shareholders in Cork. As our offer was a cash one, I dealt at length with their problem of capital gains tax, and also with their problem of reinvestment, which to my knowledge had not been raised before in this type of letter. I gave examples of alternative and better investments, drawing comparisons between the prospective income from Cork, and from these other investments. My letter also pointed out that Cork's record was cyclical, and that the long-term record was very poor. Another innovation was the use of red print to highlight salient points in the accompanying circular. I was convinced that many shareholders would not bother to read a circular letter word for word, and would only look for the key points.

Hertford Street was like a battle HQ, with everyone very excited by the takeover. We wrongly decided to post our own circular letters, instead of using a professional registrar to do it. To get the first circular out to Cork shareholders, we all stayed late one night and formed a kind of chain, with everyone doing one key task and then passing the documents down the line. I had to individually address and sign all of the personal letters and as I gradually developed writer's cramp I soon resolved never to try and do that again. Ken Meyer was provided with a large sponge and his job was to stick down the envelopes, but he was far too liberal with the water and as a result great batches of the letters stuck together. It was a bit like Dad's army, but the sense of enthusiasm took some beating. Afterwards, as we waited for the responses each morning, everyone in the office wanted to know the level of acceptances, closely following the battle in every way.

I went personally to see several of the Cork institutional shareholders, and managed to persuade some of the key ones to accept our cash offer. This boosted our overall shareholding towards the end of the struggle, and it was also important to be able to argue that knowledgeable institutions had accepted in respect of their shareholdings. On 10 September we were able to announce that 60 per cent of the share capital of Cork was in our hands, and the offer became unconditional. As a matter of interest three out of every four of the shareholders, other than the board and family interests, accepted our offer, which meant that we had won the battle of minds.

The following week was a busy one. Amongst other things I met Colonel Coote and his advisers to reorganize the board of Cork Manu-facturing and to arrange for my colleagues to start more detailed investiga-tions into the affairs of Cork, so that a full report would be ready for me when I returned from honeymoon.

Helen and I were married on Saturday, 18 September 1965, at a church near her home, and the reception was held at the Beach Hotel at Little-hampton. We had about two hundred guests in all—a mixture of family, relatives, friends and the entire staff from Hertford Street. It was a very happy occasion. Peter Walker as best man made a most amusing speech, but I was still nervous of making speeches to a large number of people and felt very relieved when mine was over. Helen and I went to Corfu for our honeymoon, and on our return we moved into my house in Esher. We had thought of buying another house to make a completely fresh start together, but after looking over a few we both decided that we liked things the way they were. The house was by no means big enough for the family we had in mind, but my next-door neighbour, who was a property expert, had given me good advice—'The position of a property is more important than its condition. You can always change condition, but you can never change position.' We both liked the position and that was what mattered. As Madame Holden had forecast, Helen and I had 'met, parted and come together again'. The second time around we clicked, and have ever since.

Soon after my return from honeymoon, on 14 October, we acted for our first merchant banking client outside the group, and helped to achieve a reverse takeover of a public company named Scottish Machine Tools. A man named Harry Creighton, who several years later bought the *Spectator*, had built up two very successful private companies dealing in second-hand machine tools. He came to see me, and asked if I could help him persuade Scottish Machine Tools to take over his companies by the issue of shares. This would give him effective control of Scottish Machine Tools. I agreed to act, and when he asked me how much we would charge I suggested £1,000. He immediately said that I knew very little about the scale of merchant banking fees, as we should charge at least £5,000. We finally agreed upon this, and the deal was easily arranged after a few meetings. This was an important and very cheap lesson for me. Merchant banking fees are substantial, as there is a considerable amount of responsibility involved in preparing and sending out offer documents, and a merchant banker needs great expertise to be successful when a takeover is contested. Because I was doing it almost as an enjoyable sideline to our main business, I tended to regard any fee as a bonus, and I had not really thought it all through carefully enough. I did not make this mistake again.

On 1 November 1965 the name of Slater Walker & Co. was changed

POSITION OF THE SLATER WALKER GROUP AT 31 DECEMBER 1965

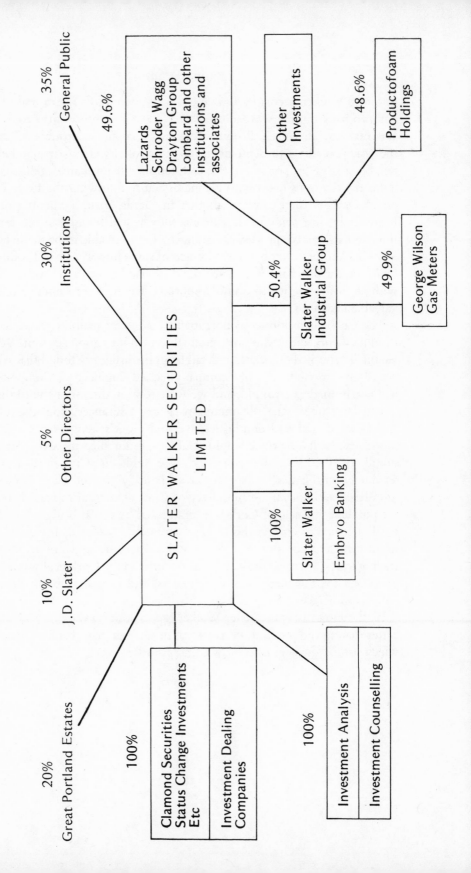

to Slater Walker Securities Ltd, and shortly afterwards the capital of the embryo banking side was increased to £500,000 to reflect the progress it was making. However, Productofoam was having its troubles. During the year preceding 30 September 1965 its profits were £107,669 before tax, but a large proportion of this had stemmed from share dealing, as the industrial divisions had been in some difficulty following the fires. Then on 17 October there was yet another fire at the main laminating plant. Fortunately, just prior to this, Productofoam had bought an old textile mill, and alternative processing arrangements were able to be made fairly quickly. Another October development of some importance to Productofoam was the purchase of Cellofoam, which had been an active competitor with licensing rights to some important patented processes and also valuable tax losses.

The Cork acquisition was potentially a move of major significance to Productofoam, and it was now essential to turn it to good account. When we finally checked out Cork in detail from the inside we found that it had been losing money. A public company named Engineering Components had nearly made a rival bid, and we were soon in discussions with them. On 14 December, after obtaining satisfactory assurances about the future treatment of staff and employees, we sold Cork's main manufacturing subsidiary, excluding the Chingford factory, to Engineering Components' subsidiary British Technical Cork. We sold the Chingford factory separately on 6 January 1966, and on 22 January we sold Flexo Plywood Industries, the other main subsidiary of Cork. The total capital profit on the purchase and sale of Cork was announced by me as being £450,000, but I later had to correct this to approximately £250,000, as we had not taken sufficient account of reorganization expenses and pre-acquisition trading losses. All in all, however, on any criteria the Cork deal was a very good one for Productofoam shareholders, and helped to boost its asset value considerably.

By the end of 1965 the Slater Walker group position was not very much better than in the previous year, except in the merchant banking field, in which it had just begun to show some promise.

SEVEN

Australian Venture

THE year 1966 started well. On 4 January Slater Walker purchased from a man named George Wiles his shares in SWIG. George, who wanted to emigrate to New Zealand, had been one of the early business associates who participated. We were pleased to buy his shares as it increased our holding to just over the magic 50 per cent level, and meant that in future we would be able to consolidate SWIG's earnings and assets.

Early in January, I was appointed a director of Walker Young & Co., which was the insurance broking business built up from scratch by Peter. Slater Walker had acquired a substantial shareholding in it, and Walker Young were handling all our insurance broking on a commercial basis. People have often asked me to describe Peter's role in Slater Walker. At this stage he was not an executive director, but he was rather more than an ordinary non-executive director. Needless to say he used to attend our board meetings, which were held every four to six weeks, and in addition he and I used to talk on the telephone for a few minutes early most mornings. I would tell him about major plans and developments, and he would give me the benefit of his advice and contacts to help wherever possible. I valued his advice, and the relationship was a pleasant and effective one.

In January we acted for a new and highly acquisitive client, Bernard Owen of British Steel Constructions, in an agreed takeover of another public company. Bernard quite soon became known as a kind of Mr Takeover because of the great string of acquisitions his companies made during the following two years. From our point of view it was very good news to have such an active client.

It was also in January, when I was interviewing executives for a job at Productofoam, that one of them mentioned to me that he had previously worked for a very profitable division of a holding company called Lloyds

73

Packing & Warehouses Ltd. I knew that the Lloyds group as a whole was not very profitable, so this encouraged me to look into it in more detail. It was in a variety of businesses such as Turtle wax, food, engineering, paper, packaging, timber, transport and travel. I had our analysts check it over, and we soon concluded that the company was a classic asset situation, with a large number of loss-making divisions as well as some highly profitable ones. Importantly, the assets were more concentrated in the loss-making companies.

Looking back on it, Slater Walker itself should have made the bid for Lloyds. However, I decided that it was a little too big for us and instead I would try to persuade someone else to take it over, sharing any resultant profits with Slater Walker. The man I had in mind was Leonard Matchan of Cope Allman, which already had packaging interests and was itself a holding company. I did not know Len Matchan, but a business contact of mine did, and he arranged for us to have lunch together at Hertford Street. When we met I simply mentioned in broad terms the possibility of doing a joint deal together. We got on well, and he was not averse to the general idea.

Leonard Matchan was an accountant who had built up Cope Allman into a successful holding company. He was a big man physically, and had an informal style of working. He owned a large Alsatian dog which was invariably with him in his nearby office, where he used to work wearing a woollen cardigan as opposed to a suit top. The dog was quite fierce, and I liked to see it well secured before I sat down and concentrated on the subject in hand. I knew Len would be difficult to negotiate a joint deal with on satisfactory terms, as he was an old hand at the game: I had to find a way of outlining the Lloyds situation without him immediately saying that he knew all about it, and that my advice was of little value. In the event I drafted an agreement between us, describing Lloyds simply as 'Company X', mentioning the extraordinarily attractive financial features of it in very broad terms only. It was outlined in the agreement that if he decided to proceed Slater Walker and Cope Allman would share any resultant profits equally. In practice this would have been a very difficult agreement to operate, as many of Lloyds' companies would have been retained by Cope Allman, and it would not have been readily possible to establish arm's-length prices for them. We therefore soon agreed that Slater Walker would act as merchant bankers only, and that the fee would be a special one of £50,000 plus all out-of-pocket expenses. For a £3m bid this was at the time a high fee, and reflected the fact that we had found the deal. As anticipated, when I told Len the name of 'Company X', he immediately said that he knew all about Lloyds; but he soon warmed to the deal and, after investigating it himself, decided to proceed.

On 11 February Cope Allman made a share-exchange offer for Lloyds. This heralded the start of a thirteen-week bid battle, which was 'like a successful West End show' as Lex of the *Financial Times* was later to reflect. Leonard Matchan and I worked well together. He had strong views, Cope Allman was his company and he called the tune. He always listened to my advice, and sometimes took it. Both of us favoured the personal letter approach, and salient points were again highlighted in colour in the bid documents. The merchant bankers on the other side were Hill Samuel, who put up a good and long fight. At a late stage there was a rival bid from AVP Industries, but Cope Allman raised its offer slightly, and AVP withdrew.

Finally, on 29 April, a further revised and final offer was sent out amounting to 36s 10½d for each Lloyds ordinary share against our original offer of 31s 0d. Hill Samuel rather grudgingly advised Lloyds shareholders that the offer for the ordinary shares 'did not adequately reflect the value having regard to the strong asset position and current level of profits'. However, in view of the 44 per cent shareholding under the control of Cope Allman they recommended ordinary shareholders to accept 'to avoid becoming minority shareholders'. The £50,000 fee was of course a very welcome and sizeable contribution towards Slater Walker's 1966 profits. It had been a bitter fight which had taught me a great deal. Now I had two hotly-contested bids under my belt, and was beginning to feel that I really knew something about takeovers.

Whilst the Lloyds bid had been going on, very little else of great moment had been able to happen within the Slater Walker group; Len Matchan had been a demanding client, and the Lloyds fight had been absorbing and time-consuming. The Slater Walker management structure was gradually being sorted out, and there were two new additions to the board announced in March: Simon Pendock, who was mainly responsible for Investment Analysis but was also helping administratively and secretarially, was a natural appointment, and the other was Herbert Despard, who had left Walker Young to join me the previous year. Herbert, who was very imaginative and could always see when a deal was possible, initially focused his activity on looking for attractive private companies which we could purchase. We always believed in paying business brokers and commission men well to ensure that the really interesting situations came our way, and Herbert Despard was their main contact at Slater Walker. In addition Dick Tarling, who had left the Leyland group and set up as an industrial consultant, was appointed to the Productofoam board in March when he rejoined me. In April Productofoam made two small acquisitions—one was effectively a small rights issue and the other was the purchase of 51 per cent of a private company named Coral Plastics. Productofoam was now very actively looking for further small private companies to take over in order to lessen its dependence upon laminating.

In July Slater Walker purchased from Adolf Rosenthal 90 per cent of the share capital of A. Rosenthal & Partners. He had been described as a one-man merchant banker, and his company had a Section 123 banking approval, which we thought would be of value to us, as it carried with it the necessary permission to lend money as a business. We increased the capital of Rosenthal & Partners to £100,000 and this was a second definite step towards our becoming bankers.

It was in late July that Slater Walker made its first contested takeover bid on its own account. I had regretted not bidding for Lloyds Packing ourselves, and had been looking for a suitable acquisition since then. Two young men, who were running a well-known unit trust management group specializing in the Australian market, had come to see me a few months earlier to draw my attention to a company named Thomas Brown & Sons Ltd. Their visit was not entirely altruistic, as their group had an 8 per cent shareholding in Thomas Brown which they wanted activated. I was a ready listener.

Thomas Brown had virtually all of its assets in Australia, and it operated principally as wholesalers of grocery, hardware and drapery. It also had interests in three small, but profitable, vaguely related companies in paper-bag manufacture, supermarkets and the manufacture of rum. The assets per share of Brown were 52s 4d at book values, whereas the market price of the shares was under 20s 0d. Brown was losing money wholesaling, but making some profit from its other interests. The net result was a profit before tax of only £90,000 in the previous year. An attractive feature of Brown from a prospective bidder's point of view was that there was a large issue of voting preference shares, which had about 30 per cent of the overall votes as they ranked *pari passu* with the ordinary shares in this respect. A relatively generous bid for voting preference shares is always difficult to resist in a situation like this, so the company was even more vulnerable to a bid than would otherwise have been the case. The other unusual feature of Brown was that the board was almost entirely made up of UK residents, whereas the business itself was entirely Australian. Since my Leyland days I had always liked Australia and felt, as I still do, that it has a great future. For all these reasons I was enormously attracted by Brown, and I asked Malcolm Horsman to fly out to Australia to investigate it on the spot.

Malcolm did some detailed research, visiting Brown's new premises at Rocklea, as well as many of its other branches throughout the country. His report made it clear that most of the premises were too lavishly built for wholesaling, which is a fine-margin operation. In addition we knew that hardly any of Brown's assets were tied up in plant and machinery; they were almost all in premises, stocks and debtors. We knew that these assets had one thing in common—they could all be turned into cash comparatively easily if the Brown wholesaling business could not be made more viable quickly.

We decided to make a bid for the company, and on 28 July offered Brown's shareholders 25s 0d per share in a mixture of shares and loan stock. We also made a generous loan stock offer for the Brown preference shares. During the preceding few months we had accumulated a large shareholding in Brown by buying in the market, and this together with the shareholding acquired from the Australian unit trust group gave us a very strong starting position. The price earnings ratio* of Brown at our offer price of 25s 0d was an astronomic 68, so there was no way the bid could be defended on a profits basis—the board of Brown, advised by Barings, had to argue on the value of the assets. Their task was a hopeless one, and only fifteen days later we sent out a revised and agreed offer of 27s 4d per ordinary share, by which time we had already bought more shares in the market to give us 29 per cent of the overall votes. I should explain here that an essential part of our tactics in an opposed bid was to buy shares in the market whenever possible. If the bid was in shares and loan stock, it was quite often possible to buy in the market for cash at the equivalent price or lower, and these purchases, taken together with our initial share stake, gave us a strong psychological, as well as practical, advantage over our opponents.

Very soon after this I asked Malcolm Horsman to fly out again to Australia, this time to investigate thoroughly Thomas Brown's business from the inside. I planned to go out a few months later, and wanted him

---

* The meaning and significance of this term to an acquisitive company is briefly explained in the appendix. In general it pays a company to issue its shares for cash or other solid assets when its price earnings ratio is far higher than the market average.

to have an action programme ready for my visit. In the meantime, in September, Slater Walker acted again for British Steel, which was successful in a bid for Tayside Floor Coverings Ltd. This was an asset situation in which Slater Walker and investment clients had built up a significant shareholding, and we had put the proposal to Bernard Owen. A few months later we again acted for his company on two further takeover bids, and, as the *Investors Chronicle* observed, he 'probably clinched the right to the title of Bidder of the Year'. Just before the Tayside bid we had decided to commission a firm of management consultants to make an independent survey of shareholders' attitudes to bids. I think we were the first firm to do this—we wanted to find out what really influenced shareholders during contested bids. The results were quite interesting.

Most shareholders felt that takeovers were good for the economy and the community at large, but that bids should be confined to companies in the same line of business as that of the bidder. There was a general preference for cash as against share offers. No more than 27 per cent of shareholders reached their conclusions on whether or not to accept a bid by relying entirely upon their own reading of the bid documents. Of the people who took advice 54 per cent consulted their stockbrokers, 26 per cent their bank managers and 20 per cent asked for the opinion of the financial press. The general press comment during the progress of a bid was also highly influential. There was a general sympathy for the possible dangers to employees in companies that were taken over, and there was also a general feeling of sympathy and shareholder loyalty towards the existing board.

I was not surprised to learn about shareholder loyalty. There is no doubt that at that time, and even more today, the man in the street's sympathies are with the incumbent board. In my view this must be wrong thinking in the case of a classic asset situation. If the assets of a company are worth significantly more than the market value, it usually means that the profits are poor in relation to those assets. This could be as a result of an unexpected or quite understandable set-back, in which case, if a bid is made, the board can explain the position and shareholder loyalty should operate to the full. Where, however, the poor profits, or in more extreme cases the losses, are more the result of mismanagement, in my view shareholder loyalty is out of place. The word 'mismanagement' is perhaps the wrong one, as often it is a case of the board not getting right the basic strategy for a business, as opposed to making mistakes in the tactics to be adopted in particular management situations. For example, in the case of Thomas

Brown, we later found that the wholesaling of grocery, hardware and drapery in Australia was simply not a viable and sensible business in which to employ capital. Many boards do not want to face up to this kind of reality.

Clearly it must be of advantage to the economy to have dead assets liberated from basically hopeless ventures, and channelled instead into other enterprises that might be more successful. It must also be to the overwhelming advantage of shareholders in the companies in question. In 1966 there was relatively full employment and therefore from a national point of view it was vital to make the best use of all of the country's existing manufacturing facilities. Indeed, at about this time the Labour Government set up the Industrial Reorganization Corporation, with a view to stimulating industrial mergers to ensure that some asset situations were rationalized by more effective management in the national interest.

The financial predator acted as a catalyst in stimulating fear within the fat and lazy managements, thereby making them more active. In some cases companies were bought by predators and then resold into stronger hands. In a sense, fear of the predator was an essential discipline for many boards, as without it they would have tended to rest upon the laurels of their predecessors.

The political climate changed as we subsequently entered a period of relative unemployment, and it was then that the term 'asset-stripping' came into use. This term tended to be used emotively when a company with large assets was taken over, and substantial redundancies were involved which in some cases were not sympathetically dealt with. Slater Walker itself always tried to deal with any redundancies in a generous way, applying Bill Black's principle of being 'considerate in execution', for example by adding to redundancy payments substantially for years of age and years of service. This was well before the Redundancy Act, and as a result Slater Walker never had any problems with unions over these matters. By the time the word 'asset-stripping' came into vogue Slater Walker had divested itself of its industrial interests, but some of the companies in which it had investments were criticized for operating in this way.

On 21 October we made an offer to all the outstanding institutional shareholders in SWIG. About a third of the offer was in loan stock, adding to our long-term borrowings. I was very keen to issue as much loan stock as possible at that time, as with growing inflation rates I could not understand why long-term fixed interest money was so cheap. For this reason loan stocks were to become a regular feature of Slater Walker bids in the years ahead. The main advantage of buying in the SWIG minority was that it would simplify our group structure. I could see that we were going to do more takeover bids like Brown, and it would then be difficult to know where to put them within the group. SWIG itself was not in a position to issue shares or loan stock, as it was a private company, and therefore could not finance the acquisition of all the industrial interests we were likely to acquire. Inevitably, therefore, this would give rise to a conflict of interest which was much better headed off at an early stage.

The most important event in my life at this time was that my wife gave birth to a daughter, Clare, in October. Several of my friends have attended the birth of their children and have told me that it was a wonderful experience. I can fully understand this, but if I had done so I am sure that the doctors would soon have had another patient on their hands. In the event the doctors and my wife were very considerate: the baby was born at twenty past five, just as our office was closing. We were both highly delighted.

In early November I flew to Australia to join Malcolm Horsman, who had been beavering away for several weeks beforehand. Malcolm and I stayed at a motel in Brisbane in Queensland, and spent most of our time at the Rocklea head office and main warehouse premises of Thomas Brown. Whoever set it all up had spared no expense; the premises were far too palatial, there was an over-elaborate computer, an automatic switchboard and every modern convenience. As Malcolm said to me on arrival, 'We are equipped here for a moon shot!' Wholesaling of grocery, hardware, and drapery in Australia simply is not the kind of business in which the margins are sufficient to afford very substantial overheads. I remember walking around the outside of the premises with Malcolm on my first full day there, in order to get a sense of perspective. After a while I said to him, 'Malcolm, four hundred people come to work here each day. Every year £10m worth of goods goes in one end of that building, and after overheads are deducted only £9.9m comes out of the other end.' It was an absolute hive of activity, with everyone working very hard, but the numbers were against them.

Malcolm drew my attention to one facet of Brown's approach to wholesaling. If there had been any kind of demand for a product it continued to be stocked for several years afterwards. One rather touching example was the French wine occasionally ordered by three doctors in

Queensland. Brown had a good range of it in stock especially for them, which was clearly uneconomic in every conceivable way, and illustrated an approach to wholesaling that was doomed to failure.

After studying Malcolm's report, he and I soon reached the conclusion that it must make sense to try and sell or close down Brown's wholesaling operation. Fortunately the major rival firm of grocery wholesalers, which was a co-operative named Foodstuffs QCT, expressed interest in the grocery side of Brown. They only wanted the Queensland operation, and we would still be left to deal with the other branches, as well as the drapery and hardware sides. They did not have much cash, so we constructed the deal to include substantial credit, and in particular we retained the Rocklea premises which was let to them on a long lease.

As far as the drapery and hardware wholesaling activities were concerned, my experience at Crossley Motors was invaluable. Here was a very similar situation—we had the stock to sell, we had the time in which to sell it and we had the premises to sell from. We advertised locally and arranged to have direct sales to the startled local population who came in their hundreds to buy, almost as if Rocklea was a vast supermarket. We sold to staff on a very preferential basis, and we also made big sales to other wholesalers, giving credit where necessary to stimulate larger sales than would otherwise have been the case.

The sale of branches in other states was more difficult. Fortunately, however, in most places there was an interested competitor, often literally just across the road. We persuaded most of them to come and see us, offering them the removal of local competition coupled with substantial credit, and before you could say 'wink' a deal had been struck. Malcolm Horsman has since told me that the most instructive sale from his point of view was to a particularly difficult wholesaler, who severely criticized the state of Brown's stocks in Darwin. I had immediately agreed with the wholesaler in question, that much of Brown's Darwin stock was in poor condition. After that he could not disagree that it could all be categorized into stock in excellent, good, poor and bad condition. I then suggested that we should adopt agreed percentage discounts for the different categories, subject to a detailed and completely independent stock-taking. A deal was soon agreed because I had leant into the wholesaler's main argument that much of the stock was in poor condition. Any other approach would certainly have failed with him. I have always believed that selling this type of concept is mainly a question of putting oneself in the position of the buyer. There they were, with across-the-road competition and very little finance, so the way we packaged our proposals was very attractive to them.

The classic case of putting oneself in the position of the buyer is told by Dale Carnegie in one of his books. He was describing in this case not a buyer but an inspector of timber. The lorry-driver who delivered the timber to the site had a very bad record of rejections by this particular inspector and usually only managed to get about 30 per cent of his load accepted. One day there was a new lorry-driver who came back from the site having had 65 per cent of his load accepted. When asked how he did this, he said that he simply reversed the usual process: he leant into the inspector's line of argument. As the inspector picked up the first log and rejected it, the previous lorry-driver would have argued with him. The new one, however, immediately said that he agreed, and grabbing the next log declared that it was not up to standard either. Before the inspector could gather his wits, the driver was on to the third log, and busy rejecting that for him too. By the time they reached the fifth log, the inspector found himself arguing against the lorry-driver that it was up to standard, and so they went on until the load was cleared. The inspector simply wanted an argument, and the important thing was to be on the right side of it. This story made a great impression on me when I first heard it, and I have always remembered it since. The principle of going along with the other man's argument is analogous to the judo principle of turning your opponent's strength to your own advantage instead of trying to resist it.

Before I left Malcolm Horsman in Australia to complete the Brown deal, we had virtually disposed of the entire wholesaling side, which left us with the three profitable subsidiaries only. We had effectively funded the entire purchase consideration for Thomas Brown, and made a massive capital profit in the region of £500,000.

Shortly before my visit to Australia, Jim Davids, a partner of Edgar Astaire & Co., the stockbrokers, had telephoned to ask if we were interested in acquiring effective control of an Australian quoted company, which had quite a lot of cash and owned a coal mine. It was a small company and seemed ideal as a potential quoted vehicle for the Australian market. There was quite a strong nationalistic feeling in Australia at this time and, as we wanted to expand there, I thought a public shareholding might help alleviate any prejudice against us as well as providing a means of making acquisitions through the issue of shares. The company was called Wancol Holdings and had open-cast collieries at Wallerawang. Malcolm Horsman and I made contact with the management in Australia, as a result of which, following my return on 2 December, Slater Walker announced the purchase of a 45 per cent shareholding in Wancol for £146,000. It was an excellent acquisition; the total cash-and investments in the company were alone worth over £300,000, and the company had made a profit before tax of £84,000 in the previous year. Wancol formed the nucleus for Slater Walker Australia, which was to become an important company in its own right.

· EIGHT ·

Conglomerate

THE year 1967 turned out to be a busy one for Slater Walker. The success of the Brown bid and the subsequent reorganization had confirmed my views that we should be looking for another asset situation.

In early 1964, while I was still writing the 'Capitalist' column, I had been challenged by one of the readers, who had run a rival portfolio against me for six months. His name was Ken Hart and he was an investment counsellor and asset specialist. One of the shares he had selected was Greengate & Irwell, which at that time were standing at 4s 4d in the stock market. Since that day I had kept an eye on them, and we had begun to build up a shareholding for Slater Walker's investment clients. They appeared to me to be an excellent investment, as the assets were worth 8s 3d a share, and earnings looked as if they could be improved. Greengate was a substantial manufacturer of industrial rubber products, and it seemed to me that there might be some scope at a later date for linking it with Productofoam. Even if on further investigation this did not prove to be a practical possibility, I was confident that we could improve Greengate's earnings, and liberate some of its capital for further expansion. Another very attractive feature of Greengate from Slater Walker's point of view was its controlling interest in Bramac, which was an Australian quoted company in the same line of business. The possibility of merging this in some way with Wancol and the residue of Brown would give us the prospect of being able to form a sizeable public company in Australia.

In the late summer of 1966 David Marshall, the chairman of Greengate, had telephoned me to arrange a meeting. He had realized that we were building up a significant shareholding, and he wanted to find out our plans. We talked in a general way about whether or not we could cooperate, but at that stage it did not lead to anything tangible.

On 18 January 1967 I telephoned David to advise him that we would be making a bid of 5s 3½d a share against the market price of 5s 3d. I knew that the extra halfpenny would not be a great attraction to shareholders, but my first offer was obviously only a ranging shot as a basis for negotiation, and I explained to David that I hoped that we would be able to negotiate an amicable agreed bid with his advisers. The bid was worth £2.3m, and included our usual element of long-dated loan stock. We soon learnt that we were up against Hill Samuel, whom we had got to know during the bitter fight for Lloyds. Fortunately, though, before we engaged in mortal combat David Marshall took the initiative and came to see me at Hertford Street to have a friendly talk about it all. He had been president of the Rubber Manufacturers' Association, and was keen on the idea of rationalizing the rubber manufacturing industry, which was very fragmented. We liked each other, and talked enthusiastically about the possibility of taking over a larger company, P.B. Cow, at a later stage. David then suggested to Hill Samuel that we should get together and try to work out a bid that the Greengate board could recommend.

I went along to Hill Samuel's offices to see Mike Andrews, who had also handled the Lloyds bid. I remember that he made me feel that my education had been sadly lacking when, during the negotiations, he referred to one point as being '*de minimis*', and at a later stage offered us a '*douceur*' to bridge a minor difficulty. I was not quite sure what it meant, but I accepted it nevertheless. Suffice it to say that after the meeting an amicable agreed announcement was made to the effect that the Greengate board would recommend our offer, which had been increased from 5s 3d to 6s 9d a share. The exit price earnings ratio was a high 19, but there was still an attractive discount on assets, which was of much more interest to us.

We were having board meetings every six weeks or so and I was finding it increasingly difficult to keep Basil Samuel, his colleague Arthur Wallace, and Tommy Walmsley of Slaughter & May in the picture sufficiently. The regular morning telephone conversations with Peter ensured that he knew exactly what was happening, but the other non-executive directors found the speed of events difficult to keep up with through relatively infrequent meetings. When we bought control of Wancol, for example, I explained that it owned a coal mine; Basil, at the other end of the boardroom table, brightened visibly and said, 'A gold mine?' 'No,' I repeated, 'a coal mine.' 'Oh,' said Basil, obviously disappointed, 'have you been down it?' 'No,' I replied. 'Quite frankly it would make no difference to the proposition even if I had, because I couldn't tell a good coal mine from a bad one'; which rounded off the discussion on a not wholly satisfactory note. Over and above all this, Basil was having some trouble with one of his other investments into which Great Portland had diversified, and more importantly the property market seemed to be picking up again. Basil realized that Slater Walker was an animal he would find increasingly difficult to keep his finger on and as a result told me one evening that he would like to place Great Portland's shares. I bought 300,000 of them, virtually doubling my own shareholding. Herbert Despard and Ken Meyer bought 150,000 shares between them and I placed the balance with institutions. Great Portland made a worth-while capital profit on their investment and our parting was an entirely amicable one. At the same time Tommy Walmsley did not seek re-election due to increased professional commitments and Ken Meyer, with a little financial backing from Slater Walker, went off to do his own thing in a private company in which we had a substantial shareholding. Dick Tarling and Malcolm Horsman joined the board, which then comprised Peter Walker and myself, Herbert Despard, Simon Pendock, Dick Tarling and Malcolm Horsman. I was chairman and managing director, Peter was non-executive deputy chairman and Herbert was deputy managing director, concentrating in the main on private company acquisitions. Simon looked after the investment side, Dick the industrial interests and Malcolm was responsible for investigations prior to acquisition and any disposals that might be necessary afterwards. In addition, Tony Buckley had been appointed secretary and he was responsible for the secretarial side as well as the accounts.

It was after the board became entirely executive, with the exception of Peter, that we changed our way of running the company to great advantage. We decided that we would have weekly meetings every Monday morning which in a sense combined management and board meetings. There was no formal agenda and we worked from the previous minutes with everyone raising points as we went along. Peter almost invariably attended the meetings, tending to listen in the main, but quite often coming in with a good point or useful observation. He was particularly good at gauging what other people outside the company would think of any proposed course of action, and this was an invaluable extra dimension to our deliberations. The meetings usually took about two hours and were fast moving and good humoured. As the company continued to grow, these meetings became more important and were my main regular medium for controlling our activities. I believe that in management meetings of this type the minutes should be brief and to the point, spelling out in particular 'who' has got to do 'what' by 'when'. We operated in this way for several years, later only modifying the concept slightly by holding a regular more formal board meeting once a month.

In April I handled an unusual merchant banking deal by advising on the sale of the *Spectator*. Through Peter Walker I had met Ian Gilmour, who wanted to sell the magazine as it was making a loss. Harry Creighton of Scottish Machine Tools was fascinated by the idea of owning the *Spectator*. A deal was easily arranged, and I did not forget Harry's advice about the fee. Other than this Slater Walker was not particularly active on the embryo merchant banking front, and my next job was to move into Greengate & Irwell to see what could be done to improve its profits. I became chairman on 12 April; Malcolm Horsman and Donald Saunders, a new executive of ours from McKinsey, also joined the board; and David Marshall, who had been chairman, became deputy chairman and remained as managing director.

David and I had got on well from the start, continued to do so and since then have become firm friends. He actively encouraged us to look at every aspect of the business, and Donald Saunders moved into the Greengate works as our liaison man. I went up there for monthly board meetings, and on one occasion spent two days looking at the buying side of the business. I wanted to try to achieve a major reduction in purchasing costs, and to start the ball rolling I selected four major items that we were purchasing in volume. The most important single one was cotton ducks (if you are not sure what they are, you are not alone), and I noticed that although we were using four or five different suppliers they were all charging exactly the same price to the fraction of a penny. I asked the buyer to arrange for executives from the suppliers to see me at hourly intervals, and to let me know which supplier he thought gave the best service. When this supplier's turn came, I advised him that in future we would be splitting the business two ways only, in the ratio of 3:1. I suggested that he should ask his board to look at our prices, with the prospect of their having no business from us at all or alternatively three times the existing volume. I wanted to know the keenest price they could quote by the next day, and I stressed that I did not want there to be consultation with other suppliers. The results were surprising, and on cotton ducks alone we saved over £70,000 per annum. The improvement in the other three supply prices was less dramatic, but altogether the improvement approached £100,000 per annum. This had to be seen against Greengate's profits of just over £300,000 in the previous year. In addition the buyer had then got the message, and promised to carry on the good work with other lesser items of expenditure.

Greengate did not retain all the benefit of the savings I had made, as we decided to have a real crack at getting a greater proportion of the vitally important National Coal Board business. They were by far the largest purchaser of rubber conveyor-belting (incorporating the mysterious cotton ducks), putting their business up for tender regularly each year. The tenders were closely contested, and the results had a very big impact upon Greengate. I felt that I was suddenly back at Park Royal tendering for London Transport's bus business again. That year we decided to look at the Coal Board business on more of a marginal costing basis, as a result of which our costings were keener, and we obtained a considerably larger proportion of the business than we had done in the previous year.

We also had a critical look at the overheads of Greengate and made a few economies as a result. It is always an advantage to be new on the scene when reviewing overheads, as anomalies stand out more clearly before you have learned to live with them. I remember Ted Needs, the chief engineer of Park Royal, saying to me when I was walking around the premises with him during my first month there, 'You see those cracks in the concrete today—after you've been here another few months you'll no longer see them.' It is the same with overheads; for this reason I think it would be a good idea for industrial firms to make a practice of asking their new incoming executives to write a detailed report suggesting improvements within a month of their being appointed.

In addition to this we cut out a few of the less profitable products of Greengate, such as rubber footwear which was sold to a competitor. We also reviewed selling prices, opened a new cable factory and generally endeavoured to improve profitability wherever possible. All in all Greengate turned out to be a very worth-while industrial acquisition which was to become the nucleus of a sizeable group in the rubber manufacturing industry.

On 9 May I saw the possibility of making a very substantial share dealing profit for Slater Walker and some of its larger investment clients, whom I had formed into a syndicate for this purpose. An electrical company named Aberdare had made what appeared to me to be a very low bid for Metal Industries. I moved into the market, and within a fourteen-day Stock Exchange account we had purchased about £1,800,000 worth of Metal Industries' shares, which gave our syndicate a vital 16 per cent of the equity. I then went to see Sir Alfred Nicholas, the chairman of Aberdare, and persuaded him to raise his bid a little and buy our shares from us at a profit. Aberdare knew that if they did not buy our shares we were likely to become the opposition; on the other hand the purchase would give them a useful platform from which to bid from strength. This deal yielded Slater Walker itself a dealing profit in the region of £150,000, and attracted a lot of publicity. It was certainly the largest account deal I have ever done.

When our syndicate sold out to Aberdare, they had agreed to give us some of the benefit of any higher offer they might accept for the shares if another bidder appeared. We had made quite a good profit anyway, so this was something that I dismissed from my mind as an unlikely bonus. A few weeks later I was on holiday with my wife in Barbados. I had agreed with her that I would not read the *Financial Times* while I was there, as it tended to impair the unwinding process, but to my mind this did not mean that I could not read *The Times*, which had substantially developed its business-news side. Accordingly I got into the habit of going off to get my wife a drink or a bar of chocolate during the afternoon at around the time the papers were delivered to the hotel reading room. She may have thought my solicitude a little out of character but she made no comment. I was highly delighted when on one of these sorties I read that there was a higher bid for Metal Industries which doubled our profit. I could not contain my enthusiasm when I rejoined my wife on the beach, but since that day all newspapers have been forbidden on holidays abroad.

On 1 July we bid for the outstanding shares in Productofoam and George Wilson in exchange for shares in Slater Walker Securities. We had decided that it did not make sense at this stage for Slater Walker to have interests in other UK quoted industrial companies for which it would be effectively responsible to the public. We had one central industrial management team, and we wanted to be able to concentrate both men and money wherever we considered the priority to be at any time. With differing percentage interests this was difficult, and in addition both Wilson and Productofoam were relatively small. Productofoam had always been troublesome on its own; its tax losses could be better used within the Slater Walker group, and there was the possibility of some integration with Greengate's activities. After this we would have one major UK public responsibility instead of three separate ones.

In August we successfully bid £470,000 for a public quoted asset situation named Constructors, which made steel furniture, factory storage equipment and car seats. Shortly afterwards, in late September, we announced an agreed bid of £350,000 for another quoted asset situation named Newman's Holdings, which made slippers. In retrospect both of these acquisitions, which were in exchange for our shares, were un-questionably mistakes, and it was fortunate that they were both relatively small companies.

Looking back on the first three years of Slater Walker's development, I had clearly made a mistake in the selection of Productofoam as my initial vehicle; it was unsuitable, I had not investigated it in sufficient detail beforehand and it was always a major headache. The fire risk alone was enough to make me regret it. After that, George Wilson was small, reasonably successful, but in essence, because of its size, irrelevant. The acquisition of Lotery itself was fortunate, as I did not know I would get the offer from P & O for the Beaufort House lease. The formation of SWIG and the investment by Great Portland were big steps forward. Slater Walker had then missed bidding for Lloyds, but Cork had been a very successful exercise for Productofoam. Brown had also been a classic and superb asset situation, followed by Wancol which was small but beautiful. The Greengate acquisition was a good one, and after that we should either have consolidated and then bought another medium-sized company in the rubber manufacturing industry, or alternatively gone for another large asset situation. To go for Constructors and Newman's was a form of midsummer madness, and it took us several years to dispose of them. In the case of Newman's we cut our losses and sold it back to a member of the original Newman family who had remained on the board.

In late September we made another sizeable dealing profit on a share-holding in a public company named Cleveland Bridge, which was finally bid for by Cementation, and in November we purchased the whole of another firm of builders merchants, Kirby Brothers, for £957,000, to add to three other firms we had bought earlier in the year. Only five months before this we had forecast profits for the year of £750,000, and now we were forecasting for the first time profits in excess of £1 million. As the *Financial Times* commented when we announced the Kirby purchase, 'It is getting hard to keep up with Slater Walker. The revised forecast indicates that profits are now running at an annual rate of £1.3 million.'

In December there was another highlight in the life of Helen and myself; she gave birth to our first son, Christopher, who true to form arrived on the scene at 5.30 in the evening. I was particularly glad when he was born as Madame Holden had been so right about everything else that

I had felt a sense of foreboding. When he caught a cold a few days after his birth I was more than usually worried, but all was soon well and Madame Holden's prophecy was finally disproved.

On 14 December Slater Walker announced the purchase, for £600,000 worth of shares, of a private company named Nathaniel Lloyd, which made tear tape. The following day Slater Walker revealed that it had accumulated a shareholding of 23 per cent in a leading firm of tanners, Barrow Hepburn & Gale, and that Malcolm Horsman and a business associate of Slater Walker's named John Bentley would be joining the board. I had met John Bentley about a year earlier when he brought to Slater Walker a very attractive share dealing situation involving a Scottish life assurance company, on which we made a substantial profit as a result of its subsequent decision to mutualize. I thought that he was able, and might be helpful to us with Barrow Hepburn. We were not sure about the quality of Barrow Hepburn's assets and did not want to make a full-scale bid, which would in any event have been fiercely contested. John Bentley soon resigned from his position as a director of Barrow Hepburn as he did not get on well with the chairman, but Malcolm Horsman stayed on the board for some years and helped the company's development very considerably.

At this stage Slater Walker itself was becoming an industrial conglomerate. Most large industrial companies are conglomerates to a greater or lesser extent, but the description 'conglomerate' was only applied at that time to those companies which were very diverse, highly acquisitive and financially orientated in their approach. In the previous five years conglomerates in America had been very much more successful than their few counterparts in the UK. Slater Walker was becoming one of the first British conglomerates to compare at all favourably with the financial performance of such American companies as Litton Industries. Conglomerates appeared to me to have several advantages over other industrial companies; they could afford to attract really high calibre management on all fronts and then select the best areas of their business to develop and expand substantially. In addition to growing organically, they were able to expand outside their industries when attractive opportunities were available. Slater Walker was, however, rather different from any other company of this kind in that we alone put much greater emphasis upon assets than upon immediate earnings. We did nevertheless share some of the inherent weaknesses of all conglomerates which were to trouble me later and cause me to change direction.

NINE

Encounter with Wolfson

I SPENT most of Christmas 1967 unwell in bed and this turned out to be the forerunner of a severe attack of infective hepatitis. I turned a very unattractive yellow colour and lost two stone in weight. When I eventually returned to the office in late March 1968 I still felt very much the worse for wear, so my doctor suggested that I should work from home on Fridays for a while. This proved to be good advice, as it enabled me to have a really good think once a week without continual interruptions, and it gave the management team a rest from me. As I recovered, I found it worked so much better that I kept up this practice for the rest of my time with Slater Walker. I have since understood that the word in the office was 'Thank God for Fridays!' Another permanent advantage of the attack of jaundice was that my doctor insisted that I should avoid drinking alcohol for some months afterwards, and that I should begin with wine-based drinks only. Again I found that I preferred these, and I have never reverted to spirits since then.

While I was at home in bed I became a millionaire on paper for the first time as a result of the substantial increase in the Slater Walker share price. Since I was still living in the same house as when I left Leyland, still had the same car, and my standard of living was virtually unchanged, it really made very little difference to me. The main benefit of having a lot of money is that you do not have to worry about minor costs. You can make long-distance telephone calls without thinking about the time being taken; send your friends flowers often; hire a car; buy more expensive Christmas presents; have better food and holidays—all without worrying about the cost. I was never tempted to buy a yacht, or for that matter a villa overseas as my wife had not travelled a great deal before we were married and liked to go on holiday somewhere different each year. We did extend our house, and in particular built an indoor swimming pool which I think was the only thing that we might not have been able to afford if I had stayed on in a senior executive position at Leyland. The fact that I passed the million pounds mark while I was very ill and in bed made me realize that it was all on paper anyway and not particularly meaningful in itself. I was in love with the game of business and, whilst personal monetary gain was in a sense the score, I was not particularly concerned about or influenced by the money itself.

My illness was a strange beginning to a year that in retrospect was clearly the most expansive and critical in Slater Walker's history. To give a general idea of the scale of the happenings in 1968: we made nine major acquisitions; the number of shareholders increased from 6,000 to 40,000; net assets from £7m to £38.6m; profits before tax from £1.1m to £4.8m; the share price from 21s 7d to 70s 0d; and the market capitalization of the company's ordinary shares increased from £12m to £107m. The main factor which helped this tremendous and dramatic growth was the sustained rise in the stock market which, coupled with growing adulatory press comment, encouraged our share price to rise almost perpendicularly.

During the three months I was ill with jaundice the Slater Walker share price doubled, and I remember thinking that as nothing had really changed within the company I must use the strength of the shares and develop its acquisition programme to the full. When our results for the year 1967 came out at the end of March, profits were £1.15m against our forecast of £1m, and the previous year's results of only £370,000. Even on these figures the historic price earnings ratio at the then share price of 33s 6d was an astronomical 39 against the market average of only 18. We were of course growing fast, but on reasonable estimates of future earnings our price earnings ratio was still a very high 26. It would therefore clearly be of advantage to the company for it to exchange its shares for hard assets, especially if these could be acquired at a discount.

One of the main factors that helped us in 1968 was that we had developed a considerable reputation for winning contested takeover bids, and that we were prepared to go where angels feared to tread. We had a young and aggressive management team who thought business was exciting and that it was great to be with a fast-expanding company which was always in the news. This excitement and enthusiasm carried us forward, and in 1968 we went from strength to strength. A further interesting point in retrospect was that in those acquisitive years there was almost a complete absence of competition. No one else, unless they happened to be in the same line of business, wanted to take over relatively large public companies which appeared to need reorganizing. It can be argued that they were right and we were wrong, but nevertheless the effect of this was that we could make our offers to the shareholders in such companies completely unchallenged by competition of a similar nature.

The combination of our very high stock market rating, our aggressive approach and the absence of competition was a formidable one. I knew that these ideal conditions would not last for ever, so it was essential to strike quickly, and to do it in as big a way as possible. I wanted to expand by share exchange on as large a scale as possible while the stock market climate was so favourable. As you will see, we progressed geometrically from a previous highest bid of £4m to £18m a few weeks later, followed by £34m three months after that. The effect upon the company's net assets was to increase them during the year by a staggering 450 per cent. Although the image was on some occasions one of a giant concern coming to take over a poor defenceless company, in reality it was often more a David and Goliath situation, and if the opposition had thought about it objectively they would have realized that Slater Walker was David.

In early April we made our first bid of the year. It was our biggest ever at £4.3m in shares and loan stock for Keith Blackman, which made electric fans and allied products. There was no fight to speak of, but when we took control we found it necessary to review in a fresh light the forecast profit. I was to find that defending boards of directors invariably tended to be optimistic. We instituted an improvement programme within Blackmans, which would have saved a considerable amount, but before we could complete it Arnold Weinstock of GEC came on the scene. He telephoned me to suggest that GEC might be prepared to buy the company from us. I went to see him to show him the detailed figures complete with the proposed improvement programme. It fitted well into his organization, and we very quickly struck a deal, as a result of which, on 28 June, GEC bought Blackmans from us for £3.7m in cash. Some newspapers suggested that Blackmans had been a big mistake for Slater Walker, but they were not seeing the wood for the trees. The *Financial Times* got it right when it said, 'Looking at it from a different angle, the effect is that Slater Walker has made a share issue for cash at 32s 10d per share against 38s 3d when the final offer was made. . . .' The price earnings ratio of our shares at 32s 10d was a high 25 and the asset backing per share was only 18s 0d. To be able to exchange our shares for hard cash therefore increased both our earnings and assets per share, as well as adding to our overall financial strength. We had not planned to resell Blackmans when we bought it, but this was a sensible way of dealing with a company that looked as if it was going to be more of a problem than we had at first envisaged. It was a classic case of a predator acting as a catalyst and transferring a company's management from weak to strong hands.

Early in the year we sold A. Rosenthal & Partners, the small banking firm we had bought previously, as we found that Slater Walker could do through its licensed dealership everything that was required of it as an investment banker. We also appointed Tony Buckley to the board of Slater Walker, together with my friend John Ford from AEC. He had rejoined me as financial director and proved to be a tower of strength.

In April we announced that the Invan Unit Trust would be launched publicly. We had formed this trust on 30 June 1967 to look after the portfolios of small clients when we raised the minimum from £10,000 to £50,000. Since its formation the unit price had increased substantially and it was thought by the press that Invan would have a very favourable initial response from the public. We hoped for £3m, but in the event it broke the previous record with total subscriptions of £8.1m. It was a very important step for Slater Walker, as it brought us right into the unit trust business in a big way, and in financial terms, after expenses, the launch of Invan must have netted the company a profit approaching £200,000. This was a sizeable sum, especially when measured against the previous year's profit of only £1.1m. Invan continued to sell well and had risen in value to over £13m by the end of June.

On 16 April the *Financial Times* featured an article by Lex showing that the average share had risen by 18 per cent in the first quarter, and that the top nine shares had more than doubled. Slater Walker was thirteenth with a gain of 81 per cent, but the interesting point, as Lex said, was that we 'already had the distinction of doubling in 1967'. By then Slater Walker had become quite a large company, and was capitalized in the stock market at £25m. To have any real impact on our assets and future earnings capacity, it was essential for our next bid to be a large one. I had already recognized my mistake in making the small, irrelevant and troublesome bids for Constructors and Newman's Holdings, and I was now looking for a company with net assets of well over £10m. Stock market conditions were very buoyant, our share price was unbelievably strong and we wanted to use this advantage to the full.

I first noticed Crittall-Hope when I was browsing through a broker's statistical survey of companies, and realized that I had found a company whose net current assets were considerably more than its share price. A company's total net assets are often more than its share price but it is far more unusual for the net current assets alone to be in excess of it. I had Crittall-Hope investigated in depth and as a result of our findings we selected it for our next target. The company was an amalgamation of two old-established firms of window manufacturers, Henry Hope and J. Crittall & Sons, which had merged a few years previously. The merger had not been a success, and they had continued to run separately as in the past, as a result of which there were still duplicated facilities, and important decisions were being stalemated. There appeared to be scope for considerable improvement. In addition to its very attractive asset value, the company had an important unquoted investment in America and a quoted subsidiary in South Africa. At this time I very much liked the concept of extending our interests abroad by buying UK based companies with overseas subsidiaries, and this was therefore an important feature of our plan.

We had been buying Crittall-Hope shares for some time in the market, so that when we came out with our bid on 25 April we had a head start. The 18m we offered was four times larger than our previous highest bid for Keith Blackman. I telephoned the chairman, Michael Hope, told him that the offer was on its way, and suggested an early meeting. I said that I would be happy to consider any counter-proposals if they did not think our terms were reasonable. We offered Crittall-Hope shareholders a discount on assets, but a high exit price earnings ratio of 28. Our bids of this kind were always mean in terms of assets, but very generous when looked at on an earnings basis. This made them difficult to oppose, as shareholders were primarily interested in their company's capacity to pay increasing dividends in the future, and this could only be paid out of increasing earnings. The bid was contested, but we sent out our offer and continued to buy in the market. During the tenure of the offer Crittall-Hope announced poor results, with considerable losses by their German subsidiary. This put them in an impossible position, the defence collapsed, and shortly afterwards, on 12 May, we sent out a revised agreed bid. It was not higher in overall price, but offered their shareholders a cash alternative to our ordinary shares, and also offered them some five-year loan stock with subscription rights, which was a relatively new concept in Britain at the time.

As Robert Heller put it in a subsequent article in *Accountancy Age*, 'The previous management had forfeited its right to remain in charge of the assets and was in no position to object to their passing into stronger hands.' As soon as our offer became unconditional I moved in as chairman of Crittall-Hope, where I was helped by Malcolm Horsman on the disposal of loss-makers, and Dick Tarling on the reorganization of their continuing industrial interests. As usual the defending board's profit forecast had to be revised downwards, and we soon found on closer investigation that the company's design and production facilities were duplicated and far too large for the steel-window market, which was a declining one. In fact, during the following four years housing starts fell by over 20 per cent and this made the metal-window business fiercely competitive. Crittall had cost us £18m but, by closing down duplicated facilities and loss-making companies and subsequently selling off its quite profitable American business, we liberated approximately £10m. We also made a further £9m out of Crittall-Hope (South Africa), which went on as Slater Walker (South Africa) to become a sizeable company in its own right.

We also decided to broaden the base of the residual steel-window business and over the following four years quadrupled the turnover in aluminium sliding windows and more than trebled the turnover in aluminium extrusions and greenhouses. The greatest growth was in double-glazing where the turnover was increased from only £21,000 to £2.2m, and this became a very profitable new division. In an article several years later I pointed out that we had dealt with redundancies that arose very generously, on a formula based upon age and length of service, and that this formula had been welcomed by the unions. In the event the turnover per employee more than doubled, hourly rates of pay were substantially raised, holidays were 20 per cent longer, and life assurance and staff pension benefits were considerably increased. A touching example of how this was appreciated by some of the employees arose almost ten years later when out of the blue one of them sent Dick Tarling a fifty-pound cheque as a contribution towards his legal costs in his fight against extradition to Singapore.

On 7 August we announced our interim results and forecast £3m profit for 1968. This put our shares on a prospective price earnings ratio of over 40, which made me keen to continue to issue them in exchange for cash and other assets. Six days earlier Slater Walker had emerged with a £6m underwritten share offer as the mystery bidder for a company named TWW, which was otherwise going into liquidation as it had just lost its Independent Television contract to Harlech Television. The main assets of TWW were £2.6m in cash and Dollond & Aitchison, the well-known optical group, which had a chain of over a hundred outlets in London and the provinces. The cash would in effect be a small rights issue for us, and we had plans to add to the optical group at a later stage. Ten days after announcing the TWW acquisition we bought 75 per cent of Carden Withers, a small Bahamian investment banking firm, for £1.6m in shares and a month later we announced a complicated £5.5m share exchange deal, whereby we acquired a 15 per cent shareholding in Wiles Group and £2.5m in cash. This exchange consolidated the already strong business links between James Hanson and myself. Some years afterwards James changed the name of Wiles Group to Hanson Trust, which has since developed substantially in America and gone from strength to strength.

Our shares were strong in the market and as we made each of these acquisitions they continued to increase in price. Usually in a neutral or bearish market shares tend to weaken when acquisitions are announced because the jobbers mark them down as they know that more will be issued and there may be sellers as a result. In a raging bull market the press and investors at large look for all the future benefits of acquisitions being announced and buy more shares in the hope of things to come. Our shares were powering upwards almost vertically and by the end of August they had reached 80s 0d. By this time I was looking for a really big acquisition to take full advantage of the strength of the share price and put the company in an unassailable position for the future.

It was during my second or third lunch with Sir Isaac Wolfson, the chairman of Great Universal Stores, that he suggested Slater Walker might take over Drages. He had built up Drages from a very small holding company into a company with net assets in the region of £30m. For various personal reasons he was contemplating selling out of Drages, so we met several times after that to talk about it further. Sir Isaac had had a remarkable career and when I met him was nearing retirement, but even then he was by far the most formidable opponent in a business sense that I had ever encountered. He was a terrific salesman. On one occasion when I arrived to see him, he greeted me with a stage whisper, 'I can see it all: it is just before the curtain is raised at Covent Garden; everyone is getting settled in their seats when they start to whisper to each other—"Who is that man who has just come in accompanied by that attractive woman in a blue dress?" "It's Jim Slater, the businessman," they say to each other. "It's good to see him supporting the opera."' This was the highly effective prelude to a request to buy tickets for the opera in aid of a charity that Sir Isaac was supporting at that time. I should have known from the start that I was going to be outclassed in any future negotiations with him.

When we started to look at the prospect of a merger between Slater Walker and Drages as a really serious possibility, Sir Isaac had two main advisers, both of whom were very able: Stuart Young his accountant, and Stanley Berwin his solicitor. I remember at one stage during a lunch, when I was enthusing about the prospects for Slater Walker shares in the years ahead, Sir Isaac stood up, put his hand on my shoulder and solemnly sang, 'Trumpeter, what are you sounding now?' He was a strange mixture, with a tough, uncompromising business-like approach which alternated with humour and warmth. I found his negotiating technique difficult to deal with. For example, to stress that he would pay cash for one part of Drages' business that I had insisted should be bought back by him, he would thump my shoulder with increasing force saying, 'We will pay you cash, cash—CASH!' I might argue back on the price, and he would then say, 'Jim, it's all for charity!' In fairness I should point out that it *was* all for charity, as almost all the Drages shares were held by the Wolfson Foundation, which is of course a leading charitable trust, founded by Sir Isaac.

I remember that just before a most critical weekend meeting with Sir Isaac I telephoned his flat to have a word with him. His butler answered and said that Sir Isaac was sleeping. Although it was mid-afternoon, I immediately told my wife that I must have a rest: I knew that I could not afford to be one down that evening. A few hours after I arrived at his flat we finalized the main principles of the deal, and the accountants and lawyers were given the job of preparing the necessary documentation. I was feeling tired, but happy, as this deal at over £30m was by far the biggest and most important one that I had ever done in my life. Sir Isaac drew me aside to another, smaller, room, where he showed me a gold key that he had been given by the State of Israel in recognition of a major charitable donation, together with several other treasures of a similar nature. Stephen Potter would have been proud of him as he put his hand on my arm and said quietly, 'Jim, this is the room I reserve for *big* deals.'

The proposed merger was first announced on 6 September, but it was not finalized for several weeks. In this interval a number of important factors had to be agreed upon: the exact price to be paid; the currency to be used to pay; whether or not the Wolfson interests would retain shares; which companies Slater Walker would prefer not to retain, and the price to be paid for those companies. These points were quite enough to keep Sir Isaac and me enjoyably busy for many weeks, and as a result at a later stage the press began to speculate that all might not be going well, and that the proposed merger might fall through. This was not to be, however, and the final terms were announced on 16 October. The total purchase consideration was £34m, and Drages' outside shareholders were offered 34s 4d worth of shares with a cash alternative of 30s 0d. Sir Isaac's interests were only retaining 550,000 shares and taking cash in respect of the vast majority. Slater Walker paid the Wolfson interests the cash of £11m, and underwrote the balance with the institutions through Sebags. At our request the Wolfson interests were purchasing several companies out of Drages, at the figures we had negotiated together, to a total value of £9.5m. The net effect of all this was that Slater Walker, by buying Drages, would acquire its banking subsidiary, which did of course have a loan book, together with cash and 50 per cent of a fully authorized bank, Ralli Brothers (Bankers) Ltd. A further factor was that the Wolfson interests had provided Drages with about £6m worth of long-term finance on attractive terms. The interest rate was raised slightly, but otherwise this continued.

I was in fact quite pleased that Sir Isaac had opted for cash rather than our shares. There would have been a temporary gain in public relations terms if he had taken more shares, but I would always have been worried about such a large holding being in one pair of hands. He could easily have decided at a later stage to start selling, and this would then have had a catastrophic effect upon the market.

Sir Isaac had outmanoeuvred me on the technical points, and I suppose that against anyone else I might have paid £2m to £3m less one way or another. However, the basic strategy of Slater Walker issuing over £20m worth of shares at 77s 0d each, on a prospective price earnings ratio of 26 and more importantly with asset backing of only 28s 0d per share, had to be absolutely right. In addition to this Slater Walker had obtained £6m worth of further valuable long-term finance, and the 50 per cent shareholding in an authorized bank. Looking back upon the Drages deal, it was clearly a good one for Sir Isaac's interests, and for the Drages shareholders who opted for the cash alternative. For the reasons I have explained it was also excellent for existing Slater Walker shareholders. The losers were in fact the institutions who underwrote the issue, coming freshly into the Slater Walker ordinary shares at a price which had already multiplied eight-fold in the preceding two years. At that time Slater Walker shares were rated far too highly by the stock market, and were discounting kingdom-come.

To put the previous nine months in perspective: we had started with the £4.3m acquisition of Blackman, which was our biggest until then. Within a month we had made an £18m bid for Crittall-Hope; this was followed within two months by a £6m bid for TWW; then £1.5m for Carden Withers, £5.5m for Hanson Holdings, and finally to cap all these a £34m bid for Drages. One of my friends used to say, 'When asparagus is in season—hit it hard!' Well, Slater Walker shares had been in season, and we had hit them as hard and as fast as we could, with the result that the company had become a giant and was completely transformed.

On 25 October we rounded off the 1968 bidding season with a £3.4m agreed share exchange for Harrisons Opticians, increasing our number of optical outlets to 175. This was followed only fourteen days later by an agreed £5.25m share and loan stock offer for Augustine Investments, which owned Hudson Verity. This brought our total of optical outlets up to 300, being about 8 per cent of the annual UK turnover in optics, and providing considerable scope for rationalization.

Our Australian company was following an identical pattern of virtually geometric progression. The name had been changed from Wancol Holdings to Slater Walker Securities (Australia) Ltd; it was on an astronomic price earnings ratio of 48 and planning to raise a further $10m by a one-for-one rights issue. After this it would be as big in stock market terms as Slater Walker itself had been at the beginning of 1967. Slater Walker (Australia) had bought the Greengate subsidiary Bramac, and subsequently another public company, Plastalon Holdings, which was in the same line of business. After this, in early 1968, there had been a fiercely contested bid for Lithgow Valley, a public company which owned a colliery near Wallerwerang. Then the residue of Brown was absorbed. At this stage Slater Walker UK had 67.5 per cent of the equity, but then we placed a large number of our shares to reduce our shareholding to below 50 per cent.

On 14 November 1968 Slater Walker (Australia) announced a bid of $34.4m for Drug Houses of Australia, which was the leading old-established firm of wholesale druggists. It had poor profits, but over $40m asset backing, and Slater Walker (Australia) had already acquired over 8 per cent of it. The market value of Slater Walker (Australia) itself was by then only $33m, so this was a very cheeky bid indeed. Dick Tarling went out to Australia to supervise the fight. The Slater Walker group borrowed locally on a large scale to finance the purchase of Drug Houses' shares, and the battle was won by aggressive stock market buying over a hectic ten-day period which gave us 51 per cent of the ordinary shares. The offer for the balance was then revised to the equivalent value in Slater Walker (Australia) shares and debenture stock, but with no cash alternative. Slater Walker Securities UK, through Thomas Brown, owned the 51 per cent shareholding in Drug Houses that had been bought in the market, and this was subsequently placed with institutions in both countries. This was a very major victory for us in Australia, and if we had simply concentrated after that on getting Drug Houses right, the company could have gone from strength to strength. Our man on the spot was thirty-three-year-old Jonathan Van Der Borgh, whom I had taken on in Britain and who had made a great success of things in Australia. For personal reasons he was, however, planning to return to the UK, and his place was to be taken later in 1968 by an Australian, Ian Murray, whom I had also taken on in Britain. Little did any of us know the terrible problems that would be in store for us.

Towards the end of 1968 I was beginning to see some clouds on the horizon for conglomerates. Some of them were beginning to fail in America, and losing their high stock market ratings, which made further acquisitions difficult. In addition they were finding that the difficulty of running very diverse activities was beyond their management capabilities. The problems seemed to come to a head with increased overall size, and I was certainly finding that the difficulties of managing a large and complex international group were being brought home to me daily. I knew that I had to find a main purpose and identity for the company, and that in preparation for this I had to simplify its structure. On the industrial side I preferred bigger units such as Crittall-Hope, Greengate and the optical group; the smaller units such as Constructors, Newmans, Nathaniel Lloyd and the builders merchants no longer had a logical place in our structure. Nathaniel Lloyd was an excellent company, but far too small for us at that stage, so I suggested to James Hanson that he should have a look at it for Wiles. On 13 December it was announced that they were buying Nathaniel Lloyd for shares, and five days afterwards we sold Metropolitan Builders Merchants for £2.4m in shares and cash to Mercian Builders Merchants. This was the start of our 'de-conglomeratization' programme, which was to gather pace in 1969; and it was also in a sense the start of the basic concept of selling our industrial interests to

(*left to right*) Sir Joseph Napier, Jim Slater and Lord Black at a Park Royal party, and below Jim Slater and another guest talking to Lord Brabazon (*centre*).

(*Previous page*) The Windermere Avenue Kid.

Blissful dog!

Lord Stokes

(*above left*) Peter Walker; (*above right*) Malcolm Horsman.

Visiting Snowy Mountain Project in Australia, 1960.

quoted associated companies. The conglomerate phase was nearing its end and the investment banking phase was about to begin.

By the end of 1968 the Slater Walker group was a totally different animal. We would never have another year like 1968, but I think I can say that we had made the most of it.

TEN

The Satellite Concept

WE started off the year 1969 with high hopes. Our share price was still surprisingly strong, considering the number of shares we had issued during the preceding nine months. The press continued to be complimentary: for example, Slater Walker shares at 71s 6d were selected by the city editor of the *Sunday Times* for his 'play-safer portfolio' for 1969 and Lex in the *Financial Times* said that Slater Walker 'must rate as a good prospect for 1969'. Press comment in the UK was therefore still on balance very good, but the problems of American conglomerates were sending me loud and clear warning signals.

It did not take us long to make our first takeover approach of the year. On 10 January we indicated interest in Forestal Land, Timber & Railways, and on 16 January made an agreed £11.7m takeover bid. As we had accumulated a lot of cash by then we offered a cash alternative to our shares from *within* Slater Walker. This meant that it would only be necessary to issue further Slater Walker shares to those Forestal shareholders who really wanted to hold them. If we had underwritten our shares with *outside* institutions in the normal way, it might at that point have occasioned quite a lot of selling by them, which would have weakened our share price.

It was Jack Dellal, the financier of Dalton Barton fame, who had first brought Forestal to my attention. At one time we had thought of bidding for it in some form of partnership, but we later agreed that it made more sense for Slater Walker to proceed alone. Forestal had very substantial tanning extract businesses in Central, East and South Africa and the Argentine, together with three excellent and profitable companies in the UK into which they had rightly diversified. These were Cruickshanks the electroplaters, Alfonal and Heath & Heather in health foods, and a chemical manufacturing company. These three companies were doing well, but all tanning extract businesses throughout the world were having a rough time, and the wattle estates and cattle farms of Forestal were suffering as a result. Our offer was 35s od a share against the asset value of Forestal of 55s od, but the real value of those assets was very much dependent upon the prices that could be realized for the vast overseas estates. We had obtained detailed reports on Forestal's businesses in both South Africa and the Argentine, and we knew that there was quite a big risk factor in buying into the company.

I am often asked by people how we did so many deals, and how we heard about them being available. The answer is that we had the right attitude of mind, and were very receptive to other people's ideas. Of course we paid business brokers exceptionally well, and we gave them quick decisions which they appreciated, so we would be amongst the first to hear of any deals that came their way. Additionally it was well known that we were highly acquisitive, and we were therefore the natural people to approach. Looking back on some of our more important deals, it is quite interesting to analyse the various sources. Productofoam was simply the smallest company I could find; Lotery came from Freddie Cheshire; Lloyds from a thought provoked by an interview with an ex-employee of theirs; Cork from an analyst spotting a very major property revaluation; Brown from a unit trust group who approached us as they knew we were acquisitive; Greengate from the 'Capitalist' challenger's portfolio; Blackman from an analyst rather like Cork; Crittall from my browsing through a stockbroker's circular—and so on. As you can see virtually all had very different origins—some came to us and others we went out to find. There was no formula—it was simply a question of keeping a completely open and receptive mind, and being alert to all possibilities.

Once we had acquired Forestal, the basic strategy for dealing with it was planned by me in consultation with Malcolm Horsman, who handled most of the disposals to excellent effect. He soon sold the Argentine assets and the three profitable British companies, all to different purchasers. The South African business was later injected into the old Crittall-Hope (South Africa), which had become an active and acquisitive public company in its own right under the new name of Slater Walker (South Africa). The Central and East African interests were sold within three months to Lonrho for shares in that company. Forestal was a classic asset situation and the overall profit—some in cash, some in shares—was in the region of £7m. It can be argued that it was a pity to dissect a company such as Forestal, but against this it is fair to say that it had no real *raison d'être* of its own and had lost its way. The assets of Forestal's various businesses were in many cases placed by us into hands that could better use and manage them, to the advantage of the employees, the shareholders, and the economies of the countries concerned.

Anyone really interested in the details of this particular reorganization should read Anthony Vice's book *The Strategy of Takeovers*, as the whole of the first chapter is devoted to Forestal. For those who would simply prefer to read about an incident from the Forestal story, I think my meeting with Tiny Rowland of Lonrho will best give the flavour of the times. I had only met Tiny once or twice before, and had found him a delight to deal with. We met at our Hertford Street offices to discuss the Central and East African wattle estates and cattle stations of Forestal, and also Ralli Holdings' interest in Motor Mart, which was a car distributor in Kenya. The book value of these assets was £6m, and profits before tax were about £550,000 per annum. To Tiny, who knew the countries involved intimately, they made a lot of sense, but for me they would always have been a problem. Lonrho's shares were flying high at 65s 0d, and Tiny knew that it was to his shareholders' advantage to issue Lonrho shares at these prices in exchange for assets. I knew that I could gradually sell the shares in the market, find a better use for the proceeds, and have several problems less. Within ninety minutes a deal was struck at £3.9m, to be satisfied by the issue of 1.2m shares in Lonrho. After we shook hands Tiny turned to me and said, 'By the way, what *is* wattle?', to which I replied, 'Where's East Africa?' For the benefit of dedicated cynics I should perhaps explain that we were both joking! Tiny does not appear to have a detailed grasp of the facts and figures concerning any deal under discussion, but in fact he can rattle them off afterwards better than most experts. More importantly, he thinks in a very big strategic way, is absolutely dedicated to Lonrho, and works all the hours that God sends. If instead of continually criticizing, more people had emulated the job he has done overseas with Lonrho, this country would be much more prosperous.

On 16 April it was announced that I would rejoin British Leyland as a director. I was delighted by Donald Stokes' offer as I liked him, and wanted to be involved with Leyland again. I was of course to be a non-executive director, but I was interested to know how effective I could be in this role. I had begun to grow very used to being chief executive, and I was not sure that I would be able to work well in a purely advisory capacity.

One of the first contributions I made was to do with a subject that many members of the public had already commented upon. It was the price of the Jaguar, which was selling so cheaply that anyone who was lucky enough to be able to buy a brand new one could resell it immediately for £400 over the list price. This had to be wrong, and I suggested that Jaguar prices should be substantially increased. There was solid opposition from Sir William Lyons of Jaguar, who argued that it would affect the order book; however, as the waiting period for a new Jaguar was about two years, Donald Stokes supported my argument and the prices were raised quite considerably. The Jaguar at that time was an engineering miracle; it was one of those unusual occasions in the car industry when everything about a new model is right. On these rare occasions it is vital to develop the opportunity to the full, as there are always losses on other models which need off-setting.

I was to find that the main difficulty of making constructive suggestions on the Leyland board was that the labour relations problem overshadowed everything else. However good an idea might be, it was always peripheral in relation to the overwhelming difficulties of getting the right level of production at the right cost. For most of the time I was on the board we were short of production and therefore overseas distributors were crying out for stock; we were short of money to finance stocks, work in progress and massive capital expenditure; and we were short of really expert management to supervise the activities of the group on a worldwide basis. At monthly board and finance committee meetings, in addition to frequently suggesting that we should increase selling prices, I used to try and persuade Donald Stokes and other members of the board to concentrate our limited resources in terms of production, money and management in a more restricted model range. In particular I argued that we should increase the production of the Land Rover and Jaguar, which sold like hot cakes at high profit margins, and eliminate from our range of vehicles some of the models that did not sell well and on which we lost money. Similarly I would have liked to have seen Leyland try to make a complete success of a smaller number of their overseas manufacturing and distributing organizations rather than spread their efforts thinly over the whole world. The essence of car manufacture and distribution overseas is that it is uneconomic unless one captures a substantial share of the market, and this can only be achieved by very considerable capital expenditure on manufacturing plants and the distribution network. In some cases it is possible to rely upon local distributors, but the best ones tend to get snapped up by the market leaders. To get really established in a new market therefore takes a great deal of money, either in direct investment or in massive help to distributors.

For all these reasons it seemed abundantly clear to me that Leyland, with its limited resources of capital, management, and effective labour, had to concentrate its efforts or die. I argued this philosophy like a theme song each month, but to little avail. Jaguar production was dramatically increased over the years, but the argument against my idea of restricting the range of vehicles was based upon the principle that distributors expect their manufacturers to offer a complete and very comprehensive range of vehicles. I do not find this entirely convincing as clearly it is not a volume manufacturer's role to make an infinite range of products to the absolute satisfaction of the ultimate customer. They should make an optimum range of products for the reasonable satisfaction of the average customer and in particular they should concentrate upon making what they are best at.

I was interested to see in a newspaper in March 1977 that the managing director of British Leyland (Switzerland) was still complaining that they could never get enough Range Rovers, Land Rovers or Jaguars. He went on to say that he could sell twice as many of each every year; but that the delivery delay for Range Rovers was eight months, and they had stopped advertising Jaguars as it was useless stimulating the demand. Although my approach would by no means have been a cure-all, I remain convinced that my argument about the model range has merit and that the policy I advocated for overseas manufacture and distribution would have been a great improvement upon the one that was followed.

The ultimate solution to the problem of British Leyland still remains an open question but whatever happens no general policy can be successful until better labour relations are developed. In my view only the Government will have any chance of solving the present labour problems, by standing absolutely firm when necessary. The last private enterprise company in the motor industry to try and do this was Rootes; they were mortally wounded as a result and this did not give onlookers much hope or inspiration for the future.

The Slater Walker results for 1968 were announced on 22 April. Profits before tax were £4.86m against only £1.15m in 1967. Such was the pace of our growth that we were able to forecast £7.9–£8.9m for 1969. The shares were 72s 0d and the price earnings ratio was 22 on the high range forecast of £8.9m. There had been a long period of dividend restraint, and after paying the maximum permissible the dividend yield on our shares was only 1.1 per cent. This was obviously an inhibiting factor as far as our share price was concerned, so during periods of dividend restraint we always indicated the dividend we would normally have paid, and would pay again as soon as we were allowed to do so. This minimized the otherwise adverse effects, as most institutional investors tended to look on

ffolkes's tycoons—14

Mr Jim Slater

dividend restraint as a passing phase. We also announced a one-for-three bonus share issue, which was something we did every two or three years, particularly when the share price was a 'heavy' one. Shares are heavy when they are priced at, say, £4 each, and then they *seem* more expensive to some investors than the shares priced at £1 or for that matter £3 each. A one-for-three bonus issue simply meant that an investor would in future

109

have four shares worth £3 each in the market, instead of three shares worth £4 each, but psychologically this was more attractive to many investors. It could be asked, why not issue ten new shares for everyone, to bring the price per share right down, but this would mean that there would be far too many shares in issue. It was necessary to strike a nice balance, and as our shares were 72s od a one-for-three issue seemed about right. It is interesting to note that at the end of April Slater Walker was capitalized at £115m, and that throughout the group we employed a total of 40,000 people. We never exceeded that number of employees, because the process of selling off our industrial interests had just begun.

At our Annual General Meeting on 5 June I was asked by a shareholder what I thought about the bearish views of our shares of some chartists. I replied off the cuff that 'chartists were people who tended to have ragged raincoats and big overdrafts'. This remark received quite a lot of publicity afterwards, as a result of which it has always been supposed that I had completely negative views on chartists. This is not the case, as I do believe that there are a few UK chartists who know what they are doing and would usually beat the performance of the average investor. I also know that most sophisticated investors like to look at the chart of the movements in the share price of any company in which they are proposing to invest heavily. My argument is that a chart is a relatively small tool in the kit and not an end in itself. Chartists do have severe limitations, which are never more evident than in narrow UK markets. They argue that when shares pass a precise limit which they have set, this may signal the beginning of a new trend. If their views had any real impact it would be only too easy, with a large line of shares to sell, to buy a few more instead, so that the shares would go up through the chartists' limit and become a chartists' buy recommendation, after which all the shares could be sold at higher levels. Unfortunately, insufficient people believe in charts in the UK for buyers to be there in sufficient volume, and for some reason, which I *have* been able to put my finger on, very few UK chartists have sufficient funds themselves. In the American market, which is much wider, some chartists seem to operate more successfully, but their charts are much more meaningful as they incorporate volume figures. An important additional factor is that more people believe in them, and that short-term success is therefore to an extent self-generating. Chartists concentrate more upon the technical supply position of shares. When a company has issued a large number of shares, the supply position becomes an important factor, influencing the immediate future share price more than the fundamental worth of the company. Slater Walker shares were at that time fundamentally stronger than they had been for some years, but there were too many shares in weak hands as so many had been issued during the previous year. At this particular time therefore, as far as Slater Walker shares were concerned, the chartists did have a point.

On 12 June I was interviewed by Chris Brasher in a half-hour television programme called *Chief Executive*. I decided it would be better not to risk doing it live my first time on television so the programme was recorded in advance and the producer agreed to give me the opportunity of having a retake on any particular part of the interview about which I might be unhappy. I was rather nervous, and although none of it had to be done again, I thought I performed rather indifferently and was relieved when it was over. There was one amusing moment which a friend pointed out to me afterwards. Chris Brasher knew that Greengate & Irwell made conveyor belting but he did not know what Keith Blackman made, so he asked, 'What do Keith Blackman make?'; to which I replied instinctively, 'Three hundred thousand a year.'

The market continued to slide during June and July, and the attractions of having cash became more apparent to everyone. In July we sold Hope Windows Inc., the American subsidiary of Crittall, for nearly $8m, and the terms for the injection of Forestal's South African subsidiary, Natal Tanning Extract Co., into Slater Walker (South Africa) were agreed with the benefit of local independent advice. By early August, in very poor market conditions, our shares, following the one-for-three bonus issue, were standing at 37s 0d, and had almost halved from their high point in late 1968 of 96s 6d. Press comment was still good however, and most commentators felt that the fall had been overdone. On 17 August our half-year profits of £4.5m were well received, and put some life back into the shares which recovered to 46s 3d.

In mid-August an interesting article appeared in the *Sunday Telegraph*, and in the long sub-headline were the words '. . . and poor Jim Slater is only worth £2¼m'. The interesting comparisons were with such men as Tiny Rowland, £17m; Charles Clore, £20m; Sir Max Rayne, £10m; Sir John Cohen, £9m, and so on. The important point was that these men had started with a higher percentage shareholding in their companies, which had grown more from within than by acquisition. They had retained much more of the equity themselves, and were a lot wealthier as a result. For anyone who is interested in accumulating *massive* wealth, it has to be right to keep a very large proportion of the equity for as long as possible, and to try to avoid diluting it in the very early stages. My route to the first million was a quick one, but after that the very substantial dilution of my percentage shareholding by acquisition made any subsequent major movement in my personal finances very difficult. For example, at that time I had one million shares in Slater Walker, which were valued at £2.25m, whereas the total market capitalization of the company was £100m. To make *my* shares worth £9m I had to make the company worth £400m, without issuing any more shares. Conversely, if I had retained 50 per cent of a company worth £4.5m, I would only have had to increase the worth of that company to £18m to make my shareholding worth £9m. There is a big difference between increasing a company's worth by £300m as against £13.5m. I have already mentioned that, to me, having a large personal fortune was all in the mind and on paper, as after a certain level it really made very little difference to my standard of living and general approach to life. At this stage I was still fascinated by the whole game of business, and the growth and success of the company itself was my main motivating force.

The acquisition of Drages had brought with it a 50 per cent shareholding in Ralli Holdings Ltd, which in turn owned 100 per cent of Ralli Brothers (Bankers) Ltd. The snag was a management agreement under which a Swiss banker, Harry Recanati, had full management powers, which made us simply passive shareholders. During the preceding few years Harry had run Ralli Holdings his way, and Sir Isaac had not interfered. I did not like this situation; I wanted to own either all or none of it. I had always been attracted to banking, and the idea of controlling Ralli Brothers (Bankers), which was a fully authorized bank, began to grow on me. I did not telephone Harry directly, but sent messages to him through mutual friends. In the event he telephoned me about a month after we had finalized the Drages deal, and I immediately went round to see him at St Paul's Churchyard. We got on well together, and agreed a half-way house—as a result of which it was announced on 28 January 1969 that Slater Walker was buying a further 25 per cent of Ralli Holdings for £4.5m in cash. This meant that Slater Walker now owned 75 per cent with management control, and Harry Recanati's interests owned the balance of 25 per cent. In addition we agreed together a put and call option scheme, whereby if Harry wanted to sell his residual 25 per cent shareholding he could sell to us for twelve times estimated net earnings, which would amount to £3m, but if Slater Walker wanted to buy him out we would have to pay half as much again.

Harry Recanati came to see me a few months later and I knew that it was unlikely to be just a social call. We had got on well together, but we had not seen much of each other and only tended to meet when there was a problem to be resolved. I was very keen to purchase his residual 25 per cent shareholding, to tidy up our financial structure and maximize our stake in the prospering investment banking side of our business. Fortunately I did not speak first, and it was music to my ears when I heard him say that he was worried about sterling (how right he was) and wanted to sell his remaining shares to us. I agreed immediately, although the acquisition was not finalized until a few months later. I saved £1.5m by waiting for him to open up the discussion, which is a clear lesson that one should avoid speaking first when negotiating the terms of a deal. Exactly the same principle would have applied if P & O had asked me how much I wanted for Beaufort House; I might well have asked for less than they offered me, as I did not know the value of it to them. Similarly, if you are buying a business from someone, *always* ask what he wants for it, *never* make the first offer. He may well quote a figure that is far too high, but there is always the possibility that he will suggest a figure that is lower than your estimated price range. In the case of a private business, the price is very much in the mind and not something that can necessarily be determined by an arithmetical formula. I should warn you however that if you meet another expert negotiator it may take quite a long time before either of you says anything meaningful.

I have already explained how towards the end of 1968 I was beginning to 'de-conglomeratize'. Now that we had control of an authorized bank I saw a way of 'creating' investment banking clients and de-conglomeratizing at the same time. I could see readily enough that the small public companies associated with us were attracting substantial market support. For example, Ralli had a substantial shareholding in Barclay & Sons, and I noticed that their shares went up in a very narrow market from 3s 9d to 6s 3d during the six weeks after we took over control of Ralli, presumably in the hope that we would activate the company. Herbert Despard left us at about this time, and moved into Cannon Street Investments as managing director, as a result of which their shares doubled within a three-week period. Slater Walker shares on the other hand were 83s 3d on 28 January 1969, and were on a *prospective* price earnings ratio of 25. With the very large number of extra shares that had been issued there was a big potential supply of our shares available for prospective buyers, and for that reason the share price was likely to be weak, which would make it difficult for Slater Walker to make further acquisitions for shares for at least a year. It is obviously much more difficult to double the size of a £100m company than a £1m company and one journalist summed this problem up with the apt saying that 'elephants don't gallop'.

These problems were in my mind, and one formula seemed to be the solution for all of them. If Slater Walker was to gradually sell off its industrial interests to smaller quoted companies for shares, this would help us to de-conglomeratize, and simultaneously provide us with investment clients. At the same time a new chief executive could be found, either from within the company as in the case of Herbert Despard or from outside as in the case of John Bentley, who could be lent money to buy shares in the company, and become responsible for its management and future development. These new small companies would, it seemed, obtain a high market rating initially, which would enable them to pursue an acquisition programme which would be good for their shareholders and at the same time good for their investment bankers. Slater Walker would make money on their shares, and on the investment banking business. It *seemed* to do everything, and this was the thought process behind the birth of Slater Walker's investment banking and 'satellite' era.

In a very low key way and with only two or three small paragraphs in the various City pages, we launched our first satellite, which was to become notorious within the following two years. On 6 May we announced that Barclay & Sons, the wholesale chemists quoted company controlled by Ralli Holdings, was purchasing J.T. Morgan & Co., who were general wholesalers, from another of our subsidiaries. Barclays were issuing 2.5m shares to pay for Morgan. John Bentley had agreed to buy 1.4m of the shares at 7s od each on completion and we lent him the money to do this. The quotation was temporarily suspended as the transaction was a large one, but when the formalities were over and the shares were requoted they immediately began to rise and had soon doubled in price.

Towards the end of June we launched our second satellite by buying 43 per cent of Kent Castings, which was a small quoted engineering company. Our third satellite was to become the largest of all, and its life really began when we purchased effective control of a small and obscure quoted company named Oriental Carpets. It was an asset situation and Malcolm Horsman was busy sorting it out, but he had become restless and had begun to want to do his own thing. He was the most able of our executives at that time, and he was very keen on the concept of building up a really international organization. We had done this more as a by-product, but Malcolm wanted to make it the *raison d'être* of his new company. His ambitions fitted in well with my concept of creating a number of satellite companies. Another advantage was that I knew that in America Litton Industries, the famous industrial conglomerate, had lost a lot of their *alumni*, who had set up their own separate organizations to great effect. In certain cases they had grown to become leading public companies in their own right. The Americans had an apt description for these people—'Litton drop-outs'. It had always seemed to me that Litton had wasted the time spent in training the executives in question, and had not harnessed these executives' talents for their own benefit. I decided that instead of their policy I would follow the principle of leaning into the other man's argument, and encourage an executive to leave once I considered he had made up his mind anyway. I coupled this with an offer of help with loans to buy shares; stakes in asset situations in which he might be interested in the future; and investment banking expertise. In addition he would benefit from the charisma arising from our interest in his company, which would help the share price. It was a formidable package, which was invariably accepted.

In the case of Malcolm Horsman, he had for some time been understudied by Roland Rowe, who was a much younger man but very able and energetic. In addition to this the disposals side of our business, which Malcolm had been responsible for, was to some extent tapering off, and we were not planning any further very major acquisitions. There was also an opportunity to turn a disadvantage to an advantage, as I wanted to dispose of the commodity side of Ralli Holdings. It was very profitable, but it also had heavy borrowings which made it potentially vulnerable. Malcolm got on well with Lord Carrick who ran the commodity business, and he too wanted to start up on his own. We agreed that we would inject the commodity business of Ralli into Oriental Carpets, change the name to Ralli International, raise money from the public by a rights issue (which was finalized in November and was nine times over-subscribed), and that Malcolm and Brian Carrick would borrow from us to invest heavily in the equity themselves.

The first acquisition made by Ralli International was a bid for Millars Timber & Trading which had many thousands of acres of land in Australia and was one of the biggest saw milling and timber operations there. Slater Walker had purchased a significant shareholding in Millars from Mr William Robinson, who together with associates specialized in building up large shareholdings in classic asset situations. William Robinson had been exceptionally successful in doing this and, for example, later became interested in Furness Withy, the shipping business. His usual technique with situations of this nature, which were loaded with assets, was to accumulate through the market a significant shareholding, obtain a seat on the board, and then try to improve the position by the application of common sense. He had become a very wealthy man as a result. The bid for Millars only a fortnight after its successful public debut helped Ralli towards becoming a large international company and maintained the atmosphere of excitement that surrounded it. That was how our biggest satellite was born and helped on its way—little did we know then that it would go on to merge with Bowater only a few years later.

Sterling Guarantee was another company which, although never quite a satellite, was nevertheless to some extent under our influence and benefited from our charisma at that time. Its life began when Jeffrey Sterling came to see me in October and offered with associates to buy shares in Consumer Growth, one of our small quoted investment trusts, saying that they intended to use it as a vehicle for expansion. I was impressed by Jeffrey and his team; coincidentally he had also gone to Preston Manor school, although several years earlier than me, but more importantly he had gone on afterwards to work for Sir Isaac Wolfson. This meant that he had learned about business in one of the toughest schools imaginable. For these reasons we did not sell our entire shareholding in Consumer Growth but retained a 10 per cent stake in the company which then changed its name to Sterling Guarantee. Within a day or so the shares had risen by over a third and were soon on a strong upward path. Sterling Guarantee, like Ralli International, was destined to become a substantial company in its own right within a relatively short space of time.

Earlier in the year we had taken control of a small quoted investment trust named Tokengate Investments, which I decided to use as a means of providing an incentive for our directors. Tokengate concentrated its investment policy in shares that were associated with the Slater Walker group, and in those heady days it was not difficult for it to perform exceptionally well. I was worried at the time about the possibility that our directors might want to purchase shares themselves in individual satellite companies in the UK, and there would have been nothing to prevent them from doing so. I therefore agreed with them that Tokengate would have in the main a general portfolio of Slater Walker 'house' stocks, and that the directors who had shares in Tokengate would not buy house stocks in the market at any time. The policy worked well, and at the time certainly seemed a much lesser evil than the alternative. It could be argued that the directors' jobs with Slater Walker should have been enough, and that they should not have been permitted to buy other shares anyway. However, the immediate growth prospects had gone from Slater Walker shares because of its size, whereas satellite share prices were doubling and trebling around us in a matter of a few weeks. In view of this it would not have been possible to retain in the central company the interest and enthusiasm of highly financially orientated people, who would otherwise all have preferred to go off into quoted companies on their own.

During 1969 Slater Walker (Australia) had a particularly active time. Looking back, this is when it started to go out of control. Its new quoted subsidiary, Mining Finance, was benefiting from the Australian mining boom which was going great guns; shares that suddenly found nickel or were thought to have found nickel, or had a vague possibility of finding nickel, were doubling in price overnight, and then doubling again the next day. Slater Walker (Australia) was also following our satellite policy and selling off some of its smaller industrial interests into quoted companies, which were performing well in those buoyant markets. The chief executive, Ian Murray, seemed to be prudently realizing some profits as he went along, the financial results looked good, and local press comment was excellent. However, Dick Tarling and I had an uneasy feeling that things were getting out of hand. During this very expansive period, we had been having increasing difficulty in our relationship with Ian Murray, who had a strong personality and wanted to be a success in his own right. I certainly did not have the time to liaise with him as frequently as would have been necessary, and he and Dick Tarling had never really got on well. In addition there continued to be a growing feeling of nationalism in Australia. We therefore agreed that Dick Tarling and myself would resign from the board of Slater Walker (Australia), and this was announced during the first few days of 1970, together with a proposal that the name would be changed to something more appropriate for the company. I thought at the time that this would make it clear to everyone that we were no longer effectively running the company or responsible for it, and the move was very well received by the Australian press.

In contrast, Michael Javett was doing an excellent job with Slater Walker (South Africa). The original Crittall-Hope assets had been sold off for cash and shares in a quoted company. Slater Walker (South Africa) had also bought Natal Tanning Extract Company from us, together with Berg River Textiles, which had been a subsidiary of Phillips Brocklehurst. In addition the company had a significant shareholding in a quoted company named Abercom, which was run by two entrepreneurs, Maclean and Lurie, who were on the takeover trail themselves. At the end of 1969 Slater Walker (South Africa) had net assets of over £11m, and during the year its shares had risen 172 per cent. It was the fourth best performing stock in South Africa, but was handsomely beaten by Abercom, in first place with a rise of 510 per cent.

Towards the end of the year Slater Walker made two bids on its own account. On 10 September we announced that we were bidding for the outstanding 60 per cent public and institutional shareholding in Phillips Brocklehurst, our quoted textile company, in exchange for £10m-worth of five-year loan stock with subscription rights in Slater Walker. There were few bargains available in textiles, and the giants Courtaulds and ICI dominated the industry. The large cash balances of Brocklehurst following the acquisition in April of Anglo-Portuguese Telephones were also very attractive to us. On 23 October we made a £6.3m ranging shot bid for P.B. Cow & Co., best known for Sorbo balls, Cow Gum and Li-lo airbeds. By 6 November the terms had been agreed at one of our shares for every two of theirs, valuing Cow at £8.5m. This was a very good acquisition and, together with Greengate & Irwell, gave us a strong position in rubber manufacturing. Cow was not an asset situation but a well-managed company, so that it was simply a question of integrating the two industrial units. Peter Fatharly, who had previously been a management consultant, was made responsible for doing this, and later became chairman of the combined group, which was floated off as a separate public company in the name of Allied Polymer.

There was a general feeling within Slater Walker that we were moving forward at a very formidable pace both at home and overseas, and that all concerned were participating in a great event. As I look back at press cuttings today it seems like a distant dream, but at the time we were all caught up in the excitement. The press had been infected by the mood and did, indeed, help to create it. For example, the *Daily Telegraph* of 4 November said, 'Master conglomerator Jim Slater's tally of bids in action reached ten yesterday when he announced. . . .' They were certainly heady times.

In late 1969 we moved into Ralli House at St Paul's Churchyard, and we subsequently changed the name to Petershill House. We were all sad to leave Hertford Street, which had great character and had served us so well. At the end of the year we also changed the name of the banking subsidiary from Ralli Brothers (Bankers) to Slater Walker. This was partly to avoid confusion between it and Ralli International, and partly to concentrate the image in one name. I was now fully committed to changing the nature of the business from an industrial conglomerate to an investment bank. It seemed to me that I had found a *raison d'être* for Slater Walker for the seventies, and that after we finished de-conglomeratizing, we would be able to concentrate on investment banking throughout the world.

At the end of the decade, which in a financial sense could perhaps have been called the 'roaring sixties', the press were in a reflective mood, and Slater Walker was featured strongly in most of the financial articles. A particularly interesting article appeared the following June in *Management Today*, under the heading 'British Business Growth League, 70', which attempted to measure the performance and growth, over the preceding decade, of Britain's largest 200 companies. They gave a growth rating to each company, based upon the percentage change in its share price, plus gross dividends received by shareholders, to establish the total percentage return that shareholders had received against their original capital investment. Slater Walker came first with an astonishing rating of 4563 and a share price that was up by 4,407 per cent. Next was Eastman with a rating of 2454, Lesney 1605, Rank 1409, quickly falling away to BSR at nineteenth with 477. I always think that tables of this kind make more interesting reading several years afterwards, but Slater Walker was ending the sixties as the acknowledged growth stock of the decade, and to me the years ahead looked full of promise.

· ELEVEN ·

Investment Banker

I AIMED during the seventies to establish Slater Walker as an international investment bank, and we were already well advanced along that road. I felt then, and still do today, that there is a vacuum waiting to be filled in international banking. The joint stock banks in this country are not prepared to even consider participating in the equity of companies that approach them for finance. The merchant banks and ICFC frequently take small equity stakes in private companies, but the scale of their participation is usually very limited. The role of merchant banks when underwriting public company shares is more that of an agent than a principal, because it is not their own money that participates but the investment funds under their management. The critical factors for the successful management of any investment bank would be to ensure that the bank itself was well capitalized, the portfolio of investments well spread and above all that on each venture capital proposition the upside potential was far in excess of the downside risk. The interesting point is that if a proposition is going to be a great success the investment bank will make many times its original stake, whereas even if it is a complete failure, provided care is exercised, the bank will only lose the money invested. The important point therefore is to get the odds right on each investment and only to invest where the upside potential is very considerable in relation to the initial finance.

Another factor which encouraged me in the belief that I was on the right track in trying to develop internationally as an investment banker was that Britain is one of the top countries in the world when it comes to financial expertise. In most other countries we have a considerable edge over local competition and only the American approach seemed to me to be ahead of our own when it came to financial problems which also involved stock market know-how.

In 1970 our satellite concept was developed substantially. As a complement to this, we had already started to build up stakes in quoted asset situations. It seemed to me, from my experience with takeovers, that it made more sense to build up significant shareholdings than to dissipate funds over a wide range of companies. The underlying principle was that it would be better to have ten shareholdings of 9 per cent than ninety shareholdings of 1 per cent. The reason for this was that a 9 per cent shareholding carried with it a measure of influence; it could be used by someone as a platform for a bid or might tip the scales at the last moment in a hotly contested takeover battle. It also fitted in well with the satellite concept, as these companies were going to be highly acquisitive. I knew how successful William Robinson had been with his asset situations, and I knew how valuable an initial significant shareholding was to a prospective bidder. For example, when six months earlier Glynwed had overbid Acrow for Allied Ironfounders, they had needed the support of our 9 per cent shareholding before going ahead. Although we had accumulated quite a large number of big shareholdings before, this was the moment when I really decided to make it a very much more definite part of our company's general investment policy.

At the time this policy was not criticized, and in fact on occasion it was praised by the press. Indeed, later in the year we launched a unit trust, and a year or so after that a substantial investment trust, which advertised to the public that its policy was to accumulate shareholdings in asset situations. It was not until 1974 that the purchase of significant shareholdings began to be described as 'warehousing', and to come under criticism. The key point seems to me to be that the undisclosed buying of shares in asset situations can only become an improper practice *after* a firm intention to bid has been formed. I agree with the April 1977 change in the law which makes the disclosure of all shareholdings compulsory when they reach 5 per cent, and obviously the shareholdings of parties acting in concert should be taken together. To my mind these measures should be sufficient to stop any abuses. As I had advocated disclosure at the 5 per cent instead of 10 per cent level, I have often been asked why I did not insist that our investment management business did this itself, to give a dynamic lead. The answer is three-fold: first, it was difficult enough to keep up with the law as it actually was, without trying to anticipate it as well; second, it would have handicapped our investment management team, who were managing other people's money against competition from other similar groups; third, it could quite easily have been open to misinterpretation, as many of our critics would have argued that we were advertising our shareholdings to influence the share prices.

On 10 January Slater Walker bought for £950,000 in shares the outstanding balance of 71 per cent of the equity of Walker Young, the insurance broking business which Peter Walker had built up from scratch, and in which he still had a significant interest. The profits for the year were estimated £170,000, and because of Peter's position on our board we asked Rothschilds to advise Slater Walker on the transaction. Peter had married a year before this, and was spending week days in London at his new house in Cowley Street and weekends in his Worcester constituency. During the week he would work for part of the mornings at the Walker Young offices, then in his political office and later in the House of Commons when it was sitting. He also had directorships of other companies, such as Adwest. At this stage Peter was preparing to leave business altogether and concentrate upon politics: he had told me from the beginning that politics were his first love and that eventually he would want to shed all his business interests. We had continued to be good friends and were still keeping in touch by regular early-morning telephone calls. Even if Peter had had a late sitting in Parliament he always seemed fresh and energetic the next morning, and I understand that he can manage with very little sleep. He still attended our weekly management meetings, but the pace of events was such that he could not really contribute to the detailed management decisions, though he came into his own on strategic and policy matters. He had a great knack of pinpointing an aspect of a problem that we had overlooked, and we were to miss him when he left to join the Government a few months later.

During the early months of 1970 our existing satellites were very busy and new ones such as Armour Trust, Priam Investments and Bodycote were being created. John Bentley had been tipped by the *Evening Standard* as the whizz kid of the seventies and Barclay had made a bid for Sebel, the Mobo toy manufacturers; both Ralli International and Kent Castings were making offers for major companies. Our activity had not gone unnoticed by others in the City, and it was at this time that something amazing happened. In early February I had been having a talk in my office with Lord Poole of S. Pearson & Son, which had only recently become a public company. During the discussion I mentioned to him that I had been negotiating with Marine Midland, a leading American bank, with a view to their acquiring a substantial shareholding in Slater Walker, when to my astonishment he suggested that Pearsons and Slater Walker might get together. As Pearsons was a company in the upper realms of the establishment the idea had great appeal for me. After Lord Poole left I had a word with all our directors, who were very excited by the prospect. We formed a small committee comprising Tony Buckley, John Ford and Bryan Quinton to get out all the necessary financial statistics so that I could take the negotiations a stage further. Lazards, which was Pearsons' merchant banking subsidiary, also had two executives working on the financial schemes that were being prepared in great secrecy. We noticed that in their detailed working papers they used the code word 'Sultana' to describe Slater Walker. We never told them, but in our own working papers we used the name 'Fruitcake' for the new combined company, as from our point of view that is what it would have been.

Another meeting was soon arranged at Egerton Crescent where I met Lord Cowdray for the first time. He was very pleasant to me, but indicated from the outset that he was going to be guided in the main by Lord Poole, who had been his chief executive for many years. The motivation of Lord Cowdray and Lord Poole was that some of the Cowdray family interests wanted wider marketability for their shares, and as Lord Poole was a few years away from retirement they were looking for a successor to him. The terms of the proposed merger were to be two of our shares for every three of theirs, and this would increase Pearsons' shareholders' earnings per share by 20 per cent. We also planned to raise the dividend to give them a 20 per cent increase in income. In addition Slater Walker was becoming quite active on the banking side, where there was obvious scope for merging with Lazards, and we had already shown the great potential for expansion internationally. From our point of view the proposal was almost dream-like—Pearsons owned Lazards, as well as very considerable general investment, property and oil interests. In addition it also controlled a very substantial publishing group which owned the *Financial Times*. The net assets of the combined group would have been a formidable £171m, against a market capitalization of £258m. Our assets before the merger were 22s 5d per share, and afterwards would have been 39s 10d against the then market price of 60s 0d. It really would have been one of the most amazing financial deals of all time, and to put it very mildly I was most excited about it.

After weeks of work in early April we were almost ready to announce the merger to what would certainly have been a startled world. We had even booked a hotel for the press conference, when just one day before the merger was due to be announced Lord Poole telephoned to say that he wanted to come round to see me urgently. I sensed immediately that something was wrong and braced myself for the shock. When he arrived he advised me that he had run into unexpected opposition from their close and important associate Lazard Frères, who did not think that the merger would be in the best interests of Lazards and that it would affect their banking business adversely. This view from such a well-respected source had caused them to have second thoughts about the whole idea, as a result of which they had decided that they no longer wanted to proceed. Lord Poole was clearly upset at having to let me down and I was too stunned to say much in reply so our meeting was over within fifteen minutes. I was left with an empty, flat feeling, but I knew that my main task was to ensure that it did not unduly impair the morale of my colleagues, so I tried to put a brave face on it. It was some weeks, however, before I could really put it behind me.

In April we announced the Slater Walker results for 1969, which were profits before tax and minorities of £10.4m. On these figures our price earnings ratio was 22, which most commentators thought reasonable. It was interesting to see that the *Economist* highlighted the move away from being a conglomerate:

> Last year Mr Jim Slater was the conglomerate king. This year his role has shifted not a little, away from industry, to finance and investment, hopefully finding immunity from the pressures of economic cycles and irrational consumers. Not entirely by coincidence, the 1969 Slater Walker results reflect the changing emphasis, with £6.1m coming in from investment banking against £4.6m from the industrial side before head office expenses.

As can be seen from the figures at this stage, we were really in a sort of half-way house, in between being a conglomerate and becoming an investment bank. At about this time one of the newspapers featured a table of British companies measured in terms of market capitalization, in which Slater Walker was capitalized at £130m, standing at 47th immediately below Metal Box and Bowater. Market capitalization was, however, an unsatisfactory and fast-changing measure, as was to be seen during the following months.

Our Annual General Meeting was held on 4 June and was well attended, with about five hundred shareholders present. I had become very much more confident in public speaking, as during the previous three years I had forced myself to take on speaking engagements with organizations such as the Manchester Institute of Directors. Also I had conducted quite a number of annual meetings by then and knew what to avoid. I had once had a strange experience at a Productofoam meeting when Ken Meyer, who was sitting next to me, had been given the job of seconding all the resolutions. I whipped through the meeting at great speed, and after I proposed each resolution he immediately stood up by my side and said, 'Mr Chairman, I have great pleasure in seconding that resolution.' This was repeated until I felt on the verge of hysterical laughter; one more resolution and I think I would have gone over the edge. After that I made sure that my seconders were all in different positions to avoid a recurrence, and also to avoid reminding me of that earlier incident. I remember too how in the early days a shareholder stood up at one meeting and asked a ten-minute question, to which I replied, 'Is that a statement or a question?' This immediately lost me the sympathy of the audience. Peter Walker afterwards advised me that I should have said, 'That's a very good question!', which would have given me a few seconds to think out the answer as well as making the questioner feel rather pleased with himself. Peter is excellent at repartee, and I will always remember a classic answer of his on a television programme. It was on a Sunday evening and he was standing in the pulpit of his local church before a congregation, being questioned by the vicar about how Christianity had affected him. He replied that it had been a great influence in his life, but then went on to say to the vicar that the Church could do more to attract people to Christianity. The vicar was slightly disconcerted, but after a minute regained his composure, saying, 'Well, Peter, I do not know if you realize it, but this church is often absolutely full on Sundays,' to which Peter replied instantly, 'Ah, but you've got such a good organist!'

I needed my experience for this particular Annual General Meeting, as a man named David Hillman was amongst the shareholders present. He and the public company he controlled had owed our banking subsidiary a very large sum of money, which was in dispute. A few months prior to the meeting he had purchased about twenty-five shares in Slater Walker and he was, as a result, fully entitled to attend the meeting as a shareholder. I noticed him in the third row just as I was about to get up to speak. He was a rather thick-set, grey-haired man of over seventy, with a very strong personality. I did not know what he had in mind and his moment arrived rather sooner than I had expected. When it came to what was usually the formality of approving the report and accounts he stood up, introduced himself and asked if we had made a provision in the accounts against the money owed by him, as he had no intention of repaying all of it. After telling shareholders a little of the background I asked our financial director, John Ford, to answer the question in more detail. He stood up and in stentorian tones told Mr Hillman that an appropriate provision had been made. Mr Hillman then asked me question after question of a similar nature for over half an hour, until another shareholder suggested that he had had every opportunity of putting his point of view. I agreed to meet Mr Hillman outside the meeting and we then moved on through the rest of the agenda. To my surprise, and to the amusement of everyone present, when it came to the vote of thanks it was David Hillman who stood up and said in a solemn voice that I should be congratulated upon the way I had handled what had turned out to be a most difficult meeting.

On 1 June the *Daily Express* had carried a critical article about Slater Walker, which included a diagram showing the complex structure of the group and our percentage interests in other quoted companies. Never in British business history, it said, had a business grown so fast; hardly a few days would go by without Slater Walker being involved in some deal, and critics were saying that the company had grown too big and too fast to keep up with its reputation. The article did not refer back to the *Daily Express* recommendation to buy the shares at a much higher price less than five months previously, when Slater Walker had been selected as one of a portfolio of seven shareholdings for the seventies. It was, I think, the first real criticism of the satellite concept; the article was to some extent trying to rationalize the falling share price, which was outpacing the downward trend of the market as a whole.

The shares continued to fall during the following months, during which there were bear raids again. The price was 37s 3d on 8 August when the half-year results were announced at £6m against £4.9m in the comparable period of the previous year. We had suffered some underwriting losses, on the Priam bid for Carlton for example, and depressed market conditions were not helpful for either dealing profits or bid activity. The *Financial Times* estimated that 1970 prospective earnings put Slater Walker shares on a price earnings ratio of 12.7, which was a far cry from the heady days of 1968. Everyone now realized that the average earnings growth rate of 65 per cent per annum was a thing of the past, and the shares were beginning to reflect this. The application of a little common sense would have made this obvious much earlier, as from pre-tax profits of £10m per annum, a 65 per cent earnings growth rate, together with shares issued for acquisitions, would have made us the biggest company in

Britain within a few years. It was the first time I had not made a specific forecast for the whole of 1970, and the *Investors Chronicle* published a cartoon on the subject.

A week later the *Investors Chronicle* carried another article which strongly recommended readers to sell their Slater Walker shares because of the adverse chart pattern. The shares had dropped to 31s 0d before the article, and as a result they dropped to 28s 0d. Chart Analysis were forecasting a drop to 20s 0d, but with uncanny accuracy they had actually found the low of the shares, and they were to be disappointed. By 26 September the shares had recovered to 37s 9d, when they were recommended as a buy in the *Financial Times*. There had been a previous interesting example of chartists' 'expertise' on 25 July, when the *Daily Mail* had published an article which gave chartists' opinions on a number of stocks, classifying them as losers—to be sold, and winners—to be bought. Only three months later the average price of the 'losers' had risen by 7 per cent, whereas the 'winners' had fallen slightly.

Our satellite policy continued and new ones included Cornwall Property, Tremletts and Sterling Land. Several of our earlier satellites were making sizeable acquisitions, but then, as a result of deteriorating stock market conditions, their share prices began to fall rapidly and they became inactive on the bid front. On 29 August the *Economist* came out with a well-argued article on the satellite concept, and identified one of the major and growing problems, which had not been touched upon before. It explained how people like Malcolm Horsman were anxious to break away from my apron strings. Indeed, only a month earlier Geoffrey Pike of Tremletts had said rather plaintively to the *Observer* that he was not 'one of Jim Slater's little boys'. The *Economist* went on to point out that there could be disadvantages in being an associate, especially if things began to go wrong with any of them: there might then be a ripple effect. The real answer to the *Economist*'s basic point was a simple one, which is as old as the hills. When a new executive joined us he would be delighted by the opportunities we gave him; he might well tackle several major industrial reorganizations under our umbrella, or alternatively help with several complex financial deals. He would then go out on his own, and at that stage would borrow money from us to buy into the equity of his new company. From that moment on he rightly no longer regarded himself as a Slater Walker man; he began to get publicity in his own right, and like most ambitious people had the natural desire to prove himself to himself as well as to the rest of the world. There were some cases in which the relationship became difficult and others in which, over a period, it became completely impossible. With James Hanson and Murray Gordon, who had been running their companies well before we became associated, there was never any problem, as they knew their own ability, had always been in command, and did not feel the need to prove anything to anybody. With them I had a simple and effective business relationship, in which they could be described better as associates than as satellites. In other cases, where I had trained the chief executive or he was a virtual newcomer, I was always very conscious of the psychological problem this posed and would treat him with velvet gloves. It was interesting to see how in some instances the relationship would improve after a year or so, when he felt he had proved himself in his own right. Perhaps a good analogy is the Commonwealth, where our relationships are better with the maturer, more self-confident members.

Looking back on it now, I can see that the satellite concept was not a mistake in itself but that I was not sufficiently discriminating in my choice of people to run the satellite companies and that there were far too many to supervise effectively. Undoubtedly the satellites gradually got out of hand, and I began to realize that I had created a monster. Some of them were becoming very sizeable companies and in certain instances the people running them were behaving like prima donnas, without the ability to justify it. A number went on to do well but others were to fail and in almost every case the man at the top was the deciding factor. If we had had, say, only four satellites in the UK, concentrating on different industries, with a really handpicked team in each case, and then supervised them more effectively, I think it would have been a different story. I do not think it is a coincidence that our two outstanding successes overseas were in South Africa and Canada, for those countries were where we had our two best chief executives. They were also the countries which I personally visited most frequently in the early stages of their development.

We had been taking steps to strengthen the banking side of our business. John Dudley, a local director of Glyn Mills & Co., and formerly the deputy principal of the Discount Office of the Bank of England, was appointed as a consultant to advise us and assist us with future development. We also opened a branch in Jersey and others throughout the country in key cities such as Birmingham; these branches simply took deposits locally and were a point of contact for people who wanted to inquire about our other services. We also strengthened our central staff to service the growing merchant banking business from our satellites and to generate ideas for the expansion of client companies and Slater Walker itself.

At the end of August we made a £2.1m cash bid for Flag Investment Trust, a quoted investment trust for which Derby Trust had made an earlier offer. I have already explained how many of our deals came from different sources, and that being receptive was the key. The Flag bid illustrated this well, as the original idea came from a young man of only twenty-two, who was the son of our solicitor and was being given merchant banking experience in our offices. He came to see me with his proposal, and got the surprise and thrill of his life, when I agreed to go ahead with it. We moved into the market, obtained 36 per cent of the equity, and after a six-week fight we were able to announce that we had control. Later in the year Flag made a £6.5m bid for Aberdeen, Edinburgh & London Investment Trust, but Cable & Wireless came to Aberdeen's rescue, so we sold our shareholding to them for a dealing profit in the region of £75,000. Investment trusts are in fact sitting ducks for takeovers, as their share prices are invariably at large discounts on their underlying and *easily realizable* asset values, but the shares are often tightly held by institutions which would frequently prefer not to be disturbed. The real answer for shareholders is to get together and at the Annual General Meeting strongly recommend to their board that they should consider the idea of converting to a unit trust, which would have the effect of raising the share price to the asset value.

It was at about this time that I began to see more of Jimmy Goldsmith. We had only had a fleeting meeting before at Hertford Street in 1965, when we had sold Cavenham an interest in a tobacco wholesaler, Singleton & Cole. Jimmy had bought this company to find that the jewel in its crown was a small snuff-making subsidiary which we had virtually overlooked. I cannot remember the exact purpose of our next meeting, but it was the first of many and we subsequently became very good friends. On one occasion, towards the end of our discussion, I asked him what he thought about the market as a whole. Jimmy is a tall and extremely dynamic man, who finds it very difficult to sit still when he is talking about something that really interests him. As he restlessly paced up and down the room he said, 'I think that next year there might be the last major bull market of our lifetime! However, the main problem is of course the ecological one.' At this time the word 'ecology' was not very widely used, and to be frank I had not come across it. As he had said 'of course' with such confidence I did not want to profess ignorance, so I thought I would keep my options open by saying something relatively neutral like, 'I quite agree that is the main problem.' He then went on to say, 'Before long there will be a shortage of water; in America the crime rate is rising at over 30 per cent per annum; within five years you will not be able to get fish from the sea; there will be a shortage of food ... etc.' I began to realize that 'ecology' might be another word for 'trouble', and I was able to join in the discussion again.

On 11 September one of the most exciting and lengthy takeover bids in which we ever participated was announced: Sterling Guarantee offered £3.5m of shares and loan stock for Gamages. Jeffrey Sterling had asked Slater Walker to act for his company because their bankers, Samuel Montagu, normally advised Gamages. Samuel Montagu had a significant shareholding in Sterling Guarantee and for this reason felt that they could not advise Gamages either. As a result Warburgs were chosen as advisers to Gamages, and they were represented by Frank Smith, who was a veteran of many takeover bids. The key to Jeffrey Sterling's plan, if he obtained control, was to develop part of Gamages' Holborn site for office use, which would result in a very sizeable potential capital profit. Gamages' results had been poor, and therefore the defence would not be an easy task. Sterling Guarantee made an initial bid of 17s 6d a share against a market price of 11s 9d. During the next few days we moved into the market and bought Gamages' shares heavily. John Lithiby of Panmure Gordon, the stockbrokers, and I were on the telephone to each other several times each day to discuss market tactics. Within five days we were able to announce that Sterling had increased their initial shareholding of 9 per cent to 30.6

per cent, and that the Sterling offer was being increased to just over 22s od a share. Six days later Gamages announced that they had agreed a bid of 27s 10d a share with St Martins Property Company. We went back in the market, and the day after that St Martins had increased its offer to 31s 7d a share. Many observers thought that Sterling Guarantee simply wanted a massive share dealing profit, but in fact they wanted to own Gamages and were prepared to go on fighting for it. We continued to buy in the market; seven days later, on 1 October, we had 40 per cent, and a fortnight after that we had just over the magic 50 per cent. A revised underwritten offer of 33s 6d was sent out a week later, and Sterling Guarantee had won.

Although we had cleared points with the Takeover Panel as we went along, it was generally agreed, after this battle, that the rules relating to market buying needed revising. The *Daily Telegraph*, in describing the fight, said, 'It was probably the most successful market operation ever witnessed—master minded by Jim Slater and John Lithiby of Panmure Gordon.' It was certainly the turning point for Sterling Guarantee, which afterwards went from strength to strength. In early December Sterling Guarantee announced that it had done a superb deal to develop the Gamages site jointly with Town & City, as a result of which Sterling Guarantee's shares began to rise strongly again, and were soon very substantially up on their price at the time the final offer for Gamages was made.

There was an incident on television during the Gamages bid that was so unfair to the other side that I felt most unhappy about it. *The Money Programme* at that time had a market section, which lasted for about ten minutes; the people responsible were keen to get in as much as possible, and it always seemed like a speeded-up film. On this occasion they featured Ronald Plumley, the chairman of Gamages, and right at the end of the programme the interviewer said to him something like this: 'Well, Mr Plumley, Sterling Guarantee have said that Gamages is out of date and badly run. They argue that it must be in shareholders' interests to explore more actively the colossal potential in the property, and that shareholders will only realize the full potential with them. What do you say to that?' Ronald Plumley cleared his throat and began to answer along these lines: 'I do not think that Sterling Guarantee have fully understood the problems of Gamages at the present time ...'; whereupon the interviewer interrupted with, 'I am sorry, Mr Plumley, that is all we have time for tonight.' They offered him more time the following week, but quite understandably he had had enough.

On 3 November we sold our optical group, which included Dollond & Aitchison, to Gallahers for £10.2m in cash. The rationalization had been very successful, and many duplicated facilities had been eliminated to advantage. Dick Harris, the chief executive who had been with Dollond & Aitchison originally, had been largely responsible for the running of the operation, and being such a well-managed group it was of great interest to Gallahers, who wanted to deversify from tobacco. The cash was attractive to us, and we were another large step away from being a conglomerate and towards being investment bankers. Our only major residual industrial interests were now the rubber manufacturing group, Crittall-Hope, and Phillips Brocklehurst in textiles. In May we had made an agreed cash bid of £725,000 for the Frankenstein group, which was also in rubber manufacturing, and the group was being rationalized with a view to floating it off as a separate entity. We thought that we might be able to inject Crittall-Hope into Kent Castings, which was getting bigger, and perhaps Bodycote would be able to take over the whole of our textile interests in due course.

In November we had another foray into the market, during which we accumulated a 12.8 per cent shareholding in Hay's Wharf, which was another potential property development situation. We sold out to Lazards and Sir Max Rayne's London Merchant Securities in just over a month, and made a profit of approximately £1.5m. The negotiations for the sale of our stake were achieved by two short telephone calls to Max Rayne, who is very decisive. I have perhaps made it all sound rather too easy: we had to have the idea; it had to be well researched; we had to have the finance and take the risk; then we had to find a buyer. We could very easily have been wrong and been left with shares at lower levels as a result. It was of course a very acceptable addition to our figures so near to the end of the financial year, although we only brought in a small proportion of the profit as revenue, and the balance was added to our reserves.

On 17 December the *Evening News* organized a Monopoly game at Browns Hotel, which was covered in the press and also on *The Money Programme*. The other contestants were Oliver Jessel, Vic Watson, Sir John Cohen, Nigel Broackes, David Malbert and Robert Morley. The idea was a bit of fun, and each of us was televized as we went in to Browns to engage in mortal combat. I have always liked Monopoly, which I used to play a lot as a boy. Although there is a great deal of luck in it there is also a modicum of skill. For example, it pays to buy the light-blue sites:

Pentonville Road, Euston Road and Angel Islington, and also the orange sites: Vine Street, Marlborough Street and Bow Street. The highest rental return on hotels in relation to the capital investment is from the light-blue sites, which average 159 per cent, followed by the orange sites at 141 per cent, falling gradually to the lowest return of only 101 per cent on Bond Street, Oxford Street and Regent Street. The way to work this out is to take the total cost of buying the sites and building hotels, which in the case of the orange sites is £2,060, whereas the rental on the three hotels would total £2,900 giving a return of 141 per cent. As it happens, I prefer these sites to the light-blue ones because I think that the difference in yield is more than made up by the increased likelihood of opponents landing on the orange sites. Firstly, there is a card in Chance which says 'Go back three spaces', and from one position this lands them on Vine Street. Secondly, the orange sites are a dice-throw away from Jail, which means that opponents coming out of it are likely to land on one of them. Thirdly, there are two other cards in Chance, one of which directs the player to 'Take a trip to Marylebone Station', and the other to 'Advance to Pall Mall'. Following these directions by-passes the light-blue sites and leaves the player with the possibility of landing on the orange ones with his next throw. It also pays to build quickly once you have a complete site, even at the expense of mortgaging other isolated sites to do so. For example, the loss of rent on the Strand would be only £18, but £100 out of the mortgage proceeds of £110 could be used to buy an extra house on, say, Bow Street. The first house takes the rent from £14 to £70 to give a gain of £56; and this rises to as much as £350 when the third house is added. Subject, therefore, to keeping a prudent cash reserve you should mortgage all isolated sites, and use the proceeds to build rapidly. As you can see I had thought it all out and was well prepared for the game. I even managed to get the orange sites and build hotels, but no one came to stay at them. It was Sir John Cohen who won easily, only to tell us that he had learned to play from his chauffeur the night before.

In November for the first time we successfully tried our hand in the new issue market with the flotation of two small companies. We also increased our involvement with two entrepreneurs, Peter Munk and David Gilmour, who, under the name of Southern Pacific Properties, had a major tourist development project at Pacific Harbour in Fiji. We had bought our first *tranche* of shares a year or so earlier, and subsequently further shares were placed with both P & O and Jardine Mathieson. Simon Pendock, the director responsible for our investment management business, had been our liaison man with Peter Munk, as he had been largely responsible for investigating Southern Pacific Properties in the first instance. Now he wanted to do his own thing, and on 24 December left Slater Walker on the best of terms to devote himself full time to his recent appointment as deputy chairman of Southern Pacific Properties. In 1972 this company was to be injected into a public company named King Fung in Hong Kong—of which more later.

Our company in South Africa continued to do well under the direction of Michael Javett. In March Slater Walker (South Africa) had announced the 1969 results of R1.38m, which showed a 321 per cent increase in earnings per share. In July it had taken over Cape Foundries, followed in August by the acquisition of a substantial shareholding in L. Suzman, the tobacco wholesalers, which was a classic asset situation. But in 1970 South Africa was the least of my worries as, with the faltering of the mining boom, all our worst fears about Slater Walker (Australia), by then called Austim, were coming home to roost.

Ian Murray had continued to expand faster than we had in the UK. He had even spread his wings to Singapore, buying 50 per cent of M & G, a quoted insurance company there, and he was also looking for a quoted company in New Zealand. Slater Walker UK had already decided to obtain a quotation for a new and separate public company under the name of Tagus, which was going to be a highly acquisitive vehicle. The chief executive, Grahame Mapp, was an Australian who had qualified as an accountant and had also been a management consultant. In November we offered shares in Tagus to the Australian public at 80 cents, and the next day they were standing at over $2.

Our success on the Tagus front was, however, happening at the same time as a number of problems were coming to a head with Austim. The Australian mining boom, which had always been rather unsoundly based, and had become grossly exaggerated, was coming to an end. At the height of the boom it had fully illustrated the validity of the old market maxim, 'Why spoil a good mine by putting a hole in the ground?' As the boom came to an end Austim's subsidiary, Mining Finance, started to make heavy losses on its investments and it also made an abortive $35m bid for Loloma, another mining company. The market price of Austim satellites began to fall sharply and there was a palace revolution resulting in Ian Murray's resignation as chief executive. Austim had over-expanded, and in fast-falling markets major problems were becoming evident to everyone inside the company. We realized that we could not leave Austim to sort itself out, and that in spite of our earlier withdrawal we still had a major responsibility for it. For this reason we moved back into the company by agreement with all concerned, as a result of which Austim made a share offer for the newly-floated Tagus. Dick Tarling rejoined the board, and Grahame Mapp was appointed group managing director. As the *Financial Review* put it in its headline, Austim was staying Australianized, but being re-Slater Walkerized. We found out subsequently, however, that it was going to need much more sorting out than we had at first envisaged, and it was a major headache for several years to come.

We had weathered some difficult storms in 1970, and we had seemed to come through reasonably intact. With hindsight I should have realized then that the problem with Austim was the forerunner of others to come, and that the satellite concept had great weaknesses as well as great strengths.

TWELVE

Opportunity Missed

TEN days before the start of 1971, Patrick Sergeant, the city editor of the *Daily Mail*, had selected Slater Walker as his share of the year. In past years Patrick had been very successful with some of his selections, as a result of which he had a considerable following. His recommendation at 35s 9d therefore gave us a good start for the year, and it is interesting to look back on his thinking at that time. He argued that 1970 had been a good year for us, and that our associates had significantly built up their underlying asset values during the year. He went on to point out that the price earnings ratio was only 11.5 (remember 1968 when it was at times over 30?), and that as we had a healthy cash position we would be well placed to take advantage of any opportunities that might arise. He was to be proved right.

On 28 January I appeared on *The Money Programme* in a half-hour interview with John Davis of the *Observer*. The interview was recorded as I was still worried about making a mistake, but I did very much better than previously. As a result I was asked to go on other television programmes, such as those covering the Budget, but I always refused because I felt that having done it well once I would rather leave it at that. At one point during the recording of the interview I replied to a question from John Davis with, 'I can put my hand on my heart and say . . .', while actually putting my hand over my heart. The chief technician was pleased with the recording, but said that when I put my hand over my heart the camera had been on my face, and he wanted me to do it again. I agreed, but found it extraordinarily difficult to do it naturally the second time. It reminded me of when I was at school acting in a short excerpt from *Macbeth*. I was Malcolm and someone said to me, 'Your royal father's murdered,' to which I had to reply, 'O, by whom?' It seemed to me a ridiculous reply and I could not decide whether to put the emphasis on the

'O' or the 'by whom?'. The more I practised saying it the more absurd it sounded.

It was in February that decimalization was announced and from this point on I will refer to prices in our present currency. Looking back upon it decimalization was one of the most inflationary moves made by any government in recent times. For a start almost all shopkeepers rounded off prices upwards, but much more importantly the psychology of the new currency was completely wrong because the new penny is so small that it seems almost worthless. Whilst I welcomed decimalization as a concept I would certainly have taken the ten shilling note as the unit, which would have meant that there would have been 100 pennies in it, as compared with the previous 120; I would also have chosen a less insignificant counter for the new penny. I am sure that as a result inflation would have been far less in the following twelve months.

I have sometimes imagined how terrible it would be to think you had won a really big prize on a football pool only to find that you had forgotten to post the coupon. Something rather similar, but far more serious and costly, happened to me during the first few months of 1971. It was at the time when licences were about to be granted for North Sea oil exploration and syndicates were being formed by the different oil companies. Jimmy Goldsmith telephoned me to suggest that I should meet a great friend of his, John Tigrett, who was a consultant of the legendary Doc Hammer of Occidental Petroleum. They were forming a syndicate and John wanted Slater Walker to participate. He explained the proposition to me, pointed out that it was a gamble, but stressed that Occidental had an excellent record of being 'lucky' in this kind of venture and that the upside potential was enormous. The cost to Slater Walker at that stage would have been in the region of £1m. I thought it over and discussed the proposition with a few of my colleagues, but eventually decided against it as I thought it was far too speculative. In the event Occidental formed a syndicate with Getty Oil, Thomson Organization and Allied Chemical and they did of course go on to find an abundance of oil in the Piper and Claymore oil-fields. I understand now that the estimated profit on that original £1m investment would have been in the region of £100m. Looking back, the basic error in my thinking was that I did not take sufficient account of the uniqueness of the proposition and its massive upside potential. If ever there was an opportunity that should have been grasped with both hands by an aspiring international investment banker—this had to be it. I have since become a good friend of John Tigrett, but even after all this time I find it impossible to meet him without feeling a terrible sense of loss.

On 1 April we announced our 1970 results, which showed profits of £12.1m against £10.7m for the previous year. Our shares were standing at 236p, and the price earnings ratio was about 15. We made it clear that we could have included £1.2m more profit from the Hay's Wharf deal if we had chosen to do so, but overall the market was still a little disappointed, as they had come to expect super-performance from us as par for the course. However, the Budget was a very favourable one for the market as a whole, and by the following month our shares had risen to 285p at which price the *Investors Chronicle* thought the market rating was too cautious.

A few weeks before our Annual General Meeting an article appeared in the *Daily Telegraph* suggesting to Slater Walker shareholders that Slater Walker should insure me for £10m at an estimated cost of £45,000 per annum. The argument was that if I died £60m might be wiped off the company's market capitalization of £150m. This proposal was subsequently put forward by a shareholder and resulted in a great deal of publicity. One city editor worked out that this made me worth two hundred times my weight in gold. In the event I am glad to say we did not proceed with the idea, as it seemed to stress the vulnerability of the group rather than bolster confidence. I see from the transcript of a Radio 4 interview that when I was asked '. . . but doesn't it please you to think that they feel this way about you?', I replied with the comment, 'Well, it is very gratifying, I suppose, that they do feel like that. On the other hand it means that I have got to make £45,000 a year more while I am alive!' It is interesting, looking back, to see that many people were conscious of this big weakness in the group then, but it did not seem to stop the shares continuing on their upward path.

The renewed strength of our shares encouraged me to make two more major share exchanges. In early May we made an agreed £8m bid for Solicitors Law Stationery Society, which was a legal and government publishing firm whose main and very substantial asset was Oyez House in Fetter Lane. Later in the same month we announced a £9.5m underwritten bid for shares and warrants for Wigham, Richardson & Bevington, the insurance brokers. Although we were bidding for the whole company, the family, who owned a substantial shareholding, retained 30 per cent of it and concurrently our insurance broking subsidiary, Walker Young, was acquired for shares. As a result of this we ended up with a controlling interest in a large publicly quoted insurance broking company, which in turn owned Walker Young. These two acquisitions considerably improved the quality of Slater Walker's earnings and the net assets per share of the company.

Earlier in the year we had started to buy shares in Cunard, the famous shipping firm which owned the QE2. We had built up a shareholding of just under 10 per cent, when shortly afterwards the company made it clear that they had capital commitments of £80m. This was several times the market capitalization, and quite enough to put me off, so I decided to cut our losses and started to sell our shares. In circumstances like these the selling might have been a difficult job, but as I started to drift the shares out they seemed to be going suspiciously quickly. Someone else was there and buying quietly but strongly. They say that it takes one to know one— I sensed that it was not an institution but another operator, who was buying our Cunard shares. I changed tack by starting to buy again, and I did not have long to wait before a stockbroker came to see me to say that he was acting for a client, who was interested in buying our shareholding in Cunard. He said that the client preferred to remain anonymous and offered me 165p a share for our shareholding against the then market price of 110p. We negotiated for a few weeks, finally agreeing on 175p. As the broker left my office I said, 'Give my best wishes to Nigel,' as I had guessed that it was Nigel Broackes of Trafalgar House who was the buyer.

On 1 July Trafalgar House came out with a £24m bid for Cunard. They had a 9.5 per cent shareholding themselves which, together with our 11.6 per cent, gave them a 21.1 per cent head start, which was a major factor in helping them subsequently to obtain control. The *Financial Times*, which covered the story well, reported:

A side issue to the main story is the interesting (although amicable) confrontation between Trafalgar House and Slater Walker. Both are market operators of proven worth, and each managed to build up substantial stakes in Cunard unbeknown to the other. It seems that this was made possible by the willingness of institutional holders to sell in view of Cunard's poor trading prospects and the share register now shows few institutions with sizeable stakes. Trafalgar House got brokers James Capel to approach Slater Walker when news of its interest leaked out. By the time that Capel had negotiated the purchase of Slater's $10\frac{1}{2}\%$ stake at a price of $175\frac{1}{2}$p a share sws had guessed the identity of Capel's principal. But it retired with a £750,000 dealing profit.

The half-way stage in 1971 is an appropriate time to catch up on what had been happening with our associated companies. I had already had a sharp lesson with Austim, which should have been sufficient to warn me about the potential hazards of the satellite system, but I may have been lulled into a false sense of security because Austim's failure had been offset by the success of Slater Walker (South Africa), which had reported record results in March, had an excellent reputation and had become one of the top forty industrial companies in South Africa. We had started to place a few of our shares with local institutions to make the company more South African in character and to provide us with cash for reinvestment. In the UK we were entering a bull market again, and 1971 was the year in which our satellites went into orbit in a big way. For example, by the end of the year Ralli International was capitalized at £45m; Kent Castings had absorbed Crittall and in its new form was capitalized at £30m; Cornwall had grown to £30m and Barclay Securities had expanded enormously ending the year capitalized at over £25m. By the end of 1971 the market capitalization of the UK companies we recognized as satellites or close associates totalled over £250m, and the market capitalization of all of our associated companies overseas totalled over £300m.

Rarely a week went by without one or more of our satellites making a bid and being in the news. On some occasions they bought companies from each other, and in some instances satellites spawned further satellites of their own. It would take too long to recount the details of everything that happened on the satellite front in 1971, so I am only going to try to give a broad picture, but from several different angles: first, the policy that I tried to adopt from the centre; second, an account of the development during the year of one of the main UK satellites; and third, a very brief note on the major developments within all the satellites.

As far as policy was concerned I was beginning to be worried about the overall number of associated companies, and encouraged a few mergers between them to tidy things up a little. For example Cannon Street took over Unex Investment Trust and Kent Castings bought Priam. These moves lessened our exposure, and strengthened the acquiring companies. After Austim I was worried about associated companies spawning their own satellites, and this really only happened in the UK in 1971 with Ralli International, which had interests in Lewston Developments and Tower Assets. In general I actively discouraged other associates from adopting this policy; each satellite concentrated in the main on one particular industry; I encouraged them to have only a few main divisions, and not to compete with each other. Barclay Securities was one of the more diverse, being involved in three main industries: advertising, pharmaceutical and toys. Other than these very general guiding principles I was attracted by size, as this often brought with it the type of company that had management in depth. I was always very concerned that efforts should be made to increase underlying asset values, and I tried to ensure that the chief executives of the various satellite companies did not fall in love with their own share prices, and start to believe all they were reading in the newspapers. As I have said earlier, in retrospect I should have radically pruned satellites to a more controllable number, ensuring that more of them had management in depth themselves, and were better supervised by us. At the time, however, I was caught up with the excitement of it all; it is only too easy to see what should have been done with the benefit of hindsight.

A fairly typical satellite was Cornwall Properties, in which Slater Walker had acquired a 40 per cent shareholding during 1970. One of our more able executives, Ron Shuck, who had joined us a year earlier and had had a thorough training in our organization, wanted to set up on his own account. Ron was thirty-three, Birmingham born and bred, and had tremendous ambition and determination. We helped him move into Cornwall on 6 February, lending him the money to buy one million shares personally. At this time the shares were 50p each against our purchase price of 25p, and the company was capitalized at £1m on a price earnings ratio of 23. At the same time Ron moved into Cornwall, the company purchased for shares one of our minor subsidiaries, Europa Merchants, and also two other property companies from third parties.

A month later Cornwall made an agreed bid worth £1.68m for Edward Webb & Sons (Stourbridge) which had interests in fertilizers, sugar beet and seeds. Cornwall also bought in parallel Worth Buildings, which manufactured leisure homes and garden sheds. The Webb deal was all in Cornwall shares which by then had risen to 60p. Only five weeks after this Slater Walker had acquired in the market over 20 per cent of a property company named Copthall Holdings, and a week after that on 5 May Cornwall announced an agreed £4.5m bid for Copthall. The offer was partly in Cornwall shares, which were by then over 80p, and partly in short-dated half-convertible loan stock, all of which was underwritten by Slater Walker. After this things naturally went a little quiet on the Cornwall front while Ron Shuck paused for breath. It was five months later, on 20 September, that Cornwall announced a £12m offer for

Alliance Property, by which time Cornwall had already acquired an initial 6.9 per cent shareholding. Cornwall shares were standing by then at 76p and the loan stock at 110p. The bid was fiercely contested by a shareholder group led by Mr Rowland-Jones, and it was not until 5 November that we were able to announce that Cornwall had over 50 per cent, and the offer was declared unconditional.

By the end of the year Cornwall was capitalized at £30m against £1m when Ron Shuck had become chief executive, and the value of Ron Shuck's one million shares had increased very considerably, making him his fortune. In addition Slater Walker had made a gain of several million pounds on its original investment plus the shares acquired through underwriting, as well as receiving substantial merchant banking and underwriting fees. This was an illustration of the happier side of the satellite concept, when everything went right.

Other satellites were also having an eventful year. Barclay Securities had taken over Chad Valley, the toy manufacturers, followed by Dorlands and General Poster, both of which were in advertising. The Dorlands' takeover was a hotly contested one, in which we played a significant role. This was when John Bentley began to receive a great deal of personal publicity and to make enemies. I have deliberately avoided writing about John Bentley at length as he has already had an overdose of publicity. I always rather liked him and thought him very able. John to some extent laboured under the disadvantage of being a very good-looking young man; one of the more amusing bits of publicity about him was when one of the girls at the *Financial Times* was asked what she would like for Christmas and replied, 'John Bentley!' Barclay Securities did of course go on to buy Lines Brothers from the receiver and subsequently ran into labour troubles with it, when massive redundancies were declared. No one seemed to grasp the point that Barclay had saved Lines from extinction earlier, and it was not a thriving company that eventually had to be closed down but one that would have gone under anyway. Barclay had simply bitten off more than it could chew.

The remaining satellites, too, had been busy. Sterling Guarantee had taken over Buck & Hickman and another property situation, Wharf Holdings. Ralli International had expanded considerably both in this country and overseas, and had taken over Duncan Fox, the general merchants. It had also announced a joint venture with Merrill Lynch, the famous American firm, which had the largest stockbroking business in the world and was known as 'The Thundering Herd'. Sterling Land had taken over Walter Thomas, and a company named Corporate Assets had been injected into it by us. The owners of this company were four well-known property experts, who had considerable expertise in that area and attracted a great following. Other satellite acquisitions included Armour Trust taking over Tizer, the well-known soft drinks company, and Griffiths Bentley, a new addition to our firmament, taking over Britax Excelsior which was well known for car seatbelts. These are only a few examples out of what amounted to a very active period.

In April six million of our shares in Ralli International had been placed by their stockbrokers with institutions, giving us an extra £5.5m to add to our cash resources of approximately £20m. This brought our shareholding down to 12.5 per cent of Ralli's total share capital which was about the size of shareholding I thought we should continue to hold as investment bankers. There was another factor in my mind—there was no substitute for a realized profit. For similar reasons I began to reduce our shareholdings in other satellites such as Barclay Securities. I remember particularly that we placed with institutions almost all of our shareholding in Sterling Guarantee during the year. By July Sterling shares had risen from 180p at the time of the Gamages bid in May 1970 to an astonishing 500p. They had just made a bid for Buck & Hickman, and John Lithiby of Panmure Gordon, the stockbrokers, was arranging to underwrite with the institutions the shares to be issued. Normally in this sort of underwriting there might have been one institution in five that would have turned it down, but after it was all completed John telephoned me to say that never in his experience had an underwriting been so easy, and that no one institution had rejected it. I knew from this that the moment had come to sell our shares, and shortly afterwards John placed almost all of them for us. The shares did not in fact improve in the market after that and we had placed our shareholding at virtually the top of the market. You might well ask why the shares did not improve as all the knowledgeable professional investors wanted to underwrite them, which meant they must have thought very well of the shares. The reason is the essence of contrary thinking—it was because *every* knowledgeable investor thought the shares were an excellent buy that they had to be a sell. By definition the market had to be overbought—who else was going to buy them in sufficient volume to put them up? I know a very successful American professional investor who simply invests in leading shares in which the institutions are not heavily invested, having checked out first that all other things are reasonably equal. His argument is that the institutions are more likely to invest in the stock in the future than to sell it. Conversely if everyone is already invested in it, sellers are more likely to appear.

Contrary thinking only works if the timing is right. It is important not to rely upon the principle until other people's thinking has reached an advanced stage approaching unanimity; otherwise you just get trampled underfoot. I saw an interesting idea expounded in a commodity magazine which took soundings each week from brokers and others in the trade to ascertain their views on different commodities. The magazine reasoned that when 85 per cent of the trade was optimistic about the prospects for a commodity it should be sold, and conversely when 85 per cent were pessimistic about the prospects it should be bought. I tested out this principle and found that it worked very well, although I preferred to adopt 90 per cent as my measure.

I have always been fascinated by the process of thinking and I like to look for extra dimensions. I very much enjoyed meeting Dr Edward de Bono, the leading exponent of lateral thinking, and we had several entertaining lunches together. Lateral thinking is a form of creative thinking which is concerned, as de Bono would put it, 'with breaking out of the concept prisons of old ideas'. He has written several interesting books on the subject in which he describes ways of approaching problems from different angles. One of his best and simplest examples is that of a tennis tournament, where there are 111 entrants. Assuming that it is a singles knock-out tournament and you as secretary have to arrange the matches, the question is, what is the minimum number of matches, excluding byes, that would have to be arranged for this number of entrants? Some people would approach this problem by drawing numerous little diagrams showing the actual pairs in each match and the number of byes, while others might try to work it out with algebra. In fact the answer can be reached without any complicated mathematics. To find the solution one must shift attention from the winners of each match to the losers, in whom no one is usually interested. Since there can only be one winner there must be 110 losers and each loser can only lose once so that must be 110 matches. The concept of lateral thinking seems to me to have much in sympathy with Dohm's maxims of trying to turn disadvantages into advantages and of approaching problems on an 'it can be done' basis. In looking for an answer one may have to think in a different dimension from the norm; the important point is not to give up immediately more conventional approaches have been exhausted.

In early June Slater Walker announced that it had bought 15.2 million shares in Haw Par Brothers International of Singapore, which had interests in banking, newspapers and the manufacture and distribution of the famous Tiger Balm medical products. The shares represented 46 per cent of the issued share capital. As this acquisition had such important consequences for both the company and myself, I should explain how Slater Walker came to be interested in the Far East.

The commercial success of Japan had made everyone conscious of the fact that the Far East was a dynamic part of the world and had enormous potential for expansion. We had only a minor indirect interest in the area through Austim's shareholding in M & G, a small quoted insurance company in Singapore. One of our merchant banking executives, Donald Ogilvy-Watson, had lived in Singapore previously, and felt strongly that we should have a direct shareholding in a more substantial quoted investment there. I agreed that the idea was a good one, and suggested that he went out to Singapore to try and find something suitable. He had gone there a few months earlier, ascertained that the Aw family's 46 per cent shareholding in Haw Par was for sale and, after investigation, we had made our offer. The Singapore Government asked us to sell the newspaper to a Singapore resident, and we also made arrangements to sell the banking subsidiary as we did not feel that we could effectively manage a bank there. Dick Tarling and Donald Ogilvy-Watson were in Singapore making all the arrangements, and they subsequently joined the board of Haw Par.

While all this was happening we took our Haw Par shareholding up to 51 per cent by purchases in the market. At one stage it looked as if the deal might be off, but it was finally confirmed. The newspaper was sold to the Aw family for £650,000 and the bank was sold to another local one for £2.97m. The Singapore Government did not like these developments. The President, in opening the second session of Parliament, said, 'Recently a British group of stock market operators quietly bought the majority stocks of a Singapore company, then sold the company's holdings in a bank and in newspapers for considerable profits, all at no risk, in little time and without much effort.' In August Haw Par bought the 54 per cent shareholding in M & G from Austim, and in October a deal was announced with Jack Chia which completely restructured the residual pharmaceutical interests. It was announced in November that Austim was taking a 20 per cent shareholding in Haw Par, in partnership with Slater Walker who retained 31 per cent. The sale of this 20 per cent to Austim reflected a prior understanding between Slater Walker and Austim.

In 1971 we were again top of the British Business Growth League in *Management Today* with a rating over the previous ten years of 2509. Second this time was Ralli International with 2257, third Blackwood Hodge 1717, fourth Rank 1021, falling rapidly to GEC at tenth with 782. Robert Heller, the editor, said at that time, 'Jim Slater has produced the most convincing proof so far in Britain, that genuine business growth can be created by in effect dealing in companies and in their securities.' I am not repeating his comments, or those of other observers, because they give me a warm glow today, but to show the prevailing attitude. Robert Heller was one of the more critical business observers of the day (he has recently written *The Naked Investor*, which debunks a number of myths about investment) but even he was moving from a negative or neutral attitude towards relative acceptance. Having gone through the whole of my scrap books for the last seven years up to this point, I would summarize the attitude of the daily and weekly press by saying that 10 per cent were neutral observers; 20 per cent were mildly in favour; 35 per cent were definitely in favour and 35 per cent were aficionados. Looking back on the preceding twelve months, it is difficult to find any adverse comment at all. Needless to say from time to time there would be a critical article on a specific news item, but this would be more than compensated for by favourable comment on other occasions. A few years later it was very tempting for members of the press to pick out isolated critical comment and maintain that this was what they had been saying all along; in fact, at the time, they were all caught up in the euphoria of a bull market. Slater Walker was a bull market stock *par excellence*, and in such circumstances it was very difficult for the press to resist the mood of the crowd. I too was getting caught up with the general feeling that the world was an oyster, and that Slater Walker would become one of the biggest investment banking concerns in the world. At that time it was difficult to envisage what could stop it.

In early September we announced the formation of Slater Walker Investment Trust. It was to start its life as a £22.5m trust with £12.5m of £1 ordinary shares, and £10m of $8\frac{1}{2}$ per cent partly convertible ten-year loan stock. Slater Walker and associates and leading institutions subscribed for two-thirds of the shares and loan stock, and we offered the balance to the public. Usually investment trust shares stand at a discount on their underlying asset values whereas in this case, because there were issue expenses, we were effectively offering shares in SWIT at a small premium. However, following the Hay's Wharf and Cunard deals, our reputation in the assets field was such that the press coverage of the issue was good, and the issue was almost three times over-subscribed.

The success of the issue had a dual effect on Slater Walker itself; firstly it increased the total funds under our management by about 20 per cent, giving us more firepower, and secondly the management fee of over £100,000 was a helpful and regular addition to our annual future profits.

By this time I was beginning to deal in millions as a matter of routine, and indeed on occasion in tens of millions. I have often been asked how this affected me as the group grew. It is interesting to look back on, say, the Cork deal, which capitalized at only £1.1m and to compare it with SWIT at £22.5m. The effort in launching the new investment trust was 10 per cent that of acquiring Cork and yet the figures were twenty times greater. The simple answer to the question is that I adjusted as I went along. When I had to make £200,000 profit in a year in the early days every £10,000 was significant, but as the annual profits increased to £12m only the half millions were particularly meaningful to me. Very soon, in a Slater Walker sense, I began to think of a million as 'one', and it was entirely logical that this should be so. An interesting psychological point is that in the City it is far easier to raise £5m than £100,000. The fact that you can be thinking in terms of raising £5m means that you are likely to be of a size and credibility that merits it, and this is more re-assuring to a prospective institutional investor or banker than something smaller and therefore apparently much more risky. The main point is that the financial unit that you think in terms of, when running a business, must be sufficiently relevant to the financial results of that business to make it worth the chief executive's personal mental effort and time involvement. After all, an extra nought on the end does not really make any difference to the basic principles involved.

On the general subject of figures, I must say that I am not entirely happy about the 'new maths' that is being taught in schools, nor the trend towards using calculators instead of mental arithmetic to solve even relatively simple problems. It would be far more helpful to many children if they were taught different ways of doing simple sums. For example, they could be taught at quite an early age to multiply, say, 24 by 11 in their heads by simply adding the 2 and the 4 together and inserting the total of 6 between them to give a total of 264. Similarly they should be taught to multiply 22 by 97 by adding two noughts to 22 and then deducting three times 22 from the answer to give 2,134. It is not so much a question of being able to multiply numbers in this way, but of the approach to the problem. Once children really *understand* numbers their ability with them will increase rapidly, and the subject of maths could be made much more interesting and enjoyable if different approaches to problems were taught at an early stage in their education.

In 1970 Michael Javett had recommended to me a friend of his, Robert Smith, who was an executive with the Thomson Organization. Robert thought he was coming to see me for a general discussion to find out whether there might be a good executive position for him within our organization in London. My motives were different however—I always associated the name of Thomson with Canada and, knowing that Robert Smith had been there on several occasions, I had him in mind for a new Canadian venture. Robert was tailor-made for the job. He was thirty-two years old, personable, ambitious, well used to business reorganization and he had some experience of arranging financial deals. My offer swept him off his feet and within half-an-hour, to his surprise, he had agreed that he would take the job.

After a brief period of induction with us, Robert went out to Canada to sniff out the ground, and renew old acquaintances. Very soon he had found a suitable small quoted company, which would serve as a vehicle for our expansion. Its name was Stanley Brock and it was, of all things, a Winnipeg-based laundry and dry-cleaning equipment distributor. In March 1971 we bought 61 per cent of the equity at $15 a share, out of which Robert Smith had 5 per cent, and we helped him to arrange the financing of them. By June the shares were $60 on a price earnings ratio of 60, anticipating things to come. We arranged a three for one split and a rights issue to make a better market for the shares and to make them less heavy. At the same time we announced plans to change the name to incorporate the words Slater Walker. The board was also changed: Robert Smith became president and John Tory, J. Pearce-Bunting, Roland Rowe and I became directors. John Tory was a partner in a leading legal firm and an adviser to Lord Thomson, and Pearce-Bunting was a stockbroker who subsequently became chairman of the Canadian Stock Exchange. The calibre of Robert Smith and the non-executive members of the board was to be an important factor in the success of the company in the years ahead.

In September I went out to Canada for a fortnight to help Robert who had been nurturing several prospective deals. At a lunch on the day before my departure I was told by a number of people that the Canadian market was not like the English one, and that it would not be possible to make many acquisitions there. That same afternoon we were able to announce two major acquisitions. We had split up into two separate parties: one to finalize the Peoples Stores deal and the other to finalize the UNAS deal. We met in the street, quite by chance, as each group was going to a separate destination, and I remember how we excitedly compared notes and checked each other's progress. By the end of the day we were able to announce that Slater Walker of Canada had acquired from the Toronto-Dominion Bank two-thirds of UNAS Investments and from Abe Gold 65,000 shares in the Peoples Department Stores. We had also agreed to extend the offer to other shareholders in both UNAS and Peoples to the extent of two-thirds of their total shareholdings. The Montreal *Star* remarked at the time, 'Almost like the old days of Bay Street . . . an asset play and the initiative coming from the staid old City of London.'

Abe Gold was a real expert in the departmental stores business. He had come up the hard way, knew the business from A to Z, and was very keen to build up a nationwide retailing organization. Two months after my visit we were able to announce that Peoples Stores were going to acquire for shares, with a cash alternative, the entire equity of Gordon Mackay, which was another company in the departmental stores business, but much more of an asset situation. Our Canadian venture was really taking shape and Slater Walker of Canada looked poised for further substantial growth.

On 5 October we moved into credit finance with the formation of Slater Walker Finance Corporation, appointing a managing director who had previously been a director of Lombank. The Government had recently removed the control of an initial deposit and the length of repayment terms in both hire purchase and credit transactions, and we were getting on the bandwagon. With hindsight this was in fact a classic case of bad thinking on my part, as I was moving with the crowd into the troubles that would certainly follow. There would be a rat-race for new business with the result that standards would decline, customers would become overextended and excessive bad debts would result. It was all foreseeable if I had applied general principles, but my enthusiasm prevented me from standing back far enough to see the wood for the trees.

Three days after forming our new credit finance business we announced that we owned $18\frac{1}{2}$ per cent of Blackburn Assurance, and that we intended to bid for the balance. We subsequently agreed a bid which capitalized the whole company at £9m and the remaining public shareholders were offered our long-dated loan stock in exchange for their Blackburn shares.

This added substantially to our insurance interests, and gave scope for integration with Pioneer, which we had acquired in July for £3.1m.

Our programme of selling off our industrial interests was proceeding well. In July we had successfully floated off to the public our rubber manufacturing interest under the name of Allied Polymer, only retaining a 20 per cent shareholding ourselves and £4m worth of partly convertible loan stock. In late October we announced that we were going to inject Crittall-Hope into Butterley Engineering Industries (previously named Kent Castings). It should be made clear that the Crittall-Hope which was being injected was a completely different animal from the original Crittall-Hope that we had taken over in 1968: the American and certain UK subsidiaries had been sold, and the South African subsidiary had been taken over by the Slater Walker group to be transformed into the nucleus of Slater Walker (South Africa). It was therefore only the slimmed down residual operating companies that were being sold into Butterley. In exchange we would receive £9.25m of which £4.4m would be in a 10 per cent partly convertible loan stock, and the balance would be in Butterley shares. Dick Tarling was going to be chief executive of the new group, but would retain his seat on the main Slater Walker board and his responsibility for our investments in Australia and the Far East. As *The Times* said, this 'effectively completed the transformation of Slater Walker from an industrial conglomerate to an investment bank'. All that was needed to add the finishing touches would be to place enough shares in Butterley to de-consolidate it from our accounts and to sell off our relatively minor residual textile interests.

In early 1970 I had delivered a speech at a Manchester Institute of Directors' lunch before a few hundred people, and it had gone down well. There were a number of questions asked afterwards, and I always found that once a dialogue got going the atmosphere became much livelier. Sir Richard Powell, who was Director General of the Institute, was present, enjoyed the speech and had the idea that I might be a suitable person to speak at the Institute of Directors' Annual Conference at the Albert Hall on 2 November 1971. The committee approved his proposal, and after thinking it over carefully I accepted. It was a big challenge, as the audience was to be in the region of five thousand and the other speakers would be Lord Goodman, Sir Christopher Soames, Tony Barber, who was then Chancellor of the Exchequer, Lee Kuan Yew and Billy Graham.

I put a lot of work into preparing my speech. The essence of it was that commercial greatness was within Britain's grasp. I argued that we needed to be more adventurous than our international competitors; to form a new relationship between management and ownership; to have more youthful representation in our boardrooms; to continue with the fundamental reform of taxation; to have a more enlightened approach to industrial relations, and to develop a positively international approach to doing business. I went on to say that I believed that there was strong evidence that managers were at their most efficient when they had some form of capital stake in the business they were managing—for example, the average director's shareholding in the six best-performing companies was ten times that in the bottom six. I then gave the arguments for share option schemes, and for interest being chargeable for taxation purposes against the funds borrowed by a manager in buying shares in the company for which he worked—this, I said, gave him the owner's eye, and the stick of downside risk as well as the carrot of upside potential. At this time no eyebrows were raised—this was Slater Walker's well-known and well-advertised policy—but years later in more bearish markets many people seemed surprised that money had been borrowed by directors to buy shares and that there were incentive schemes within the group.

In the event, as the *Economist* said, the content of my speech was good but it was 'drably delivered'. I had by this time become quite effective when speaking to five or six hundred people, but there was, I found out, a big difference between five hundred and five thousand. To put it mildly the atmosphere was rather less intimate. In addition, because the occasion was important to me, I read my speech as opposed to speaking from brief notes which I normally did. There is a well-known saying that the worst spoken speech is better than the best read speech. Whilst I do not entirely agree, I think that the general principle is sound.

Lord Goodman started off and spoke brilliantly with no notes for about forty minutes. He was most entertaining and had the audience in the palm of his hand. I came next and was followed by Tony Barber, who spoke about the future of the capitalist system. Then came Sir Christopher Soames with whom the audience were naturally in sympathy as he was the man who had been very helpful in our relationship with France prior to the successful Common Market negotiations. His speech was excellent and he told a number of good stories. He began by saying that he would not take long as he had never forgotten a terrible experience in New York, when an after-dinner speaker took as his text the word 'Yale', which was where the speaker had been educated. He said Y stood for youth and gave

them ten minutes on that; A for ambition; L for leadership; E for enterprise, and they were treated to ten minutes on each of these as well. As he
was drawing to the end of E for enterprise a voice from the back said,
'Thank God he didn't go to the Massachusetts Institute of Technology!'
The remaining speakers, Lee Kuan Yew and Billy Graham, both acquitted
themselves very well. All in all I found it a very levelling day and realized
that while my public speaking might have improved considerably, I had
been completely out of my league.

At the end of November we bought the leasehold of the Galeries Lafayette
property in Regent Street for about £1m. A few months prior to that we
had spent £3.7m on the Westland Helicopter factory at Hayes in Middle-
sex. We subsequently successfully redeveloped this site and realized a good
profit in doing so. These two relatively major purchases were symptomatic
of many other property purchases of a less newsworthy nature. We had
recruited a team of property executives and, in addition to our indirect
interests in property through our quoted satellites such as Argyle, Cornwall and Sterling Land, we were building up a significant property portfolio both at home and overseas. Credit was easy to obtain and in particular we could borrow dollars apparently very cheaply on a medium-
term basis. Our expansion in property, like our entry into the credit
finance business, was very much stimulated by the availability of easy
credit. With growing inflation rates the mood of the country was that it
was better to have money in things than in cash and this mood did of
course fuel the stock, land, property, picture and commodity markets. It
would have been too early to apply contrary thinking as the view was not
approaching unanimity. Money was still to be made, but with hindsight
it was getting dangerous to be a buyer, because if the mood changed it
would be difficult to change tack, realize profits, and degear. I did not
appreciate this at the time and as a result I was still intent on building up
our property interests at full speed.

As was to be expected Austim had had a difficult year following its period
of over-expansion and the sharp fall in the mining market. When their
results were announced in late April they were described by the *Financial
Review* as a 'grim—but frank—tale of woe'. Profits had shrunk from
$3.8m to $434,000 net assets were written down from $44.7m to $24.9m
and there was to be no final dividend for 1970. To deal with Austim's
problems Grahame Mapp explained that the share portfolio had been

liquidated, investment banking activities severely curtailed, speculative mining ventures stopped, and head office overheads halved. Two months later they also announced offers for the outstanding shares in their four main satellites and a rights issue which was underwritten by Slater Walker. In addition Austim had come into partnership with Slater Walker in the purchase of a 20 per cent shareholding in Haw Par, which was to prove to be a very lucrative investment for it. The name of the company was changed back to Slater Walker (Australia) Ltd, and this was very well received by the Australian press, one newspaper commenting, 'The prodigal son has returned. Rejoice, kill the fatted calf, let us give him back his parents' name.' We knew we had taken on a major problem when we first moved back into Austim, and it had already taken a lot of time and money to get it back on the right road. Some big problems remained, but at least its survival seemed to be assured, and we were hopeful that in the longer term, with Grahame Mapp's help, we could restore it to a state of reasonable prosperity.

At the end of 1971 the overall funds under our management, excluding Slater Walker's own resources, amounted to £130m. This was to some extent due to the rise in the market, but other important factors were the extra funds raised by the Slater Walker Investment Trust issue and the success of Flag Investment Trust. In the previous year only our High Income unit trust had done exceptionally well, coming top of the league tables, and this was largely due to Ian Wasserman who, in 1971, joined the main board and handed over the management to concentrate entirely on corporate finance. After Simon Pendock left, Jim Nichols took over as chief executive of the investment side and worked in partnership with Brian Banks. Both of them had come from National Provident Institution and they worked hard to improve the operation as a whole and to make the overall performance of funds under our management live up to earlier promise. They succeeded, and I was very pleased to see that in 1971 we had two of our unit trusts in the top ten, and that we were selected as managers of the year by both the *Daily Express* and the *Observer*.

On 20 December Patrick Sergeant reviewed the progress of Slater Walker, which had been his share of the year, and had risen from 175p when he selected it to 319p, with a gain of 82 per cent against a 41 per cent rise in the market as a whole. He remained optimistic about our future prospects but recommended another share as his selection for 1972. Patrick Hutber, the city editor of the *Sunday Telegraph*, also wrote an interesting article in December under the title 'Slater's Magic Wand'. He commented, 'The magic of the Slater Walker name is still the most potent way to put up the price of a share,' and went on to say:

How far can Jim Slater create values? I sometimes imagine him standing in front of a complex glass apparatus, the sort of thing used in fifth form science. Through it goes a flow of cash, of propositions, of buying opportunities. He turns a tap underneath and out into one of a row of beakers comes capital appreciation. And yet the process is by no means as irrational or as easy as the metaphor may suggest. The plain fact is that the Slater satellites have done extremely well till now, with Sterling Guarantee up eight times, Barclay Securities up a similar amount and the group of satellites as a whole showing a growth of something like 165% per annum. It is also true that Slater is not yet apparently in a position to be able to afford to let a satellite fail. If one falters, as Austim did, there is no alternative but for the head office team to move in, take over and sort it out. With this providing a floor, it is not surprising that 'the premium for hope', i.e. the rise in price that the announcement of an association with him brings, is liable to be in the region of 100% or more. Certainly there has not yet been a case in which those who paid the premium regretted it.

At the end of the year the *Investors Chronicle* featured a review of the best and worst share performances during 1971. Their main comment was that looking through the top twenty-five companies they were struck by the number of shares in which Slater Walker had had some influence. Indeed, they said that the market-dealing activities of Slater Walker had been one of the highlights of 1971. Our share price on 30 December 1971 was 329p, and we were ending the year with our charisma at its highest. I was very optimistic about our prospects, but at this point a really good contrary thinker would have known exactly what to do.

· THIRTEEN ·

Far Eastern Visit

THE first press comment of any interest in 1972 was in the *Financial Times* of 3 January under the title 'Oh Mr Slater! Yes Mr Heath?' It referred to a dinner at Chequers the night before, which had also been attended by Jacob Rothschild, Malcolm Horsman and some other young businessmen. There had been two senior members of the civil service present and Ted Heath had used the occasion to try and spark off some useful ideas. My main recollection of the dinner is that when the cheese barrel was passed around I dug the spoon rather too forcefully down the edge of the cheese, and some of it came out in a fine spray; to my embarrassment it landed on Mr Heath, who was sitting next to me. I recovered quickly and said, 'Would you like some cheese?', to which he replied, 'Thank you—but not this way!'

I had met Ted Heath a few years earlier while he was in the Opposition and living in chambers in the Albany. I had advised him on his personal financial affairs and as a result had got to know him quite well. As there has been some publicity on the subject I should like to make it clear that Ted Heath had no knowledge of the detailed investments made by Slater Walker on his behalf. His merchant bankers, Brown Shipley, handled the administration of his portfolio and Slater Walker recommended the investments. On several occasions I had lunch with Ted Heath at the Albany, but I found him difficult to relate to easily, as he had a disconcerting habit of switching off in the middle of a discussion. I would be waxing eloquent on a subject which I thought would be bound to interest him, when I would notice that a very remote look had come into his eyes which indicated that the conversation was at an end.

After Ted Heath became Prime Minister I continued to see him socially, and my wife and I were invited to dine at Downing Street on two occasions, on one of which the guest of honour was Lee Kuan Yew. We were also sometimes invited to lunch at Chequers which is situated just north of Aylesbury and is about an hour's drive from my home. The road is a long and winding one and the turning off for Chequers is very easy to miss, as it is not signposted in any way. Nearer the house itself there is a check-point with police on duty and other policemen can occasionally be glimpsed in the very extensive grounds.

The house was originally made available to the Prime Minister of the day by Viscount Lee in 1917. Ted Heath refurbished some of the rooms and had the panelling in the main reception hall stripped, as a result of which the woodwork was a much lighter tone than the original sombre dark brown. Although I thought this was an improvement I would have felt that I was tampering with history. Ted Heath might have been encouraged by Churchill's example. In the same reception hall there is a very large oil painting which features a lion and a mouse. Churchill considered that the mouse was too small in relation to the lion, so he painted a new and larger mouse over the old one. I doubt if any other Prime Minister would have been capable of doing this, and as a result it has become a feature of Chequers and somehow seems entirely in character.

I can vividly recall an occasion when Ted Heath telephoned one Saturday morning to invite me for lunch at Chequers. Someone else had let him down and we would be on our own. The idea was very appealing, but it was my elder daughter's first speech day and my wife insisted that I went to it, as there was a strong possibility that my daughter might be presented with a prize. It was an absolutely perfect day and I remember how I kept thinking that I could have driven to Chequers in an open car and had lunch with the Prime Minister of England. As it happened, my daughter did not get her prize, and after the speeches were over, as I was walking around the school thinking of the opportunity I had missed, I suddenly tripped over and severely sprained my ankle. It was so bad that I had to go home immediately, and it gave me trouble for at least two weeks after that. There's no justice!

The success of the flotation of Slater Walker Investment Trust, which invested in the prey of acquisitive companies, had made me think that there might be scope for an investment trust which invested in the acquisitive companies themselves. There was no doubt that satellite stocks were performing exceptionally well, as Patrick Hutber's December article had made clear. The prospective investor always had the difficulty of choosing the right satellite, and I thought that many people would prefer simply to invest in the average one through the medium of an investment trust managed by Slater Walker. To attract two different types of investor there could be capital shares with rights to all the capital growth, and income shares with rights to all the income. From the Slater Walker point of view our percentage shareholdings in many of the satellites were too high for investment banking purposes and I usually aimed to lower them to about 10–15 per cent. The extra cash we would raise by an issue of this nature would also be very helpful in the expansion of our banking and property interests, which were gaining momentum. These were all the ingredients which helped me to conceive the Slater Walker Dual Trust.

The final structure was 15 million capital shares and 15 million income shares. The Slater Walker group retained 49 per cent, investment clients and directors retained a further percentage and the public were offered the balance of just over 5 million capital and 5 million income shares. As this trust came in for criticism later and with the benefit of hindsight was obviously a mistake, it is interesting to see what the press said at the time. In the main it was neutral to mildly bullish, pointing particularly to past performance and the pulling power of the Slater Walker name. The *Sunday Times* warned of the dangers if the market turned and a few months later, in an article criticizing our dealing in the shares of satellites, referred to the group as 'a seething pyramid of escalating paper'. The *Investors Chronicle* also had a double-page article under the heading 'Slater's high risk proposition', which advised against investing in the Dual Trust. Looking back on it the article was a well-reasoned one, pointing to the fact that the Dual Trust was highly geared and therefore dangerous if the market turned. It also went on to say that the Dual Trust was an exercise in pyramiding, which, whilst useful in raising cash in the short term, could dramatically accelerate the down-turn if the market should begin to move against Slater Walker companies.

The offer in January 1972 attracted a total of over £23m, but in early dealings the capital shares went to a small discount, and it was a few weeks later that the Dual Trust acquired its nickname of the 'Dustbin Trust'. The market did in fact move against Slater Walker companies later in the year, and although the trust performed reasonably well in the circumstances it was always a failure in terms of investor appeal. I was to find later that it also had another less obvious disadvantage. When I wanted to move much more positively into cash I was unable to sell many of the underlying investments because I had to preserve the tax status of the trust; important tax privileges available to its shareholders would have been lost if more than a small proportion of its portfolio had been sold during the first year.

At this time I was in contact with David Frost whom I had met about twelve months earlier when he had telephoned to arrange a breakfast meeting. I think he must have picked up the business breakfast habit in America. I never liked the idea myself but it seemed to be the only time that we could both manage easily. We had met at the Savoy, where a few other people were eating their bacon and eggs or kippers in a desultory way. David seemed at first to be very like the man one saw on television, with a breezy, larger than life 'hello and welcome' approach, but I soon found that he had a very quick grasp of figures, a warm personality and a keen sense of situation humour. I liked him very much and although our first meeting had proved abortive we kept in touch, as he was keen on the idea of injecting his business interests into a suitable quoted company at an appropriate time. He was earning colossal fees for regular appearances on American television and wanted to use them as an earnings base upon which to build a worth-while company in the entertainment industry. I soon found a suitable quoted company—Equity Enterprises—and both Slater Walker and David purchased a significant stake in it. We planned to use it as an acquisitive shell to build up the asset base, and then in due course to examine the possibility of injecting David's other business interests into it.

My meeting with David broadened my life, as he had a very wide range of friends and acquaintances. Another interesting by-product of our meeting was the film *The Slipper and the Rose*. My wife had frequently complained to me that there was nothing really suitable on at the cinema for young children during half-term. At that time there seemed to be a dearth of family films, and I could not understand why there was no good film of Cinderella. It seemed to me to have all the ingredients—the stepmother and the ugly sisters representing evil, the fairy godmother representing good, and the prince and Cinderella providing the romance. The moments of fantasy, like the changing of the pumpkin into a coach and Cinderella's rags into a beautiful ball gown, would be a film technician's dream. I suggested to David that a film of Cinderella would be a winner, and he agreed to get something moving by arranging for the Sherman brothers to write the songs. He then told me about his ideas for the film, which I thought were in danger of losing the essence of the story. I therefore opted out at that stage and David continued alone, subsequently linking up with Naim

Attallah on the production side and with Bryan Forbes as the director. I must confess that I thoroughly enjoyed the film when it was first shown in 1976 and thought it a great improvement over anything I had had in mind.

In early March I went to Singapore, Hong Kong and Australia. It was a very rushed trip because it had been delayed by my having influenza, and it was to have fateful consequences. I went first to Singapore for three days —my one and only visit—to give a talk to an Investment Seminar. I also attended several social functions and met Lee Kuan Yew. The meeting was a very brief and formal one during which we exchanged a few pleasantries and, amongst other things, I explained to him the difficulties we were having in obtaining work permits for our key staff. A few hours before we had gone to see Lee Kuan Yew, one of the Chinese employees in the office had said to Dick Tarling in a rather embarrassed way, 'I hope you don't mind me saying so, but my Prime Minister would not like your long hair and I suggest you have it cut.' Dick did wear his hair rather longer than most people and Lee Kuan Yew had brought to Singapore an appearance of puritanism by encouraging shirt-sleeve order, no smoking and frequent hair cuts. He had also closed down all discotheques and brought in harsh legislation to discourage litter in the streets.

Although the population of Singapore is over two million, of which three-quarters are Chinese, the city-state island is only a third bigger than the Isle of Wight. There is a facade of freedom in that there is a Parliament, an electoral system, and an opposition to the ruling People's Action Party; at first sight the press do not appear to be controlled and there seems to be an excellent and impartial legal system. But just under the surface it is very different: in Parliament the PAP holds all sixty-nine seats; electoral votes are numbered and members of the opposition are frequently arrested. The Government has effective control over the press through printing licences, and journalists who step out of line are arrested and detained without trial. The legal system also has important defects: the jury system was abolished years ago when the Government found that they were not getting the decisions required in political cases, and recently lawyers have also been arrested. The trappings of freedom are all there but underneath it is an absolute dictatorship.

Interestingly, the casual visitor to Singapore would at first be impressed by the imposed puritanism, but just beneath the surface it is again different. The contrast is most evident in the infamous Bugis Street, where I went to one of the open cafes for a drink one evening. Here small children go from table to table trying to play you noughts and crosses for money, but the main feature of the street is that there are an astonishing number of brothels and the numerous very colourfully dressed prostitutes are, in the main, young male transvestites. I have travelled several hundred thousand miles but have never seen anything quite like Bugis Street.

From Singapore I went to Hong Kong where again there were many social functions. I also put into effect the Spydar share incentive scheme and left the administration of it to be set up by one of our executives, a solicitor, in liaison with Deacons, who were Haw Par's solicitors. I enjoyed Hong Kong. At that time it was an exciting place to be in business. The Stock Exchange was just beginning to come to life and was to increase in value six-fold in the following year. After Hong Kong I went on to Australia and it was there that I concluded an £8m deal with Sir Douglas Clague to exchange shares in Slater Walker and Haw Par for shares in the Hong Kong based Hutchison International. In the event, this turned out to be a very profitable investment for us.

Our results for 1971 were announced following my return in late March. Profits before tax had advanced from £12.16m to £16.28m which was ahead of general expectations. Other financial groups, such as Dalton Barton and Vavasseur, were also reporting excellent results. The *Investors Chronicle* referred to us as being 'a sleek financial group specializing in merchant banking, property and insurance instead of as a conglomerate with only limited industrial logic'. They concluded by saying that the price earnings ratio of 22 was taking a relatively undemanding view of the future. In early May when the full Report and Accounts was sent to shareholders I was optimistic about our future prospects and we also announced a one for three scrip issue. The shares by then had risen to 412p; the market capitalization was £225m and underlying assets at market prices about £100m. The press was generally bullish and Lex's views that there seemed 'little reason to think that the goodwill element of the share price was vulnerable' summarized the feelings of most observers. The shares were in fact virtually at their all-time high at this point, which, in view of what happened afterwards, is another classic illustration of the effectiveness of contrary thinking.

I was beginning to be bearish about the market and I had started to turn some of our quoted investments into cash. This gave us a strong short-term cash position but we were still borrowing money long term to invest in property and to expand our banking and overseas interests. In retrospect I should of course have applied the policy of going into cash right across the board. Instead, like everyone else in banking at that time, we were busy actively *seeking* opportunities to lend more money. A few months earlier we had taken on two new senior banking executives to help us extend the purely commercial side of our banking business: one to concentrate on building up the branch network and deposit getting, the other to expand our loan book. This policy was a cardinal error on my part because the pure lending of money is a highly professional business. It is quite different in investment banking, where in parallel to a commercial loan one is also taking an equity stake, on which the upside potential could be very considerable. In pure lending the upside potential is only the 'turn' on the interest receivable, less the cost of borrowing plus overheads, which in our case probably worked out at about 2 per cent per annum. Bearing in mind that the downside risk on any loan is 100 per cent the odds were substantially against our being successful, especially as we were going with the crowd and actively competing for business.

There were a number of other developments of significance in the first half of 1972. In February we added to our long-term borrowings by raising £9.8m by the issue to institutions of £10m-worth of $9\frac{1}{2}$ per cent unsecured loan stock, and we successfully handled our first takeover defence when we warded off a bid for AAH. In May, Hanson Trust finally called off their attempt to take over Costains, and Slater Walker raised approximately £15m by the issue of Sterling/Deutschemark bonds and convertible dollar loan stock to finance the acquisition of our initial investments in quoted companies in France, Belgium, Holland and Germany, where we planned to expand substantially. In June we floated a new £6m Far Eastern investment trust and arranged a successful new issue of shares for Leisure Caravan Parks. These were only the major events and each one of them would have been of great significance to us two years earlier, but by that time they had become almost routine. Both the breadth of our activities and the speed with which we were dealing with problems generated a great feeling of excitement within the company. As one newspaper commentator said at the time, 'However heavy weight the volumes of future historians might be none would be able to catch the breathlessness of the pace.'

Dr Channon of Manchester Business School prepared a case study on Slater Walker for the year 1972, and the details of it give some idea of our offices and work style at that time. We had about 150 people in our head office at Petershill House. The investment side, which employed approximately 40 people, was quite separate at Leith House nearby, and the insurance-company staff of about 100 were located initially at Oyez House and subsequently at Shepherd's Bush. Head office concentrated on accounts, secretarial, banking and property, and contained the central executive with their supporting staff. Among other things Dr Channon said:

> Individual offices were relatively small yet functional and furnished in spartan fashion. Mr Slater's own office was not large and was furnished in similar style containing a desk, chair, telephone table and cloak cupboard, together with a small table and chairs at which discussions took place. Only the reception rooms contained any semblance of luxury, principally from the hanging of original oil paintings, many of which formed part of Mr Slater's own collection. By comparison with other leading merchant banks the atmosphere in the company was very informal and most of the executive team was very young, including members of the main Board. There was a strong sense of pride and confidence in the organization's capabilities and people thought of themselves as part of a successful team. Mr Slater deliberately fostered the atmosphere of informality tempered by a search for excellence in professional standards. Commenting on this, he added: 'Political intrigue is relatively low here and I deliberately discourage it. For example, if anyone starts talking to me about somebody else behind his back I say "Hang on a minute", and call the other chap into the room. Then I invite the first chap to say what he has to say in front of the individual concerned. As you can guess it doesn't usually happen more than once. Decisions are the things that are important to me, and I don't want to know any tittle-tattle. What we have here is a sort of earthy meritocracy.

Dr Channon went on to describe the feelings of one of the executives he interviewed with the words, 'First, there is an enormous *esprit de corps*, which should not be devalued. People working at Slater Walker really do believe they are part of one of the fastest moving groups in the country. The pace is quite tremendous. The group is young, alive, open to ideas and there is never a dull moment. Everything takes place at enormous speed.' One of our key overseas executives commented, 'The most impressive fact is the speed of this thing. Whenever I have consulted London about any matter, I have never waited more than a day for a reply after giving all the details. Most companies I have worked with would have a board meeting and I'd get an answer in three days time to say they've a board meeting on Wednesday week and they'll let me know then.' It was all happening at that time and certainly the morale in the group was very high.

I was following with great interest the build up to the World Chess Championship which was due to take place in early July. I had stopped playing chess after leaving school as it took too much time and concentration while I was studying accountancy. In the early days at Hertford Street, Herbert Despard had rekindled my interest by asking me to teach him to improve his game. I had enjoyed playing again and for a short while I joined a London club. I soon found, however, that I preferred correspondence chess, which could be played much more conveniently when I got home in the evenings. After dinner I would sit watching television with a chess board by my side, and I did quite well in my correspondence club, going up a few grades until I reached a level at which it became quite hard work. I had maintained a link from boyhood with Leonard Barden, who had been British champion and is today a leading chess correspondent. With his advice I had started to help British chess by subsidizing the annual Hastings Tournament, with a view to expanding it, so that our leading young players would have a chance to qualify as international masters. They could only do this by playing in tournaments of sufficient calibre, and as our best was Hastings, and that was not big enough, their opportunities were severely limited. Other countries would not invite them to play in their tournaments until they became international masters, so they were in an impossible situation. The small amount of help I had given to Hastings had been arranged in a very low-key way, and had attracted very little publicity. The World Chess Championship proved to be a completely different proposition.

For the previous two decades the Russians had dominated world chess, and then the West produced two exceptionally good players, Bobby Fischer of the USA and Bent Larsen of Denmark. In particular Fischer had fantastic potential, but was handicapped by being extremely temperamental. He was in a sense to chess what Nastase was to tennis at one time. The World Championship qualifiers had got to the last eight players and in the quarter-finals Fischer was paired with Taimanov of Russia. They were playing the best of ten games, and normally the kind of result that might be expected would be six draws with three wins to one player and the remaining game to the other. At this level there were frequently many

163

agreed draws until Fischer came on the scene—he disliked agreeing draws and played to win. He went through Taimanov like a knife through butter and won six games to nil. In the semi-final he was paired against Larsen, and although Fischer was favourite it was thought that it would be a battle royal. In the event Fischer won again six games to nil. This had never happened before in world chess, and for the first time it looked as though the Russians were going to get a run for their money. In the final qualifier Fischer came up against Petrosian, a brilliant defensive player, who had been world champion before Spassky. Fischer won the first game but lost the second. The next three games were then drawn and it looked as though Fischer had faltered. It was said by some that he had had a bad cold, and everyone in the chess world wondered if he would regain his earlier momentum. They were not to be disappointed: after his momentary relapse he resumed his winning streak with four successive wins against Petrosian. This result made Fischer the challenger against Spassky. Spassky too was a brilliant attacking player and had been a chess genius since early childhood, so it promised to be an exceptional match.

While preparations were being made for the World Championship in Iceland, Fischer started to complain about the proposed match conditions and in particular the prize money of £50,000, which he thought should be doubled. I was driving into London early one Monday morning in mid-July feeling very disappointed that after all this build-up Fischer might not be taking on Spassky, when it suddenly occurred to me that I could easily afford the extra £50,000 personally. As well as providing me with a fascinating spectacle for the next few weeks it would give chess players throughout the world enormous pleasure for the match to proceed. As soon as I arrived at my office I telephoned Leonard Barden, and told him that I would be prepared to double the prize money. Leonard telephoned Fischer's lawyer, who passed on the message. I also telephoned David Frost who in turn contacted Henry Kissinger, who then also telephoned Fischer urging him to play and assuring him that my offer was a bona fide one. That afternoon, to my surprise, my offer was the main headline of the *Evening Standard*, and for the first time the whole idea of the match caught the imagination of the world. About four o'clock in the afternoon my wife telephoned me to ask what I had been doing, as the house was swarming with reporters and photographers. I told her that I had had a good idea on the way to the office.

The match between Fischer and Spassky was a most exciting one and fully up to everyone's expectations. Spassky won the first game after a blunder by Fischer and he then won the second by default as Fischer did not turn up for it. This gave Fischer a very big handicap to overcome because he was then two games down, and as the challenger he had to win $12\frac{1}{2}$ points out of the remaining 22 games. It was in the third game that Fischer came into his own. He was black playing a Modern Benoni, when on the eleventh move he played a new and brilliant departure from the more accepted and conventional move that Spassky would have expected. Fischer fans felt that the moment they had been looking forward to had finally arrived, and so it proved to be: Fischer never looked back and went on to win the match by $12\frac{1}{2}$ games to $8\frac{1}{2}$. I have often been asked why I helped Fischer by doubling the prize money as to most people he seemed ungracious and rude. In fact I was not helping Fischer as much as I was helping the game of chess. The winner received five-eighths of the prize money and the loser three-eighths. The extra £50,000 was therefore split between Fischer and Spassky in those proportions. Another factor that made me want to help to ensure that the match took place was that I strongly believe in encouraging excellence. Provided there is equality of opportunity it seems to me that the encouragement of excellence is an essential feature of a healthy society. Fischer's chess was unquestionably excellent, and markedly better than anyone else's in the world at that time. That was what mattered to me, and whilst I had not liked to hear about Fischer's tantrums I could put up with them (at long distance) because of the quality of his play.

In making the £50,000 offer I had overlooked exchange control regulations. There was likely to be a question in the House about it and there was newspaper comment on the difficulties that might arise. At one time, when it looked as though the permission might not be given, a senior Bank of England official telephoned me to discuss the problem. He began by explaining how difficult it all was, especially as sterling was particularly weak at the time, and obviously controls were controls and had to be maintained. I suggested to him that it had to be good in prestige terms for someone in this country to come to the aid of the World Chess Championship, which had by then caught everyone's imagination. I went on to offer a solution by saying that I was sure that I would have no difficulty in persuading a wealthy American philanthropist to come to the aid of the chess match, and that I would in reciprocity give £50,000 to any charity he nominated in this country. We both agreed that this would be technically in order, but that the consequences would be adverse in terms of prestige. He concluded on the note that he was certain that there would be no trouble in obtaining the necessary permission after all; sure enough it was received soon afterwards.

A few months later, in an endeavour to stimulate our young players, I offered on behalf of the Slater Foundation to give a prize of £5,000 to the first British grand master and £2,500 to the next four. I am pleased to say that Tony Miles has won the £5,000, and others look like qualifying for the remaining prizes. British chess has advanced very considerably since that date and we now have one of the strongest teams of young players in the world.

As part of the process of moving into cash I began to realize that in addition to selling individual shares in the market and placing them with institutions I would have to sell whole companies, if I was to make any real progress. At this time Jimmy Goldsmith had a very high flying vehicle in the form of Anglo-Continental Investments, which was quoted on a price earnings ratio that had lost all touch with the facts of life. He was the first to realize that it made sense to Anglo-Continental shareholders for the company to issue its shares for hard assets, and that his company was in a very strong position to do this. By that time we were dining together about once a fortnight and during one of those dinners in early July the first large deal was struck, as a result of which Anglo-Continental bought two of our satellites, Thomas Stevens for £9m and Tanker Investment Trust for £8m. There was also a complicated deal which resulted in Anglo-Continental acquiring effective control of our property satellite, Argyle Securities, although we retained an interest in it. Slater Walker ended up with three satellites less, a lot of cash and a few Anglo-Continental shares; whereas Jimmy had very substantially boosted the underlying asset value of Anglo-Continental by issuing its shares for relatively hard assets. It had of course been necessary for Anglo-Continental shares to be underwritten institutionally in exactly the same way as I had arranged for Slater Walker shares to be, when we had acquired Drages in 1968.

After a few games of backgammon at his home, Jimmy Goldsmith and I usually dined at Wiltons in Bury Street. At that time that great character Mr Marks, the proprietor, was still alive, although I would guess that he was about ninety years old. He was very fond of Jimmy and when he made his rounds of the tables he would often linger at ours. I remember one occasion when he achieved the near impossible and left Jimmy almost speechless, and definitely one down. We were sharing a small pot of caviar and enjoying it with some hot toast when Mr Marks came to our table.

He stopped with us for a moment and said, 'Ah Mr Goldsmith, I am glad to see you here. Nice to see you enjoying the caviar.' As he moved away he added, 'Of course, your father always used to have a large pot.'

Our other big deal of that year was in August and totalled £43m. Most of it was conceived in Wiltons on a pad of paper lent to us by a waitress there. There were three basic deals that made up the package: Anglo-Continental were to acquire Wigham Richardson and two of our investment trusts—Flag and Irish. Slater Walker at that time owned approximately 44 per cent of Wigham Richardson, 10 per cent of Flag and 42 per cent of Irish. All three offers were to be half in Anglo-Continental shares with a cash alternative and half in a $9\frac{1}{2}$ per cent Partly Convertible 1982 Loan Stock. If the loan stock had held par we would have sold the two investment trusts at a small premium over asset value, as against the very substantial discount that they had been standing at in the market, and we would also have made a very sizeable profit on the sale of Wigham Richardson. In the event the loan stock fell to a discount but nevertheless the overall effect of the deals was excellent for Slater Walker and added substantially to our cash balances, especially as we placed out quite a lot of the loan stock within a few months. The effect on the underlying fundamental worth of Anglo-Continental was extremely beneficial to that company, but the share price never recovered from the weakening of the technical position occasioned by the issue of so many new shares. The subsequent rapid fall was also hastened by the fall in all financially orientated shares, which happened a few months afterwards.

In July I had talks with Warburgs about the possibility of a merger. I had always been an admirer of the founder, Sir Siegmund Warburg, and we had had talks together on several occasions. In mid 1969 we had a number of meetings together to see if a sensible working arrangement could be evolved. I remember that Sir Siegmund had asked me as a preliminary to write in my own handwriting a sentence like 'Banking is not easy but it can be fun.' He was a great believer in handwriting analysis and immediately sent this sample to an expert in Europe, who subsequently came over to see me. She thought Sir Siegmund and I could work well together, and more detailed meetings then took place. Sir Siegmund's idea in 1969 was for Warburgs to take a significant stake in Slater Walker and for Slater Walker to do the same with Warburg's master company, Mercury Securities. The banking and financial services side would then be concentrated in Warburgs and Slater Walker would be responsible for the industrial and overseas interests. I did not like this concept very much, so did not pursue it with much enthusiasm. After a few months we mutually agreed to take it no further and parted on amicable terms.

In mid 1972 I had lunch with Sir Siegmund, as a result of which we resumed discussions, but this time we were both contemplating a full merger. The negotiations reached quite an advanced stage but when I raised the subject at our board meeting I found everyone very unresponsive. Slater Walker was doing exceptionally well at that time; everyone was thoroughly enjoying it, and they felt that our work styles would be incompatible with those of Warburgs and that this would impede future progress. Wrongly, I did not press my colleagues, and as a result we again broke off negotiations on an amicable basis.

When Sir Siegmund had tested my handwriting three years earlier I had thought it was a very strange thing to do. However, a year later an associate had sent off a sample of my writing to another expert for analysis and then forwarded the results to me. I was very impressed, made contact, and after that used the expert extensively myself. I found that with executives he would frequently pick up a key weakness or strength that might otherwise not have been readily apparent. Nine times out of ten he would be spot-on in character analysis, to such an extent that I would regard it as an intrusion into someone's privacy to have their handwriting analysed by him without their permission.

On 11 August our half year results showed profits before tax up from £6.68m to £8.09m. The press thought the results were reasonably good and that the shares at 275p were fairly priced on a price earnings ratio of about 17. In August, *Management Today* came out with a City Growth League and Slater Walker were again top over the previous decade with a rating of 2,986 per cent. Ralli International was top of the separate business Growth League and Robert Heller said that this 'again confirms the unassailable lead which the Slater operation has established in perfecting its peculiar financial art form'.

During 1972 the satellites and associated companies were even more active than in the previous year. It would be boring to recount even brief details of the many bids that were made, but to give a general idea of the level of activity, I have reproduced opposite the events that were highlighted by the *Investors Review* in an article about Slater Walker at the end of the year. By this time individual bids were receiving my personal attention only when they directly affected Slater Walker itself or were of really major significance. The satellite bids were growing in size and the companies they were bidding for were therefore becoming rather better known. For example, Sterling Guarantee took over the company which controlled the exhibition site at Earls Court; Combined English Stores bid for Fentons; Barclay Securities bid for British Lion and Wrenson for David Greig in supermarkets. Ralli International had also had a very active year starting up in Switzerland and taking over the British Cotton

THE SLATER WALKER CALENDAR 1972

It has been a hectic year for Slater Walker. Here we list some of the main activities of the group over the year. Few of them are dramatic but taken together they add up to a formidable achievement for any investment bank in a single year.

January 14.—£30 million Dual Trust is launched. Investment policy is to concentrate on "young financially-orientated aggressive companies" and it acquires much of SW's holdings in satellites. Soon dubbed the "dustbin trust" it was not an unqualified success.

January 15.—Slater Walker reorganises its unsecured loan stock and increases its borrowing powers.

January 25.—Bids on behalf of Martin and Peter Green for Wrensons Stores. Offer is worth 55p in cash, and shares are now 300p.

February 3.—Reorganisation of main board of SW—Tony Buckley becomes managing director, Rowland Rowe deputy managing director and Michael Booth becomes a director.

February 9.—Slater Walker South Africa announces it owns 920,000 shares in BG Shoes and makes a bid for the rest.

February 10.—SW and David Frost buy stake in Equity Enterprises.

February 14.—Slater Walker South Africa bids for Hesperus Holdings and Hesinca, reducing the parent's stake in the South African offshoot to 38%.

February 29.—The major moves in Hong Kong begin: Haw Par buys 70% of Kwan Loong, which will soon be renamed Slater Walker Hong Kong.

March 8.—Issues defence document on behalf of AAH against bid from Tricentrol which is eventually repulsed.

March 9.—Further Hong Kong moves: Haw Par buys 65% of King Fung Development.

March 9.—Slater Walker Overseas Investment Trust launched in Hong Kong.

March 13.—Slater Walker South Africa makes another bid, this time for Norbank.

March 13.—Bid on behalf of Hanson Trust for Richard Costain (not successful).

March 14.—A bid in Canada: by Peoples Department Stores, controlled by SW Canada, for Gordon Mackay.

March 23.—Offer on behalf of Sterling Guarantee for Earls Court.

March 26.—Another Hong Kong move: a link with Hutchison International.

April 1.—SW Insurance Annuity Income Bond is launched.

April 17.—Offer by Wrensons for Redman.

April 20.—Offer on behalf of Argyle Securities for Circle, which brings Charles Spreckley into the stable.

April 24.—Singapore move: Haw Par bids for Island and Peninsular and Austral Malay Tin.

April 24.—Offer on behalf of Barclay Securities for British Lion.

April 26.—Thos. Stevens, a quoted property satellite, bids for James Howell.

May 8.—Offer by Dundee, Perth & London for Falkland Islands Company.

May 10.—Raises some foreign capital —$20 million in convertible bonds and £8 million in Deutsche mark bonds.

May 15.—South African bid: BG Shoes for Stanoptical.

May 15.—In Hong Kong, King Fung is successfully reversed into Southern Pacific Properties.

May 18.—In Canada, SW Canada and Unas Investments amalgamate. SW already owns 66% of Unas.

May 23.—Southern Pacific Properties makes a partial bid for Travelodge Australia.

May 25.—Peoples Department Stores links with Marks and Spencer in Canada to form jointly-owned St. Michael's Shops. First-ever joint venture by M & S on this basis.

May 26.—SW Australian Investment Trust offer for sale.

May 26.—The build-up in Hong Kong continues: Kwan Loong bids for the Sun Company, a stores group.

May 27.—SW Professional Trust launched.

June 7.—SW Far Eastern Investment Trust launched.

June 8.—Haw Par buys 30% of Edible Oil in Malaysia.

June 20.—SW Canada acquires 75% of Venus Esterbrook.

June 26.—Wrensons bids for David Greig.

June 29.—New issue: Leisure Caravans.

June 30.—The European build-up begins: acquisition of 82.9% of Cogefon in Belgium.

July 3.—Acquisition of 55.8% of C. F. Haussmann in France.

July 6.—Thos. Stevens and Tanker Investment Trust sold to Jimmy Goldsmith's Anglo-Continental.

July 6.—Argyle Securities buys Renslade, then SW's key stake in Argyle sold to Anglo-Continental. SW buys back 30.8% stake in Charles Spreckley, owned by Argyle. This is a complicated deal that takes the City weeks to work out and causes Anglo-Continental to start falling.

July 7.—Further foreign capital raised: 50 million Swiss francs and 60 million Dutch guilders.

July 19.—Joint merchant banking offshoot formed in Hong Kong with Hutchison, called Slater Walker Hutchison.

August 1.—The Solicitors Law Stationery Society floated off—not a great success.

August 9.—Office building bought in Amsterdam for £2.5 million.

August 24.—Further sales to Anglo-Continental: Wigham Richardson, Flag Investment and Irish Investment Trust.

September 1.—In Australia the old troubled Mining Finance offshoot is revamped as property company and renamed St. James Properties and begins building large property portfolio.

Septembers 26.—Slater persuades Malcolm Horsman of Ralli to merge with Bowater and then persuades Bowater to agree. Bid announced.

October 2.—Back to Hong Kong, where Kwan Loong acquires Mandarin Textiles. Plans for integrating Hong Kong interests under Kwan Loong, to be renamed SW Hong Kong, revealed.

October 5.—Another European takeover, this time in Holland: 62% of Hellingman acquired.

October 25.—In Hong Kong Kwan Loong bids for Stelux Manufacturing.

October 26.—Slater Walker Bank AG formed and becomes a member of the Frankfurt Stock Exchange.

November 16.—In Holland, Hellingman bids for Park Hotel.

November 17.—Frankfurt banking subsidiary buys 75% of Steingutfabrik AG, Colditz.

November 21.—Charles Spreckley bids for ADH, another SW satellite.

November 23.—Offer for sale of Whinsparken Investments—success.

November 27.—First regional office of SW opened in Birmingham.

December 2.—SW Insurance launches Increasing Income Bond.

December 7.—Acquires 500,000 shares in James Finlay.

December 15.—Bids for Lampa Mining.

December 19.—SW Canada buys 75% of Immobilia Inc.

December 20.—Haussmann bids for France Bureau.

These are only the main events in the calendar and exclude most of the bread-and-butter merchant banking deals which are too numerous to list here. They also exclude most of the major property deals done during the year: purchases of the Galeries Lafayette in January, of Oyez House in July, of the Westland Aircraft site in September and of Armadores House in December (dates of completion).

169

Growers Association in this country, followed by a £12m rights issue. All of this was, however, *de minimis* (with acknowledgements to Mike Andrews) when compared to Ralli's great fight with Trafalgar House over its plan to merge with Bowater. This merger was the largest ever achieved by a satellite company, and the fact that it could even be seriously considered by the investment community and the press illustrated the fantastic growth that Ralli had achieved in only three years since we had offered its shares to the public.

Slater Walker had built up a significant shareholding in Bowater after my attention had been drawn to its strong asset position. In April I had offered our shareholding to Nigel Broackes and suggested that Trafalgar House should consider bidding for it. He had turned it down so I had continued to buy without a specific bidder in mind. It then began to occur to me that it would be a natural for Ralli, and when I suggested the idea to Malcolm Horsman he was immediately enthusiastic. We agreed that it would be better to try a friendly approach, especially as it would otherwise have increased the risk of a reference to the Monopolies Commission. I had got to know Sir Kenneth Keith and Bob Clark of Hill Samuel quite well, and as they were Bowater's advisers and Bob Clark was a director of Bowater, I thought that it would be best to approach them first. I went to their offices one evening in late September and they reacted favourably to the idea, although they did not want Slater Walker to become dominant shareholders. I therefore agreed that I would be prepared to place half of our overall shareholding through them at a later stage. We then arranged for Malcolm Horsman to have a meeting with Martin Ritchie, the Bowater chairman, and shortly afterwards the proposed merger was announced. It was to be effected by Bowater bidding £80m for Ralli which would make the market capitalization of the new company about £180m.

Shortly after this Nigel Broackes had second thoughts about Bowater and decided that after all Trafalgar House would make a bid for it. On 1 November they announced their offer, which was worth £126m, and a lengthy battle ensued in which the Slater Walker shareholding was an important factor. The proposed merger with Ralli International won the day and on 20 November Trafalgar gave up the struggle. Martin Ritchie resigned as chairman of Bowater on 6 December, and Malcolm Horsman became chief executive of the non-paper side of the new combined group. The outcome was a very satisfactory one for Slater Walker as we had underpinned the assets per share of Ralli International in which we had a substantial holding; activated our shareholding in Bowater; realized about £11m in cash by the sale of shares to Hill Samuel and earned a sizeable merchant banking fee for advising Ralli on the merger.

As a result of all Slater Walker's activity and perhaps the chess prize, I was beginning to become much better known. In September I appeared on the cover of *Time* magazine along with seven other European bankers and industrialists, one of whom was Jimmy Goldsmith. Also, *Vogue* asked Cartier-Bresson to take some photographs for a series of articles they were covering on what they called 'Power People'. More significantly, in late October I was invited for the first time to the Lord Mayor's Bankers Dinner at the Mansion House, which is a kind of status symbol in City terms. When I first started Slater Walker I actively sought publicity to develop the company's business, but after a year or so it became more a question of trying to avoid excessive publicity. This did not mean I became a recluse and obviously if an important magazine like *Time* wanted to do a feature on European entrepreneurs I had to consider seriously the advantages and disadvantages of appearing in it. We were just on the point of starting in America and therefore it was a net advantage on that occasion. As far as *Vogue* was concerned, almost certainly the disadvantage was greater than the advantage, but I wanted to see Cartier-Bresson in action. He did not arrive with a lot of paraphernalia like many photographers, but with only a very small hand camera, and while I was having a conversation with someone in my office he took several very natural photographs. Like most things in life—it's easy if you know how.

There was no doubt that I had begun to believe some of my own publicity. I was constantly reading in the newspapers how clever I was and on many occasions being referred to in the city pages as 'the master'. It was very heady stuff and without doubt it affected me. On the other hand I did not really enjoy a high social life: I tended to go out no more than twice a week. I have always spent one evening a week with my mother at her flat in Richmond; on other evenings I would dine with friends like Jimmy Goldsmith or Gordon White of Hanson Trust, and in the Esher area we also had many good friends whom we liked to see often.

On Fridays I worked from home and this enabled me to keep the weekends completely free to be with the children. By this time we had another boy, Mark, and a second daughter, Jennifer. Most Saturday mornings I would take them shopping, when I always bought the greengroceries: it has always been one of my delights to go into a really good greengrocer and stock up with fresh vegetables and fruit for the weekend. After shopping I would have a few games of table-tennis with a neighbour, followed by a swim. I learned to swim on honeymoon, when Helen shamed me into it, and I feel that I have been catching up ever since for all the pleasure I missed through not having learned as a boy. The rest of Saturday would fly by doing nothing in particular, and on Sunday I would often play tennis with a friend, followed by another swim and a few games of backgammon. Then on Sunday evenings we would quite often have a kitchen supper with some close friends, and that would conclude what for me was a thoroughly enjoyable weekend.

An interesting example of how the press operates occurred on 17 September. On this day there was a three-page article on satellite companies in the *Investors Review* under the title 'Is the Game Over?'. In its conclusion it said that it would be a real loss 'if this means that the slumbering dinosaurs of British industry frittering away inherited assets in a low wage/low growth/high directors' perks operation can sleep more easily in their beds'. On the same day, in the *Investors Guardian*, there was a two-page article under the title 'City turns against the high fliers' which included the words 'as far as the stock market rating is concerned it is rapidly becoming bad news to have the tag asset stripper attached to a company and the frenzy that made investors think that almost any price was too low for these operations has disappeared'. The *Investors Chronicle*'s four-page article was headed 'Go-go shares when the going gets rough' and opened with the accurate observation: 'Financial shares traditionally lead a bull market up and they also lead it down.' The significant point is that the three weekly investment magazines came out simultaneously with their articles because they were simply reflecting the mood of the market and, in effect, reporting upon something that had already happened. It was because their writers and editors felt strongly enough about the subject to feature it so fully in each magazine that the prices of the shares in question had already come down in anticipation. The herd had begun to move, and I knew then for certain that the policy I had been following during the previous few months of liquidating major share positions had been the correct one. The *Financial Times* 30 Share Index was about 500, but I felt that it would be at a much lower level before the following year was out. What I had not realized was that this would also apply to property values, as otherwise I would have called a complete halt to our expansion in that area as well and begun to reduce our property portfolio.

In December we bought a substantial shareholding in James Finlay, the merchanting and banking group, which appeared to be a classic asset situation. We decided not to make a bid for the whole company but instead by agreement our financial director John Ford joined the board to represent our interest. In contrast to this, in July we had sold 45 per cent of Solicitors Law to the Thomson Organization and in October we offered 44 per cent to the public, retaining approximately 10 per cent as a continuing investment. By agreement with the Thomson Organization we had taken out Oyez House, and it was the operating company alone that was being offered to the public. Overall, Slater Walker made a capital profit in the region of £5m out of the whole transaction, and I am pleased to say that Solicitors Law has continued to prosper since then.

We ended 1972 on a mixed note. We had established a good platform for expansion overseas, particularly in Europe and the Far East. However, whilst some of the satellites in the UK had done very well, others were beginning to experience problems and market sentiment was definitely turning against them. In a market that had risen about 7 per cent during the year, Wrenson Stores had increased in value by over 500 per cent and Equity Enterprises by over 450 per cent. On the other hand, Barclay Securities was down by 25 per cent and both Armour Trust and White Child and Beney by over 40 per cent. The newer satellites were still faring exceptionally well in the market, but some of the older ones were not holding all of their earlier gains as they grew bigger and issued more of their shares.

FOURTEEN

Hill Samuel Merger

IN 1973 the stock market as a whole was to fall by a third and our shares were almost to halve in price. It was to be the year when we nearly managed a massive merger, and also the year of the Arab oil crisis.

It all started well enough, with the *Financial Times* suggesting that the fundamentals of Slater Walker had at last caught up with the share price of 260p. Very early in January we opened the bidding season for the year with a £13.5m agreed bid by David Frost's company Equity Enterprises for Hemdale. As the *Evening News* said, 'Hello Hemdale, super to see you!' A large part of Hemdale's income stemmed from the earnings of such well-known stars as Susannah York, Glenda Jackson and Peter Sellers, and it also had interests in film productions, music royalties and betting shops. Tony Buckley became non-executive chairman and David Frost and John Daly of Hemdale became joint executive deputy chairmen. We all hoped that this merger would create a company that would become a real force in the entertainment industry. A few days after this, Hanson Trust made an £11m bid for BHD, the engineering group, and I began to feel that in spite of my forebodings about the market we were going to have a busy year.

On 24 January I was having lunch at our office with Patrick Sergeant, the City Editor of the *Daily Mail*, when he asked me what I thought about share prices. The *Financial Times* 30 Share Index was standing at 478 and I said that I would be surprised if it was over 425 by 30 June. I also said that I would advise selling on rallies, and that for the time being I thought cash was the best investment. Patrick did not mention to me that he intended to write a full-page article about our discussion, so I was surprised the next morning to see the headline on the City page of the *Daily Mail*, 'Jim Slater says, shares are still too high.' I had not asked Patrick to keep my views confidential, and there was therefore no breach of etiquette on his part, but if either of us had known the storm that would be created by his article we would both have thought twice about it. That day the index fell 16 points as a result of a wave of selling by small investors. In the following day's press and the following Sunday's, I was criticized by

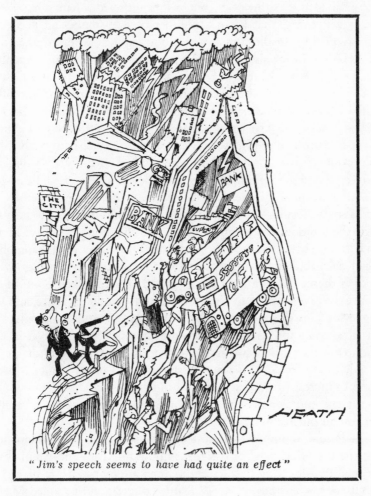

" Jim's speech seems to have had quite an effect "

almost everyone for being irresponsible and causing the market's reaction. The *Economist* was the only magazine to suggest that perhaps investors had been given some excellent advice, as in the event that is what it turned out to be. On reflection, I am sure that I would have been much wiser to have kept my own counsel, and I resolved there and then that I would never again make a pronouncement on the state of the market while I was actively engaged in the business of investment management.

At the end of January I went into hospital for a gall bladder operation. I had had no particular problem health-wise until the previous November, when I was playing tennis, and felt a sharp pain in my shoulder. I thought I had sprained it in some way, but as it continued I had some X-rays taken. It was found that I had a number of gall-stones and needed an operation quickly. At the same time I had my appendix removed, and ten days after that I was also operated upon for a hernia which had been troubling me. When I came out of hospital about a month later I caught 'flu and it was the end of March before I finally returned to the office.

While I was still convalescing at home in early March, the *Guardian* published a series of articles about the working conditions of African workers in British companies in South Africa. Apparently only Shell, Unilever and ICI—out of one hundred companies—were paying all employees above the minimum subsistence level. There was a front-page picture of a woman with her sick baby on a wattle estate owned by our quoted associate Slater Walker (South Africa). I was horrified to hear that this was the position. Critics immediately said that I ought to have known about it, but on my few trips to South Africa I had never left Johannesburg and had delegated the management of the industrial companies to our executives there. After reading the *Guardian* article I asked Rod Taylor, a senior executive of ours, to come down to my house in Esher, and then arranged for him to fly out to South Africa to institute an investigation into the position and to make recommendations to improve it in conjunction with the local board. As a result of this less than a month later we were able to announce a nine-point improvement programme, which in addition to increasing wages 50 per cent in 1973, included free milk, free clothes, new houses and schools and also the appointment of welfare officers on all our farms.

A Trade and Industry Committee was appointed by Parliament to investigate the position of British firms in South Africa and we of course cooperated by supplying detailed figures and attending before them. The Committee was chaired by Mr William Rodgers, and included Mr Joel Barnett. I went before them on 13 June together with Rod Taylor. The chairman was soon on the attack, saying that the figures we had supplied were 'meaningless'. In fact, we had checked with the Secretary of the Committee a week beforehand in order to ascertain if they were exactly what they wanted, and we were reassured by him that they were completely in order. We offered to let them have any further figures they required, and then we moved on to an extraordinary dialogue about whether or not the chairman of a quoted company controlled the company. I found myself explaining that the chairman of a public company like ICI does not control the company. I said, 'In my view—I put this very happily on record—the chairman of a company, especially if he is a chairman with a very small holding, and you mentioned the chairman of ICI for example, most categorically does not control the company.' Mr Barnett responded, 'He does with his board?'; to which I replied, 'Absolutely not. He is elected by his board. He has a casting vote if there is a difference of opinion.' I went on to explain that whilst I had considerable influence with the board of Slater Walker (South Africa) and could try to persuade them to take a given course of action, any major financial change would have to be approved by them, as they represented all the shareholders and were not just responsible to Slater Walker in the UK. In spite of my explanations, I was left with the distinct impression that some of the members of the committee were still firmly convinced that, as a chairman representing a 28 per cent shareholding, I could have arranged for Slater Walker (South Africa) to give away an unlimited sum without the local board, some of whom were major shareholders themselves, having any say at all. In fact, the whole improvement plan had to be negotiated with them in detail as there would have been no point whatsoever in turning the company into an instant loss-maker, thereby endangering the jobs of many thousands of people including the African workers.

During my convalescence from my operations I was able to do a lot of thinking at home, which enabled me to get a better sense of perspective. I decided among other things that I no longer wanted to run a large public company. I did not have a very constructive alternative in mind, but one of my thoughts was that I would diversify into pleasure. It is always difficult to recapture an exact state of mind at an important turning point in one's life, but in this case there were a number of factors which all seemed to coincide. First of all, the operations had left me feeling rather washed out, and I had also begun to feel that I should see much more of my family, especially while the children were growing up. I had never really enjoyed travelling and the problems of running a large and complex international company were in my weak state quite mind-boggling. Also, I had begun to feel very bearish about the general financial climate, and the outlook for the more aggressive forms of capitalism. I felt that there must be something more worth-while to do in life, and even if I could not put my finger on it at that time, I felt sure that I would soon find a more constructive concept for the future.

They say that the thought is father to the deed and so it proved to be. My first idea was to merge Slater Walker with Bowater and become a non-executive director of that company. Malcolm Horsman had banking aspirations, was attracted by size and internationalism, and had both the energy and the ambition to take the company on to greater things. I had a word with him in late March from my home and we arranged a meeting with his executives, together with Tony Buckley and John Ford, at an hotel near Esher. The idea had many attractions, but in the end we decided not to proceed as we were all worried about the possibility of a reference to the Monopolies Commission. The main drawback of this would have been that the Commission tended to be a dead hand, taking so long to reach a decision that in the meantime both businesses would have died on their feet.

The Slater Walker results for 1972 were announced on 28 March. The net profits attributable to ordinary shareholders came to about £12m against £9.3m in the previous year and the shares fell a few pence as the market was rather disappointed. However, when the full report and accounts was published on 25 April, the asset position was seen to be very considerably improved. The *Financial Times* commented: 'To the reported figure of 160p a share for net worth (up from 99p) you can add a further 30p odd for the end year surplus of quoted share values over book, and speculate that a price of 241p and an historic price earnings ratio of 13.5 involves precious little goodwill—whatever the one man image of the group.'

In the course of the early negotiations with Malcolm Horsman I had had a discussion with Sir Kenneth Keith and Bob Clark of Hill Samuel, who still advised Bowater and had a large shareholding in it. As a result of this both of them knew that I would be in a highly receptive mood to merger proposals, and be prepared to take a relatively back seat in the resultant company. For some time Hill Samuel had been thinking of different ways of substantially increasing their net asset value and they had recently failed to arrange a merger with MEPC, the property company. The idea of getting together grew on Kenneth Keith, Bob Clark and myself, as all of us felt that to succeed in international investment banking it was vital to have a large asset base and that there was considerable scope for rationalizing our banking, investment and insurance interests. Hill Samuel had the professional banking expertise and name, and were members of the exclusive Accepting Houses Committee, whereas we had the assets, a fast growing merchant banking business and a network of international companies. This time the Slater Walker board were enthusiastic about the concept and authorized me to finalize negotiations.

The proposed merger was finally announced to the world on 26 April 1973 and was front-page headlines in all the newspapers and the main news item on both television and radio. The new company would have been the largest merchant bank in the City with gross assets in excess of £1,500m and net assets of over £150m. One of the reasons the merger was such big news was the special place that Slater Walker had in the eyes of some of the media and the investment community themselves, perhaps best illustrated by the normally phlegmatic *Financial Times*' leading article, which included the words, 'But while Hill Samuel is leading towards a breakdown of tradition, Slater Walker has from the beginning carved out its own traditions. There have been success stories in the City before and will be again, but never has there been anything quite so big, so successful, and so singular as the growth of sws.'

The initial reaction was favourable but then there were some calls for a reference to the Monopolies Commission. In the event this was avoided by Kenneth Keith giving the following three undertakings to the DTI:

1. It is our intention to develop on the lines of a European Banque d'Affaires and our policy will be directed to the long-term improvement of profitability, with due regard to the interests of employees, rather than to the realization of short-term gains;

2. We shall not without previous reference to your Department enter into any transactions which indirectly or through *de facto* control of companies create a situation that, if it had been created directly, would be within the terms of the Monopolies and Mergers legislation;

3. In respect of disclosure of shareholdings of 10% or more of the voting capital we shall adopt a broader definition than that contained in the Companies Act 1967; we shall include in calculating the aggregate holding falling for disclosure shareholdings of investment trusts and unit trusts managed by the Group and of full discretionary investment clients together with our direct holdings.

When the merger was first announced Slater Walker shares were 240p, but by the end of May they had fallen to 206p. Whenever a company plans to issue a large number of shares the natural market reaction is a downward one as the jobbers reason that some of the new shares to be issued will be going into unwilling hands. This means that there will be sellers around for some time and little hard news for a few months to cheer the market up again. For this reason, jobbers usually mark down the issuing company's shares the day a proposed merger or major takeover is announced. The reaction in our shares had however gone further than would normally have been expected, reflecting a growing feeling of unease about the merger. This gathered momentum in June when the *Sunday Times* came out with a series of four articles criticizing the merger proposals and Slater Walker in particular. The attack centred around the quality of Slater Walker's profits, which they suggested were mainly as a result of share dealing; the 'vague' nature of the assurances given to the DTI; and the complexity of the Slater Walker group. They argued that in view of all this the proposals should be referred to the Monopolies Commission. There was an underlying element of fair comment in their observations but the method of attack was of low calibre. For example, in mid-June they gave a nine-point examination paper to prospective Hill Samuel shareholders, which included questions about the aims of the Slater Foundation and also asking if they knew about the Slater Walker health club. The Slater Foundation was a charitable trust founded by me and nothing whatsoever to do with the company, and the Slater Walker health club was formed for employees at Petershill House, which had in the basement a small gymnasium and sauna to help keep executives fit. The idea was, however, to create unrest in the minds of Hill Samuel and Slater Walker shareholders and in this the *Sunday Times* succeeded. I suppose that they would argue that the end justified the means, but this seems to me to be a dangerous philosophy for a powerful newspaper which, with the best will in the world, might on occasion have a wrong objective.

The *Sunday Times* articles were undoubtedly the major single factor that contributed to the merger being called off only a few days before the closing date for acceptances from shareholders. There were, however, a number of other factors, and I have often wondered since if it would have gone ahead even if there had not been so much adverse comment. In endeavouring to arrange for the merger to take place I had deliberately given way on most of the major negotiating points. For a start I had readily agreed to the name of the new group being Hill Samuel, and for Sir Kenneth Keith to be chairman of it. I had also agreed to Hill Samuel having board control in terms of number of votes and to Slater Walker bidding for Hill Samuel, thereby giving their shareholders a small premium. All of this had to be seen in the light of Slater Walker being by far the bigger company at the time—our profits after tax were £12.2m against their £5.2m and our net assets were £113m against their £40m. I had agreed to become deputy chairman and Tony Buckley was to become joint managing director with Bob Clark. It was generally understood between us that Bob Clark would dominate the banking side of the new business, and that I would run everything else with Kenneth Keith having the final say when necessary.

As we began to run into criticism, and our share prices continued to weaken, tempers began to wear a little thin. Sir Kenneth Keith is a tough and able man who has a strong physical presence; I knew that, whilst I had enjoyed meeting him for lunch and at an occasional City cocktail party, I would not enjoy working for him, as I also liked my own way most of the time. I had hoped that all would be well, though, because my underlying objective was not to dominate any more, but to take life more easily and to 'diversify into pleasure'. However, during the two months after the initial announcement was made I was recovering physically and it was beginning to dawn on me that all was not going to be sweetness and light in the years ahead.

As usually occurs in these kind of situations, there was a flash-point; Kenneth telephoned me at home while I was having breakfast the last Saturday morning before the closing date for the bid. He complained that I had not kept them fully advised about placing a large number of Slater Walker's shares in Bowater, which we had agreed to liaise about, as they also had a large shareholding following the Bowater deal with Ralli International. As the merger was only a week away from completion I had acted on the assumption that our shares were their shares and that the earlier understanding on Bowater was outdated by the merger proposals. I can see now that they would have been upset to be told for the first time by the newspapers about the placing of the shares, but I did not like being taken to task over my breakfast and made this very clear to Kenneth. By the time the telephone conversation had ended so had our plans to merge. I would like to make it absolutely clear that our talk together was only a symptom of what had become an incurable disease. If it had not been an argument about Bowater shares it would have been about something else of a similar nature. Our work styles and approach were different and I am sure by that time there was a feeling of relief on both sides when we decided not to proceed.

Several observers other than the *Sunday Times* were saying that they thought the merger should be called off, but when the break-off was finally announced a few days before the deadline date both Sir Kenneth Keith and myself were accused of an ill-judged bid and the general feeling was that we should both have known better. We said in the agreed press release on 19 June that 'full discussions had revealed fundamental differences of work style and personalities, which both boards considered could prejudice the successful implementation of the merger'. This very aptly summarized the problem, which in retrospect was one which both of us should have seen before we made our plans public. There are times when companies benefit very substantially from having chief executives who are quick and decisive; unfortunately this was one of the occasions on which the disadvantages were more apparent.

Hill Samuel arranged a £10m rights issue very quickly after the merger proposals fell away. This solved their immediate problem, but we were left with a credibility gap, especially as we also had to cope with the problems posed by the sustained criticism of the *Sunday Times'* articles during the previous month. I arranged a board meeting in a private room in the Dorchester Hotel to discuss the position fully, away from the office and day to day pressures. As a result of this we decided that we had a number of immediate objectives:

1. To improve the quality of our profits and lessen dependence upon investment dealing.
2. To improve our general level of disclosure on the investment and accountancy side to ensure that it was beyond reproach.
3. To endeavour to simplify our financial structure to the maximum possible extent in the hope that it would then be better understood.
4. To continue to go liquid to meet the coming financial storm that I was getting more worried about daily.

To meet these objectives we agreed to stop investing in property and to start selling it as quickly as possible. We also planned to liquidate the majority of investment dealing positions, and to concentrate instead upon building up a few longer-term shareholdings in established companies such as Rockware and Costain, which we planned to equity account. Our more complicated tax-saving schemes would be abandoned; we would bid in the Dual Trust and also endeavour to eliminate any unnecessary subsidiary companies. On the banking side we planned to stop *trying* to lend money actively and instead to gradually contract our loan book in preparation for the financial crisis that loomed ahead. In parallel to this we also agreed to publish a monthly statement showing the full details of our investments in UK quoted companies and to include unit trust and investment clients' shareholdings as well as those of Slater Walker itself. We were fighting back to improve our image and to bridge the credibility gap; as the *Financial Times* put it at the time, the group was 'oozing Dunkirk spirit'.

There were a few other developments of importance during the period of the attempted Hill Samuel merger. On 27 March we had announced that we were going to tender for 65 per cent of Franklin Stores at $21 a share in a move designed to acquire control of our first publicly quoted company in the United States. Buying orders flowed in from both UK and Canadian investors with the result that the shares soon developed a healthy premium.

The name was then changed to Slater Walker of America, and I planned to visit New York later in the year to arrange our first acquisition.

Shortly after I returned to the office in March I went to Canada for a week to see Robert Smith, to review the progress made by Slater Walker of Canada and also to speak to the world-renowned Empire Club. There were six hundred people at the lunch and my speech seemed to go down reasonably well. I see from the text that to illustrate my point that business could be fun, I told this story about one of our first acquisitions in Canada:

'Two years ago Robert Smith, Roland Rowe and I were negotiating here in Toronto with Alan Lambert's representatives to acquire control of Unas from the Toronto-Dominion Bank. We wanted to purchase two-thirds of the company and leave Toronto-Dominion Bank and the general public with the remaining third. It was therefore essential to impress on them that we were bright fellows and worth backing. We came to the stage of calculating the provisional purchase consideration. The calculation was two-thirds of 283,362, multiplied by $18. I turned to my two colleagues and in clipped tones said, "Check me." Each of us worked out the calculation separately, and to my acute embarrassment we came up with three different answers. Fortunately, Alan Lambert's representatives thought this was most amusing and we all burst out laughing. In a sense it helped to cement the deal in human terms and I am glad to say that since then it has worked out well for all concerned.'

Another story that I liked to slip into speeches whenever appropriate was that of the chicken and the pig. This story illustrates the difference between a takeover and a merger and in particular how important it is not to be lulled into a false sense of security by being told that it is a merger that is being proposed. The chicken said to the pig that bacon and eggs were very popular and they should get together to arrange a merger. The pig readily agreed, but then came back to see the chicken and said that he had been thinking it over; he said, 'It's all right for you, because you just lay the eggs, but to provide the bacon I get carved up.' 'I know,' said the chicken, 'you would never have agreed if I had called it a takeover—that's why I suggested a merger!'

I had continued going two or three times a year to the dining club formed by Peter Walker from the people who were featured in the *Evening News* series of articles on the 'Under-Forties'. A few new members had subsequently joined and usually there were about thirty or forty people at the dinners, as every member was entitled to bring one guest. Every three or four years it became your turn to be chairman, and when this happened you had to make all the arrangements and also find the guest speaker. It was to be my turn on 31 July, and as there had been a very serious tone at the last two dinners I thought I would give everyone a complete change by inviting John Aspinall, whom I had met originally playing backgammon and who had since become a good friend of mine. I asked John to talk about gambling.

John began his speech crouching like a gorilla, with his hands resting on the table before him. He speaks extremely well and is a brilliant *raconteur*. He was explaining his theories about gambling, saying how he admired people who persisted, and how important it was to make the most of a winning streak. At this point someone's guest interrupted and asked if after making a fortune it was a good idea to put something on one side before progressing further. John swept away the interruption with a dismissive gesture, and explained how having made a million he admired a man who went on to make five and then ten. This was too much for the guest who interrupted again and said, 'Mr Aspinall, after having made five million wouldn't it be sensible to put, say, a million on one side?' To which John replied in an exasperated tone, 'Oh all right, if you are a *family* man, you could *garage* a million!'

During the second half of 1973 a number of apparently separate happenings had in fact all formed part of the four-point plan that had been conceived and agreed at our July board meeting at the Dorchester Hotel. As I have already said we had bid in the balance of the Dual Trust and also started to disclose all of our investment holdings on a monthly basis. In parallel to this, when we announced our half-year figures, we gave a complete and detailed analysis of the various sources of profit and we also showed clearly the amounts transferred to inner reserves. Although profits before tax for the half year were up from £8.1m to £11.9m the market naturally added back the previous half year's £8.2m transferred to inner reserves and compared the £11.9m with the total of £16.3m. The shares fell from 169p to 160p on the announcement. The price earnings ratio on an annualized basis was only 8, but the market was now in a bearish mood and no one was interested. Investment dealing profits were £4.8m for the half year, but these were now regarded by most investors as low quality profits. Gone were the days when many newspapers had been extolling the virtues of our shares on a multiple of over 20 knowing that the results included dealing profits from the Cunard and Metal Industries type of deals.

We had also started to move into cash in a really big way. We sold our entire shareholding in Sterling Land by accepting Town & City's share offer. A few months afterwards we placed all of these shares with institutions to yield us over £10m in cash. We also accepted Argyle's offer for Cornwall and we sold our shareholding in Charles Spreckley. Unfortunately in this last case we made a loan to finance the acquisition, and that loan subsequently became a bad debt when the property boom came to an end. Concurrently with selling off our shares in quoted companies we also began to sell off individual properties. Unfortunately we were late in doing this and many of the contracts were never finally exchanged. One of the big problems with property is that because it takes so many weeks to finalize a deal you have to wait a long time to receive the cash. For this reason deals frequently tend to go off mid-way and verbal agreements are often not honoured even at a quite advanced stage. Although I had seen the fall coming I was not quick enough, and we had gone on investing in properties too long. Another factor which did not help was the old problem of staff morale. We had built up a very good property team who would naturally all have been very upset to be told to stop investing and liquidate all our property positions, thereby putting themselves out of their jobs. In the event this unfortunately happened to them anyway and I should have grasped the nettle earlier, as a few months would have made a great deal of difference to the company.

We were able to sell one property at a quite remarkable price. It was Granite House in the City which we had bought for Slater Walker Insurance Company in three separate parts for a total of £9m. There was no doubt a substantial marriage value in adding the three parts together, and there was then also a rarity value in a freehold City property, which was available for occupation. We had an unexpected offer for it through an estate agent and the final negotiated price was a staggering £22.4m. This valued the property on a $3\frac{1}{2}$ per cent yield and at about £25 a square foot. The buyer was the Singapore Monetary Authority which we understood wanted the property for its own occupation. The price was of course a remarkably good one; they had bought a relatively rare object at the *absolute* top of the market. As it happened they never occupied Granite House and at 1977 property values the unrealized loss must be about £12m. I have since understood from reading both the *Daily Mail* and *Daily Telegraph* that the authorities in Singapore were very displeased by

their error of judgement, which undoubtedly helped to add to the growing feeling of dislike of all things Slater Walker in Singapore. At the time
I was delighted by the sale as the profit from it enabled us to offset substantial investment losses in our insurance company.

Also, in furtherance of our July board meeting, on 13 September I
joined the Costain board to represent our 20 per cent interest in the company and on 5 October John Ford joined the Rockware board to represent
our 29.7 per cent shareholding in that company. Both of these moves
meant that we were able to bring into our accounts the relevant proportion of those companies' profits each year, which made us that much less
dependent on investment dealing profits.

I left for New York in early November and stayed for just over a week
at the Carlyle Hotel. Jimmy Goldsmith was also staying there, arranging
for the Grand Union deal with Cavenham, and James Hanson and Gordon
White were in a nearby hotel making plans for Hanson's further expansion
in America. New York has a dynamism that is difficult to define, but
which can definitely be felt soon after you step off the plane, and certainly
as soon as you step into a New York taxi.

When I arrived at the Carlyle Hotel I had a shower and changed and
then went up to Jimmy's suite. He welcomed me and immediately suggested that he take me out to a typical American dinner. We found a taxi
and went to Gallahers, where we were ushered into red-leather corner
seats. Jimmy said he would do the ordering, and suggested we have T-bone
steaks, salad with Rocquefort dressing, and Michelob beer. I said that it
sounded good to me and that I was ready for it. We waited a few minutes
and then Jimmy tried to catch the waiter's eye; he was unsuccessful, so I
piled on the pressure by emphasizing how hungry I was and how much I
was looking forward to the steak. Jimmy is not a very patient person at the
best of times and after ten minutes he was becoming very agitated. He
started to wave his arms to attract attention and then began to call out to
the waiter 'I say, I say.' After a few more minutes of this one of the waiters
came over to our table, looked hard at Jimmy and then said to him, 'What
do you say, bud?' Jimmy laughed nervously and quietly gave his order.
When the waiter had gone he turned to me and said, 'See, I told you it's
very primitive and exciting here!'

There is a totally different approach to business in America, where it is
regarded as something worth-while and where the rewards of success are
much greater. The study of business management and methods is an
industry in itself, and the whole approach is much more professional than

in Britain. The problem in America is that, if anything, it has become too professional, and as a result relatively simple transactions require teams of lawyers. For example, shareholders can sue directors by means of shareholder suits, anti-trust laws are very complex, and the Securities and Exchange Commission regulations are a life's work to master. Certainly most English businessmen have found it very difficult to be really successful in America for all of these reasons, and also because the competition is that much harder and tougher.

The share price of Slater Walker of America had performed quite well as a result of support from Canadian and UK investors. At an early stage we almost took over a property company which appeared to be a good asset situation, but the deal faltered at the last moment. After that we rather lost our way, and were too choosy in looking for the next deal, as a result of which our own share price fell below our acquisition cost and we missed the boat in stock market terms. We had chosen a rather bad time to start as, coincidentally, this was about the same time as the beginning of the Arab oil crisis which adversely affected world markets. Unfortunately, therefore, Slater Walker never really got off the ground in America. However, I understand that both James Hanson and Jimmy Goldsmith are well pleased with their companies' developments there, and they seem to have found ways of mastering the many problems to which I have referred.

Our other overseas associates suffered in stock market terms with the general decline in world markets, but their underlying financial positions were reasonably sound and gave no particular cause for alarm. Both our South African and Canadian companies turned in record results, and towards the end of the year, as part of our liquidity drive, we placed 10 per cent of the share capital of Slater Walker of Canada with Lord Thomson's family interests. This placing had the added advantage of making the company more Canadian in character.

In the Far East Haw Par had acquired from four London institutions 29 per cent of London Tin Corporation, and obtained board representation. This was a very important step in its development and as a result gave Haw Par considerable influence in the Malaysian tin industry. In November, as part of our more general plans, we also simplified the financial structure in the Far East. After this had been finalized Slater Walker owned in excess of 20 per cent of Haw Par, which had wholly-owned subsidiaries in both Singapore and Hong Kong, and Haw Par was very clearly designated as our main quoted associate in the Far East. Slater

Walker lent a substantial sum to Haw Par to assist it to carry out the necessary transactions, and that loan together with a subsequent one later became the subject of a major dispute. The Hong Kong market continued to slide and Haw Par's portfolio of quoted shares and properties suffered considerably as a result. When the Singapore authorities looked at this transaction two years later they considered that Haw Par's assets had been depleted by the purchase of shares and properties from Slater Walker. In fact the transactions had been cleared by the Singapore Stock Exchange and the Singapore Monetary Authority and indeed Haw Par had also received independent merchant banking advice. It was rather like the way they looked at the Granite House purchase after the London property market had crashed. Most people can 'job backwards' but it is taking the right view at the time that counts.

In Europe our quoted companies had made a few minor acquisitions: in Spain, Belgium and France property companies had been acquired, and in Holland and West Germany we had acquired some small industrial companies. None of these was particularly exciting or on a sufficiently large scale to capture the imagination of the investment communities in those countries, and the share prices of the European companies were beginning to suffer in line with the general decline in world markets, making future expansion much more difficult.

Things were very quiet on the satellite front during the last six months of 1973. The state of the market made share acquisitions very difficult, and there was a growing awareness that cash was not to be parted with lightly. Most of our merchant banking activity was therefore confined to selling companies such as British & Canadian, Tower Assets, Cornwall, Spreckley and Slater Walker Far Eastern Investment Trust. We also sold our shareholdings in such companies as Bibby, Nairn & Williamson and Crosfields & Calthrop. The *Sunday Telegraph* in mid-December referred to all of this as 'Jim Slater's Christmas sales'. In fact I was feeling anything but Christmassy as by then the Arab oil crisis was in full swing and I could see the market, at about 350 in December, halving within twelve months.

I have often been asked why Slater Walker was so badly affected by the fall in the market, and the generally adverse financial conditions of late 1973–5, if I saw most of it coming. The reasons are complex, and I have touched upon them to some extent already, but I think the time has come to explain them more fully. The first main point to grasp is that when the Arabs through OPEC more than trebled oil prices they changed the world. Previously Western Europe had been relatively wealthy, and taking the

British economy as an example, we had enjoyed a good and growing standard of living, while at the same time gradually improving working conditions and shortening working hours. Our balance of payments deficit was usually quite manageable in real terms, hovering between £100m and £300m per annum, sometimes even going into a small surplus. Suddenly we were faced with an extra cost of £2,500m per annum which, if it had not been for North Sea oil, would have put us out of business in a financial sense. As this extra annual cost almost equalled the country's total financial reserves, the money to finance this great shift of wealth had to come from somewhere, and it was obvious to me at the time that the pound would for several years ahead be a very doubtful currency. After all, if Great Britain had been a quoted company, who would have invested in such a company with its uncertain management, difficult labour force, very large overdraft and enormous yearly losses? Western Europe and Great Britain in particular would reel under the shock for some time to come, and currency exchange rates would be very uncertain. This would be very good for gold, and that was the reasoning process which enabled Slater Walker in 1974 to make very considerable dealing profits from that source. It was quite obvious also that there would be a horrible period of several years, while we in Britain waited for North Sea oil to come on stream, and that during this period things would become very black indeed. Stock markets would obviously be very depressed and would take a long time to find the bottom, as indeed would the property market. It was to be a completely new ball game for the Western world.

Even all of these future horrors would have been relatively containable from Slater Walker's point of view if we had had £85m of assets and no borrowings—but that was not the case. We had very considerable borrowings which meant that the effect of any fall in stock and property markets would be very exaggerated for us. These borrowings were the main single factor that prevented Slater Walker from being relatively unscathed by the coming holocaust.

The main advantage of financial companies in good times and the main disadvantage in bad times are their borrowings (frequently called 'gearing') of all types—long, medium and short. Most financial companies are *highly* geared and that was one of the reasons that Hill Samuel wanted to merge with Slater Walker. At the time their net assets were £40m and their total assets were well over £1,000m. The difference between total assets and net assets is simply borrowed money, which in the case of most bankers is in the form of deposits. Slater Walker was not particularly highly geared in relation to most merchant banks, but its assets were invested comparatively aggressively, and in large lumps as opposed to being widely spread over a lot of small shareholdings. The approximate position at the end of 1973 was that our gross assets totalled about £550m and that our net assets totalled £85m taking quoted investments at market values. The difference of £465m was made up of £130m of *long-term* loans and about £335m of *short-term* borrowings in the form of creditors, deposits, loans and bank overdrafts. In other words our gross assets were more than six times our net assets and a 20 per cent fall in our gross assets would have cost us over £100m and made the company insolvent. As I thought the market was about to halve, it should be sufficient to explain why I did not feel in a particularly Christmassy mood.

I have of course over-simplified the position and there were other important factors to consider. First of all, to some extent as a result of massive sales of shares, we had cash balances totalling £125m. This meant that gross assets could be reduced by that figure when assessing how vulnerable we were to any further fall in the market, and the resultant figures were net assets of £85m and gross assets down from £550m to £425m. This residual total of £425m contained a high element of vulner-ability as the figure could again be broken down to £200m in debtors, loans and advances; about £100m in quoted investments; £100m in property and out of the balance of £25m there was £17m in our insurance companies and £8m in plant, machinery and stock. I had begun to realize too late that not only shares were dangerous assets to hold, but that in a real blizzard properties and loans were also very vulnerable. After all, the main security for loans is usually either property or quoted shares and since these were going to fall in value the loans to which they related would be insufficiently covered by security. I looked at the figures again and after registering that we only had £85m with which to resist the coming storm I reviewed our assets, which suddenly and for the first time looked very fragile.

When the outlook is good and you consider a property or a share you can think only of the good things that can happen to it. Taking a property, for example, you relish the prospect of buying the one next door which might be for sale, and almost add into your valuation the potential marriage value. You budget for a high rent and a high price per square foot, and then you envisage selling the property on a very high multiple of the rent to an institution. When the outlook is bad, on the other hand, you can only consider the bearish factors—cash might be in short supply, property values are already astronomic, yields are ridiculously low, you might not get a tenant and so on. I looked in this new and bearish light at our property portfolio and my heart sank. I could see £20m coming off the £100m value very easily. I then looked at our £200m of debtors, loans and advances remembering with horror how we had been competing to lend money. A prudent reserve would be 10 per cent which accounted for another £20m. After this I came to my first love, our quoted Stock Exchange investments, and it did not take many seconds to realize that in spite of all the sales we had made we were more vulnerable in this area than anywhere else. If the market was going to halve and we moved in line with it we stood to lose £50m. I had now reached a total of £90m against our net assets of £85m and this was only after looking at properties, loans and investments.

Our insurance companies were also vulnerable, but the Granite House sale had secured the immediate position. There were two extra bonus factors which were in our favour—first of all our long-term loan stocks were mainly quoted and if the market continued to fall we would be able to buy them in cheaply with a resultant major boost to our asset values. If, for example, we bought in £10m worth of loan stock for £7m this would add £3m to our net assets. I calculated that this factor alone was worth about £15m to £20m to us, and it proved to be a vital buffer. The second important bonus factor was that I was still alone in being *highly* bearish, and was in fact due to run into considerable press criticism a few months later because of our headlong dash into cash. This would give us valuable time during the coming precious few months when we could still achieve major reductions in the level of our loans, properties and investments.

At the end of 1973, therefore, I had realized how vulnerable we were, and I was making every effort to go into cash as quickly as possible, but as the stock market continued to fall and the property market began to crack it was becoming increasingly difficult to make significant sales. The year had been a difficult and defensive one, and the alarming consequences of the Arab oil crisis had made me realize for the first time that because of our substantial borrowings we would be fighting for survival in the future.

FIFTEEN

Drive for Cash

O N I January 1974 the *Financial Times* 30-Share Index stood at 344 and Slater Walker shares were 140p. By the end of the year the index had dropped to 163 and our shares had fallen to $35\frac{1}{2}$p. 1974 was to be the year of the hurricane with a vengeance.

I continued to urge, within the company, a massive liquidation pro-gramme, and in the first four to five months of the year we managed to substantially lessen our vulnerability. This was during a period when the index fell only a further 15 per cent and before anyone else became seriously alarmed. In fact we achieved so many major sales that the press began to wonder what was happening. In February we managed to sell Crittall-Hope to Norcros; in April we sold our two industrial life assurance companies Pioneer and Blackburn for nearly £8m in cash, and we also placed with institutions our residual shareholding in Slater Walker (South Africa); in May we sold our interest in Slater Walker of America and also our entire shareholding in Slater Walker (Australia).

Quite a number of the sales of companies such as Crittall-Hope would be announced to the world in a few short lines of a press release after the terms had been finally ratified by all concerned. What is not generally realized is that for every deal which is actually done an average of two to three fall through for some reason or other. I had, for example, reached quite an advanced stage of negotiation with James Hanson, as Hanson Trust had also expressed interest in taking over Crittall-Hope. In the end they decided not to proceed, but several weeks were spent in giving them detailed figures, having discussions and examining all the implications of the proposal. The completion of these five very major transactions was therefore the result of several months' concentrated effort not only on the successful deals, but also on several abortive ones.

We were also successful in disposing of a number of smaller properties, and very fortunately we managed to sell for £10m the Westland Industrial Estate, which we had redeveloped. In addition we bought in the balance of Slater Walker Investment Trust for cash and loan stock, and then began to liquidate the underlying portfolio, at the same time unitizing our only other investment trust. All of these moves added approximately £50m in cash to our liquid resources, and gave fuel to bid rumours and speculation that I might be trying to liquidate the whole company to make it into an attractive rights issue for another financial group. The most prevalent unfounded rumour at the time was that National Westminster Bank were interested in taking over Slater Walker, and this persisted until they finally had to issue a denial a few months later.

Our results for 1973 were announced in late March and pre-tax profits were £23.4m against £17.6m. Attributable profits were £12.8m against £12.2m, but in the previous year we had transferred £3m to inner reserves so on a strictly comparable basis the results were not as good. Because of the bid rumours the shares at 140p were quite strong in relation to the market, and on a price earnings ratio of 8 most observers thought that the shares looked attractive.

It was after our results came out that newspaper comment started to build up, querying why we were continuing to move into cash in such apparent haste. The only *positive* things we were doing with the proceeds of sales were to buy gold shares and gold, which did very well for us, and also to buy in our long-term loan stocks at a big discount on their par values, with a consequent substantial addition to our own assets. The rest of the cash we were storing away to meet the coming storm. The failure of so many fringe banks and other financial companies did mean that deposits were more difficult for us to obtain, and it was also becoming very difficult to obtain substantial funds in the money market. This meant that some of the cash proceeds were already being sucked into our banking subsidiary and I was sure that the rest and more would be needed soon. The press comment gathered momentum in May and the tone of it can best be judged from the City editor's article in the *Daily Telegraph* a week before our Annual General Meeting; in one paragraph he said:

Why has Slater Walker divested itself of so much equity all over the world in recent months? Unless Mr Slater gives an acceptable reason at the company's annual meeting next week, what started out as eyebrow-raised interest in Slater Walker's tactics could turn into genuine apprehension.

In seeking a rational explanation, he concluded:

If the 'sell all' theory is correct, Mr Slater may know something the rest have yet to realize. In his city career Mr Slater has usually been a good six months ahead of the pack. If he is right to be a determined seller of shares at in some cases rock-bottom price, while the *FT* Industrial Ordinary Index is 300, what horrors does he think are in store? Are the Four Horsemen of the Apocalypse about to ride down Throgmorton Street?

The short answers to his questions were that I did think I had seen something that most people in the investment community had not yet fully realized, and I did think that Throgmorton Street was about to have a visitation from the Four Horsemen. Following my warning about the market the previous year and Patrick Sergeant's by then famous article, I had resolved that I would not give my views on the state of the market or the future as I saw it. The continued press comment was, however, alarming our shareholders and I realized that as a result I would have to give them as full an explanation as possible.

The build up of publicity before the Annual General Meeting was quite extraordinary. As the *Sunday Times* remarked, there would be an air of electrical suspense. Patrick Hutber of the *Sunday Telegraph* summed up his editorial on the subject with this observation:

At the moment he is cursed by his reputation for prescience, though in my experience it is hair-trigger reactions rather than prescience that are his real strength. Is he gathering in cash, they ask, for fear that property failures will set the fringe bank scene alight once more? Or does he foresee a horrendous economic or stock market crash? And so stock-brokers, with insufficient business to occupy their minds, shudder to each other. That is why the heat is on him to speak at Thursday's Slater Walker meeting, thus ensuring further publicity. Knowing him, and remembering the violently hostile reaction to his prediction of a market fall last year, I should think he will be reluctant to say very much. But silence from him, or gloom, will knock the market just as much as optimism could set it temporarily alight. He is paying the price for those happy years of headlines.

Over one thousand people attended the meeting at the Connaught Rooms on 30 May and we had to have an extra room in which some shareholders could hear only through a relay system what was being said in the main hall. As I went into the meeting I was asked to give interviews for both radio and television. I had been on holiday for a fortnight beforehand and I was feeling very fit. I had given a lot of thought to what I was going to say and, whilst I sometimes felt a little tense, I was no longer particularly worried about public speaking. I decided to take the bull by the horns and gave shareholders a brief outline of the company's history, followed by a short lecture on investment principles, the general financial position of Slater Walker, and the world outlook. After the historical review, I explained that it was essential for a financial company to reduce its gearing if it was to avoid crashing during a bear market. I went on to say that there were three basic scenarios for the world economy—hyperinflation, single-figure inflation or world recession. I then explained that there was no proof that hyper-inflation was good for equities, and that if there was a world recession, cash would obviously be very attractive. If there was going to be a neutral phase of single-figure inflation, there would be plenty of time to wait for that trend to develop, and the most we would lose would be part of a gain we might have made. In addition the yield on cash was very high when compared with equities. Cash, I explained, was a highly flexible asset which could easily be switched into other things such as property or shares, but it was not always as easy to switch out of these assets into cash. In the statement we published for the press we concluded with the words: 'Cash remains the optimum investment for the major part of your Company's available resources. In addition to being high yielding, cash is also a very flexible asset. Your Company is therefore now in a uniquely strong position to take advantage of favourable investment opportunities whenever they arise.' In answer to a question, I admitted that I had lost some of my early enthusiasm for business, which was partly explained by the financial outlook, increasing government control and the changing social climate. Shareholders received my general remarks on the outlook well and so did the press. The mood of the meeting was perhaps best captured by *Accountancy Age* which reported, 'When the curtain fell on a memorable performance even the hardened pressmen applauded enthusiastically. Afterwards, in the bar, regret was expressed that it couldn't happen again.'

The press was full of the subject during the next few days and it stimulated a great deal of editorial comment. No one seemed to disagree with the philosophy in strictly financial terms, but it did of course raise questions about what would happen if everyone followed my lead, and it also raised questions about the social justification of Slater Walker itself. As I hope I have made clear, I was not trying to give everyone a lead, but had been forced into making this statement by continued press comment that had unsettled shareholders. In fact if everyone followed my lead it would only make my job more difficult. The company itself was also *forced* into its liquidation programme as otherwise it would have rapidly followed the First Nationals, Cannon Streets, Triumph Investment Trusts, Vavasseurs and Jessel Securities of this world, which were falling like flies around us.

Most people outside the City did not realize what was happening as the financial crisis continued to gain momentum. Industrial companies could carry on relatively unperturbed even if they were not making much profit, because at least, in most cases, they were unquestionably solvent. Even if assets such as plant and machinery were not earning much money they would remain in the balance sheets at their cost less depreciation, but the assets of financial companies such as shares and dealing properties had to be written down to their market value. This put enormous pressure upon financial companies, as their assets were literally disintegrating before their eyes. To appreciate the scale of the financial disasters that were becoming commonplace it is worthy of note that two years earlier the market worth of the financial companies mentioned in the paragraph above was in the region of £400m and this equity value had been virtually eliminated in that short space of time. In May 1972 the *Financial Times* Ordinary Share Index stood at 543 and at the low of the market, when the crisis of confidence was at its peak, on 6 January 1975, it had fallen to 146. This was a drop of 75 per cent and tens of thousands of millions of pounds had been wiped off share and property values as confidence reached its lowest ebb. The market, adjusted for inflation, fell during the last nine months of 1974 to a lower level than during Dunkirk, when many thought that it was unlikely that Britain would survive the war against Germany.

As all this happened the assets of major insurance companies and pension funds fell alarmingly, but their liabilities were in many cases increasing because of double-figure inflation. In addition, the whole banking system was put in peril because traditionally bankers have always considered properties and shares to be the best collateral to lend against. As the markets in both fell almost perpendicularly practically every bank in the country experienced extreme difficulties. At that time the average capital and declared reserves of the banks was only 6 per cent of their total assets so none of them had a sufficient buffer against a major collapse in the value of the security they held against loans. Imagine, for example, a large merchant bank with £50m of net assets and £1,000m in gross assets. Assume that £300m is in cash or quickly realizable assets, leaving £700m locked up in loans. In a blizzard as much as 10 per cent of the loan book could prove worthless and the bank would be insolvent if prudent and realistic reserves were made against those loans. It has to be borne in mind, as I have said, that the main collateral against loans would be in the form of quoted shares or properties. At one time some merchant banks would lend against a good property with only 150 per cent cover. In other words a good property of £150,000 would secure a loan of £100,000. Between the top and the bottom of the market, properties more than halved in value, and that would therefore have uncovered many loans. Similarly a large number of loans were secured against quoted shares, and many entrepreneurs were to see the whole of the equity value of their shares disappear before their eyes, while their bankers looked on help-lessly.

If the old established banks were having bad dreams you can imagine that the newer financial companies were having nightmares. Companies of the nature of Slater Walker, Triumph and First National succeeded exceptionally well in good times as was shown year after year by *Management Today*'s League Tables. They were all highly geared, invested aggressively and took risks, which in bullish climates tended to succeed more often than not. Usually they survived the normal bear markets that happened every few years, but they were simply not equipped to survive the extreme bear markets that happened every fifty years or so. The 1929-31 market crash was one of these, and 1973-4 was probably worse.

It is important to understand that the Slater Walker balance sheet was *not* a highly geared one for a banking organization. Many banks were geared several times more than we were, but their loan books were of higher quality and better spread. In addition their parent companies would not have invested in property and quoted investments which were much more vulnerable than loans. Their sources of funds, too, were compara-tively secure as the deposits of joint stock banks do not fall away in bad times, whereas any company whose name is in the *slightest* doubt finds the going very rough. The older established banking companies usually have substantial hidden resources, a wider-spread loan portfolio and are strengthened by being members of the 'club'. By this I mean that there is an unspoken understanding that if in trouble members will help each other. To take an extreme example: it would be very bad news for Midland Bank and for everyone else in the banking world if, say, Lloyds

Sir Isaac Wolfson

Sir James Goldsmith

Tiny Rowland

With Sir Kenneth Keith, 1973.

Behind the scenes with David Frost.

(*left to right*) Jim Slater, Oliver Jessell, Vic Watson, Sir John Cohen, David Malbert, Robert Morley and Nigel Broakes in the Great Monopoly Game.

Celebrating first salmon.

One of the Cartier-Bresson photographs.

Bank could not meet its commitments, and it is quite right that they should all recognize that in terms of confidence they depend upon each other. The joint stock banks and the accepting houses also have the great advantage of the implicit backing of the Bank of England, which, if necessary, would instantly support them.

The Bank of England's role during the financial crisis deserves the gratitude of us all. By forming the 'life-boat' and helping the smaller secondary banks which could not meet their commitments they stopped panic growing to uncontrollable proportions. It was a sign of the times when later in the year the largest clearing bank, the National Westminster, had to announce publicly that they were not in trouble and were not receiving support from the Bank of England. If more of the secondary banks had been allowed to fail in this climate, and depositors had lost their money as a result, the general public would rightly have asked themselves where they could put their money and sleep at night knowing that it was safe. There could then have been massive withdrawals from the banks and the whole system would have been put in extreme jeopardy.

It might be asked why the newer financial companies took risks by making sizeable investments and why they had less well-spread loan portfolios. The answer is simple—they had less experience in banking and had to compete for business against the established banks. They would always get second best in choice of loans to be made, as the natural first choice of most customers would be their joint stock banks. The newer financial companies, including Slater Walker, had to be more aggressive while the going was good in an attempt to build up great financial strength for the future. Most of them would have survived a normal bear market, but the 1973–4 crash was of such intensity that the policies they had followed proved to be extremely vulnerable and, in almost every case, fatal.

The social justification of a company like Slater Walker at this particular point was not readily apparent. We were liquidating investments simply to survive. To find a social justification in the longer term would have required a stable period during which the company would have had to establish a real identity and role in the business and investment community. We were, however, at this time much too busy fighting for our lives to worry about more academic problems of that nature, which were essentially longer term. The real question was whether or not there was going to be a longer term for us. There was a very good letter in *The Times* on 27 June which put our point of view in the growing debate which had by then become a quasi-political one. Among other things, the writer said:

For the benefit of the uninitiated, not one penny appears to have been withdrawn by the company from industry. Taking an unfavourable view of the outlook, the company sold in the market a large quantity of United Kingdom equity shares last year, these being bought by other people. It so happens that the company's action last year saved it losing many millions of pounds, to the benefit of its shareholders and its employees. Would its action have been less anti-social in the eyes of the politicians if it had sold only half as many shares and avoided losing only half as much? Or, in order to receive full political approbation, would it have been necessary for the company to have misread future events, taken no action at all and gone bust like a number of others? Optimism is probably a prerequisite for a successful politician. Unfortunately this same optimism operating in Government finance is the cause of countless millions being poured into bottomless pits in the name of wealth-creation. The nation cannot afford that those who are really responsible for the creation of its wealth should be wrong quite so often.

In complete contrast to my growing worries about the financial climate I was introduced in June to a new and delightful pastime. Earlier in the year Slater Walker had bought as an investment the Tulchan Estate of over 20,000 acres in Morayshire, which had amongst its many sporting facilities four salmon fishing beats on the River Spey. We were getting the lodge ready for the coming shooting season, and I thought I would go and have a look at it all and try my hand at salmon fishing. I went up there for a few days, staying in the factor's house with my friend Mike Allan, who was an excellent shot but had never fished before. The weather was poor and it was not a particularly good week for fishing but I managed to catch an 11 lb salmon and three small sea trout, and Mike also caught a sea trout. Later in the year we had four days together on another estate, and to his great delight Mike caught a $17\frac{1}{2}$ lb salmon.

Fishing is a pleasant, relaxing pastime. You are in the open and in wonderful surroundings; the ghillie is invariably a man of few words and great character; you see herons flying past, an abundance of oyster-catchers and an occasional osprey. You wade in water which is sometimes thigh-high taking a tentative step forward after every cast. There is great pleasure and satisfaction in making a good cast and in the moments of expectation while you watch it drift down river. There always seems to be plenty to do, so there is not much time to think about anything else. Time flies, and you live in hope for most of it. Maybe two or three times a day you get a sudden pull on your line which tells you that there is something very alive on the other end. A salmon 'take' is quite unmistakable and the ensuing fight is usually exciting. Since that first day I have been fishing six times altogether and I have caught only twelve salmon in all; I have only once caught two in a day, and my largest so far is a fifteen pounder which gave me a twenty-minute fight that I will never forget. My idea of a perfect week is salmon fishing on the Spey, and whenever I am there I wonder why I spend my time doing anything else.

Another of the great attractions of a few days' fishing is the good company. Over picnic lunches and in the evenings, during the hour or so when you are not on the river, fishing stories abound. One of my favourite ones actually happened to me quite recently, when I was the target of a conspiracy. In early 1976 I took my two boys Christopher and Mark, who were at that time seven and eight, up to Tulchan for four days. They were both very keen on bird-life and I had arranged for them to be shown the nests of some seagulls, oyster-catchers, sandpipers, curlews and a large variety of other birds. They were also going to learn to fish for the first time and we had all looked forward to the visit with mounting excitement. I was very keen to do some salmon fishing again and I had arranged with the factor, Andrew Coombs, for one of the best pools near the lodge not to be fished during the day, so that it would give me maximum chance on my first evening.

Andrew met us at the airport and we drove to the lodge which took about an hour. During the journey he explained that Gerald Panchaud, the new owner of Tulchan, was more in favour of spinning than fly fishing in the particular conditions on the Spey at that time. He had, according to Andrew, only fished for a total of four hours in two separate sessions since his arrival and he had caught an astonishing eight salmon. To the consternation of the ghillies he tended to fish pools that were generally out of favour and always seemed to catch fish, whereas other fishermen on the same beat were having a very lean time of it. Andrew told me that Gerald had agreed to come down with me that evening and show me his special way of spinning. I was very excited by the prospect of being taught how to catch salmon in poor conditions at the rate of two an hour, but I told Andrew that nevertheless I preferred fly fishing and would like to try that first before resorting to spinning. When we arrived at the lodge I saw through the dining-room window that Gerald was just finishing his dinner, so I raced upstairs to put my two boys to bed, following my wife's detailed instructions to the letter. By the time I had done this and changed into my fishing gear and got all the necessary equipment to hand, Gerald had already gone down to the pool. 'Oh dear,' said Andrew, 'I hope he hasn't started to fish. He's very impatient and once he gets going there's no stopping him.' I almost ran down to the river, because if someone takes a spinner over a fly-fishing pool it can ruin it for fly fishing for several hours afterwards. In addition, if Gerald was so lethal there would be no fish left if I did not hurry. By the time I got there I could see that he was already half-way up the pool and on the side of the bank there were *two* gleaming silver salmon. To put it mildly I was terribly disappointed and for a few moments felt that I could have pushed him into the river, spinner and all. I braced myself however and, in a not very successful attempt to hide my true feelings, uttered a heart-broken 'Well done'. At this point they both broke down with hysterical laughter and it was a few minutes before Andrew was able to tell me that the fish had come from the refrigerator and were ones that had been caught by Gerald with his spinner on the previous day. There was an even happier ending to the story, as to Gerald's surprise I managed to catch a very nice 10 lb salmon on my third cast and he then, for the first time since he had bought Tulchan, tried his own fly rod and soon afterwards got another one of a similar size.

When I returned from my fishing trip in June 1974, the debate about whether or not cash was the best investment had simmered down. We continued with our programme of liquidating investments and in early June we sold our interests in Germany to Bowater in exchange for a medium-term loan note. The name of our quoted associate was Colditz and the apt newspaper headline was, 'Slater escapes from Colditz, but cash still locked up'. We also sold for about £10m our entire shareholding in Haw Par to a syndicate which included Ivory and Sime and Charter Consolidated. As part of the negotiations with them we had agreed to make a substantial dollar loan to Haw Par. I thought at the time that I had said 'good-bye' to Singapore but it was in fact the forerunner of a much more unpleasant 'Hello again!' During these and other realizations the market was falling rapidly but our shares were still standing up relatively well. By the end of July they were 127p against 140p at the beginning of the year, whereas the market had fallen by a third.

On 8 August John Ford, our financial director and my very good friend, died at the age of forty-eight from a heart attack after running up the steps at the memorial of the Battle of Waterloo. I was on holiday with my wife and family at Studland Bay near Bournemouth when I heard the news and I can still vividly remember my sense of shock. I had known John since AEC days, had introduced him to his wife Maureen, and we had always kept in very close touch. Since John had joined me at Slater Walker six years earlier he had been a tower of strength. He was a very hard worker, had great clarity of thought and a delightfully keen sense of humour. I was to miss him badly as a colleague, but much more as a valued friend.

There were a number of other changes on the Slater Walker board as Roland Rowe had left us in June because he wanted to try something different and his job at Slater Walker was gradually disappearing as our various overseas interests were sold off. Dick Tarling also left us to join the Allied Polymer board after we sold out of Haw Par. We had already sold our interests in Crittall-Hope which was his other main area of responsibility, and as a result there was simply nothing left for him to do. Robin Whitten, who had previously been deputy to John Ford, then became financial director of Slater Walker. In the same way that some of our directors were to find themselves out of a job, so were a number of our staff. On the property side quite a number of people naturally drifted away as we concentrated upon selling our existing property portfolio without making any further purchases. We also cut down on the insurance and banking sides of the business, though to a much lesser extent.

Our interim results were announced in August and profits before tax were £10.1m against £11.9m for the comparable period of the previous year. In spite of very poor market conditions, dealing profits had totalled £6m, a large part of which had come from gold mining shares and gold. Profits from other sources such as merchant banking fees were naturally well down. Our shares had by then dropped to 96p. The most important factor about our figures was that the 'footage' of our balance sheet had been substantially reduced from £587m to £476m and this of course reduced our overall vulnerability.

A few months earlier Jessel Securities had failed and, because we had similar businesses, this affected both the market in our shares and confidence in our insurance company. Jessel, like us, had been very active in the sale of income bonds to the public. The failure of London & Indemnity made many other income bond holders feel uncertain and as a result we encountered a wave of redemptions, which continued at a high level for several weeks. Our shares began to slide drastically and by mid-October had dropped to 48p. By this time everyone had the jitters and the bear market was in full swing. We had to make a reassuring statement about the cash balances of over £20m which we had built up within the insurance company, and in addition to this we also increased its share capital by a further £5m.

In early September I acquired personally a substantial interest in another small quoted company, Lubok Investments. I did this simply and solely to try to make some money to repair my shattered financial position. Like Slater Walker itself I had been very highly geared as an individual. Most of my money had been in my two million Slater Walker shares and I still had substantial borrowings against some of these. I had also invested extensively in both farmland and paintings; most of these purchases were made on borrowed money: there was a £2m ten-year loan to finance the farmland and a £500,000 medium-term loan to finance the paintings. The problem with my borrowings was that the interest charge had increased very considerably with rising interest rates, and in some cases had almost doubled. The interest had to be paid regularly and in cash, especially as the value of the security was falling fast. Taking the Slater Walker shares alone, over £4m had been wiped off the capital value during the previous two years, and farmland and pictures were beginning to look much more fragile investments than in the past. I therefore acquired control of Lubok with a view to filling up the holes that were beginning to gape in my personal exchequer. The shares in Lubok immediately went to a very substantial premium over net asset value and within a few months Lubok had acquired control of two other quoted companies and purchased two more outright.

Earlier in the year over a broker's lunch in the City I had suggested, in answer to a question from a fellow guest, a joke portfolio to meet all impending disasters. I had said that it should include tins of baked beans; a bicycle; Krugerrands and a shot-gun. The rationale was that the baked beans would help to feed you if hyper-inflation developed; the bicycle would get you around if the flow of oil from the Middle East stopped; the Krugerrands were internationally accepted currency if sterling failed or there was any other emergency; and the shot-gun might be necessary for self-defence in case of insurrection and mob rule. One of the guests must have mentioned this to a journalist because within a matter of a day or so it was featured in a newspaper, and after that quite often referred to. In November Margaret Thatcher got into hot water by admitting that she had stock-piled enough tinned goods to last for years. When criticized for helping to induce panic buying she replied that she thought everyone was doing it, and that the idea was recommended by me.

In November we sold our interests in both an overseas investment trust and our banking subsidiary in Hong Kong to Hutchison International. This completed our withdrawal from the Far East and added a further £5m to our much needed cash balances. By means of a complicated series of deals with Jimmy Goldsmith's French company we had also sold a proportion of our French and Dutch associated companies, which left us with very little in Europe. The only positive move we made in November was later in the month when we bought the management company of the unit trust side of the Jessel group for £1.58m. The funds under management totalled £40m and this acquisition nicely complemented our own unit trust group, which had performed exceptionally well during the year because of its high degree of liquidity. The *Daily Express* rated us the Managers of the Year and the *Observer* gave us second place.

In December we also sold our shareholding in Costain to Arab interests for £4.2m, which resulted in a loss of £3.2m, but this had to be looked at in conjunction with the use of the proceeds, which was to buy in at a substantial discount approximately £10m worth of our unsecured loan stocks. The gain on this redemption more than offset the loss on the sale of the Costain shares, and the two moves together did of course improve our annual rate of cash flow as well as further reducing the footage of our balance sheet and our vulnerability.

The general weakness in the Slater Walker share price at this time has to be seen in the perspective of a bear market of almost unparalleled sharpness and intensity. There was a real crisis in the financial community and shares of old established companies such as Hambros had fallen by an even greater percentage during the year. As I have mentioned, at one point even National Westminster Bank had to make reassuring noises to convince people that they were not in trouble. It had been a frightening year and it was obvious that for many years to come the investment community in the City of London would have a lingering memory of its horrors. I have often been told by businessmen who lived through the 1929 slump that it had changed their approach to financial problems. After 1974 most people who were active in the financial world would look at things very differently for the rest of their lives.

SIXTEEN

The Spydar's Web

THE *Financial Times* 30-Share Index had closed on 31 December 1974 at 163 and our shares had closed at $35\frac{1}{2}$p. By March 1975 the index had doubled and our shares had nearly trebled. The market had reached a completely over-sold state and rose almost perpendicularly during January and February, with giant rises of 15 to 20 points on the index in a single day. It is important to realize that a fifteen-point rise on an index of 150 is the same as a thirty-point rise on an index of 300. It was one of those market movements which caught most people, including myself, by surprise. It was all over almost before it had begun; each day one waited for a set-back and buying opportunity, but instead there was another significant rise. Usually the market takes a long time to consolidate at new levels and most people expected it to pause at around 180 to 200 before testing higher ground. Instead it turned on a sixpence and caught us all by surprise by continuing straight on upward through 200 and on to 250, all in the space of a month. This was a great pity for Slater Walker as I could easily have made a very valuable £10m or more by a modest reinvestment programme within the company and another £5m or so by reinvesting some of the substantial cash resources of the insurance company. Instead I stood by and watched it all happen like the proverbial hypnotized rabbit.

We did make one excellent positive move in early January by buying for £1.2m the National group of unit trusts from the receiver of Triumph Investment. This added £60m to the £80m of unit trust funds we had under management and made us the third largest group of unit trust managers in the country. The 2 per cent of funds under management that we had paid to buy the management company compared very favourably with the average of well over 5 per cent paid when other unit trust groups had changed hands during the previous five years. In addition we had purchased when the market was at a low and, within two months, as a result of the market doubling, the effective price had dropped to only one per cent. Our investment management business had become the strongest part of the group at that point, a fact that was becoming generally recognized. For example, a review in the *Investors Chronicle* in early February selected Slater Walker Growth as the strongest performing unit trust over the previous five years, and in two out of the previous three years, Slater Walker Investments had been chosen as Managers of the Year by the *Observer*; the overall track record was becoming hard to beat. We had an excellent team at Leith House led by Brian Banks, and above all in the last few critical years they had managed to get the major market movements right. It does not matter too much whether you invest in either GKN or Tube Investments, if the market is going up: the important point is to be fully invested in good quality stocks. If, on the other hand, the market is going down it is important to be liquid. In 1971 the market had risen 40 per cent; in 1972 it had stayed static; in 1973 it had fallen 30 per cent; and in 1974 it had fallen 50 per cent; so overall it was more important to be right about being in or out of the market, than to be worried too much about fine tuning.

During the first few months of 1975 I would still have liked to sell off the whole company. Obviously in its fight for survival Slater Walker had to a large extent lost its *raison d'être* and no longer had a worth-while role to play. If we survived we would have to find a new identity, and it would take years to build. The failure of so many of the secondary banks and finance companies such as Jessel Securities, First National, Triumph and Vavasseur would make investors and the City community continue to worry about a company such as Slater Walker for many years to come. I had lost my early enthusiasm, and felt that it would be much better for shareholders and for employees if a different solution could be found.

Over the previous year or so Jimmy Goldsmith had built up a substantial shareholding in Slater Walker, and he was the obvious person to talk to about the company. The bear market had, of course, also affected his financial companies, and as a result he did not have enough energy to spare to be of real help with my problems at that time. We had several general talks about the possibility of his master company, General Occidentale, acquiring Slater Walker, and we also discussed the idea of General Occidentale and Slater Walker equity accounting each other, but all of this came to nothing. In addition I had talks with Tiny Rowland of Lonrho, and we almost arranged a merger, which was called off at the last moment, a few months later, because of the Singapore affair. Adnan

Khashoogi, the wealthy Arab financier, expressed interest in buying a substantial shareholding in Slater Walker and we had brief talks together in
early 1975, but we were unable to consummate a deal as he was experi-
encing some problems with a recent investment in America. I kept trying
to find a complete solution to the problem, but could never quite bring it
off, and there was therefore little alternative other than to battle on.

In mid-February we sold our residual shareholdings in both Slater
Walker of Canada and Solicitors' Law, and used the proceeds as usual to
redeem large quantities of home and overseas Loan stocks. We were also
successful in selling off our credit finance company, Slater Walker Finance
Corporation, to an American company. While this transaction was being
negotiated I met Lord George-Brown for the first time, as he was a member of the board of the company's British subsidiary. I found him very
likeable, and almost exactly as I had imagined from reading about him
over the years. The sale of the credit finance subsidiary had the wonderful
effect of reducing our balance sheet footage by a further £40m, and
substantially lessening our vulnerability as a result.

The 1974 results were announced in late March with pre-tax profits of
£14.5m against the previous year's £23.4m. In the Report and Accounts
which followed in early May, I explained that we had sold £140m worth
of assets since the beginning of 1974. Our shares stood at just under 100p,
which was near net asset value. I subsequently explained at the Annual
General Meeting that profits for 1975 would be at a very low level, and
that 1974 had essentially been a year of survival. I went on to say (too
optimistically as it turned out) that we planned to sell off our remaining
£65m worth of property, and to use the proceeds to continue to buy in
our loan stocks. The Annual Meeting took place on 5 June, which was
Referendum day for the vote on whether or not Britain should remain in
the European Common Market. I had always been in favour of our entry
and I remember that when I was asked my views by a shareholder I
replied, 'When Enoch Powell, the Communist Party, Wedgwood Benn
and the National Front are united against a given course of action, I find
that the alternative demands serious consideration.'

Meanwhile, my new vehicle, Lubok Investments, was moving steadily
ahead. It had acquired control of Salect, a small public company in South
Africa, and this in turn acquired control of two further quoted companies
during the following months. All of them developed healthy premiums on
cost prices and their future looked very bright indeed. When Lex reported
upon Lubok's results in early May he observed, 'The transformation of

Lubok Investments has been an exercise in sheer nostalgia—establishing goodwill, and turning it into assets through a string of takeover deals.'

Most of my life I have been keen on games and usually have a current favourite. When I was at Hertford Street I was very fond of scrabble, and then chess took over again for a year or so. I was introduced to back-gammon in 1968, and played a little with Gordon White who was good at the game. I then went on to play with Jimmy Goldsmith, who was even better, and after that I played quite regularly with players of high calibre. I became above average at the game myself, and found that it really fasci-nated me, so I decided to apply the Zulu principle to it. I had been introduced to Joe Dwek who was at that time, and still is, the best player in Europe, and he agreed to give me a series of lessons. Joe is an interesting man who went to Harvard business school and was in stockbroking before he became a professional backgammon player. He has an absolute mastery of the odds and a clear, incisive way of explaining problems. The lessons Joe gave me improved my game a great deal, and he subsequently wrote an excellent book based upon them, entitled *Backgammon for Profit*. Backgammon is a delightful game—a nice mixture of luck and skill, quick, aggressive and sometimes very exciting. It can be played for love, low stakes or high stakes and is certainly one of the best gambling games.

My craze for backgammon has passed. I love playing it still, but I have got it back into perspective and now find that I prefer bridge. In 1975 I joined the Portland Club, where bridge is the main game and back-gammon, although quite popular, takes a back seat. I have since bought a few bridge books, and I have learned a little more about it. It is a wonder-ful game and the luck element in it is less irritating than in backgammon. Bill Black told me a story about bridge when I asked him if he played. He said that he and his wife had played frequently in the early years of their marriage but tended to have too many inquests, and after a major disagree-ment over one particularly difficult hand they decided to call it a day. He went on to say that on their twenty-fifth wedding anniversary they were driving home in reflective mood, when his wife remarked on how few arguments they had had during their marriage. He agreed and said how glad he was that they had stopped playing bridge, reminding her of the particular hand fifteen years earlier that had sparked off this decision. She immediately recalled exact details of the hand and before long they were arguing about it again. Bill concluded, 'That's why I don't play bridge— do you know by the time we got home we weren't speaking to each other!'

In May I visited Tulchan again which by this time was in full swing and heavily booked for the months ahead. The other members of the small fishing party were Angus Ogilvy, Jacob Rothschild, Jimmy Goldsmith and Selim Zilkha. There were very few fish around, but we all had a very enjoyable few days together. According to one of the newspapers, its 'man in the rushes' had reported that Angus was the only one of the party who looked right in tweeds.

On 6 June there was the Nuneaton train crash, and my great friend Michael Allan was one of the four passengers killed. Mike lived in Stoke D'Abernon with his wife, Meg, and their five children. Most weekends we used to meet to have dinner and play some tennis and backgammon. He was great company and I felt a terrible sense of loss when I heard the news and still do today. There is no way of rationalizing a happening of this nature, and all one can do is try and pick up the pieces and carry on. Following the death of John Ford a year before, it certainly made me feel that it was vitally important to rethink my life and get my own thoughts and beliefs into proper perspective. As always, however, there is invariably very little time to do this, as events have a habit of overtaking us. Certainly a large part of my life has always been taken up with dealing with the current crisis, and in recent years very little of it has seemed optional.

Slater Walker continued with the sale of strategic shareholdings throughout the summer months, for example, its stakes in Grampian Holdings, Whitecroft and Permali. On the more positive side we had seen that the merger of the Lowson Trust interests would bring a lot of new shares on to the market, and that it would be a good opportunity to purchase a strategic stake at well below asset value. When the scheme was announced the new master company was to be Estates House Investment Trust, and we had soon acquired a very substantial shareholding in it. If all had gone well, at a later stage I would probably have bid it in, and I also had plans to bid for Trust & Agency, which had substantial unrealized profits which I planned to offset against some of our tax losses. We had also started to purchase some blocks of flats at bargain prices, were making sizeable profits dealing in sugar futures, and were just beginning to reinvest in shares with the substantial liquid resources of the insurance company. In most other respects, though, our approach was still fundamentally a defensive one.

During the ravages of the bear market the price of the shares of some of our satellites such as Equity Enterprises and Adda International had slipped to a few pence. The main problem was their high borrowings and so much damage had been done that some of them would never recover again. The jobbers and brokers in the stock market frequently nicknamed shares very aptly, and one of the best ones I can remember was the name for Adda during the bear market, when its price was falling daily: they called it 'Subtractor'.

In July we announced a scheme to reorganize our four different outstanding long-term loan stocks by replacing them with another new long-term loan stock which would have a much higher interest rate, but a lower capital value. Whilst this would cost us more in interest each year it would also have the effect of increasing our net asset value. When we first announced the scheme it was quite well received, and the *Investors Chronicle* commented that we had retained our knack of financial one-upmanship, referring to the scheme as ingenious and suggesting that imitations were probable. A little opposition built up during the following months and in the event holders of about £17m out of the £31m of outstanding loan stocks accepted the offer, as a result of which £8m was added to Slater Walker's net asset value.

It was at about this time that I met Clement Freud for the first time. I have always enjoyed his sense of humour, and remember particularly his coverage of the World Cup in the *Financial Times*. When England played Brazil he wrote an extensive piece on the match, but only the last three paragraphs described the actual game. The highlight of his article was that a very large green and yellow dragonfly had settled on his typewriter. As he said, green and yellow were the colours of Brazil, and this gave him a sense of foreboding for the rest of the day.

Clement had come to see me about a charitable proposition, which did not come to fruition as we were pre-empted by events. After we had discussed the detailed figures he asked me if I played draughts, monopoly and gin rummy. I said that I did, and he said that he knew I played backgammon and table-tennis, and would like to agree five games so that he could challenge me to a pentathlon. I accepted the challenge and a week or so later he arrived at our offices and we went down to the basement, where there was a table-tennis table. He changed into a bright red track suit, and we began the pentathlon. We only played the table-tennis and backgammon, but that was sufficient for me to realize that he could have taught Stephen Potter about games.

In mid-July I attended the final stormy British Leyland Extraordinary General Meeting to consider the Government's offer to shareholders of 10p a share, which would have the effect of nationalizing the company. The meeting was very crowded and there was organized opposition to the proposals. Many shareholders were naturally extremely disappointed, and felt that the company had been grossly mismanaged during the previous ten years. The main mistake that Leyland had in fact made was in taking over the British Motor Corporation, and from that moment on, taking a ten-year view, the company was a dead duck in financial terms.

The home markets of most European companies are simply insufficient to provide the volume to cover the high cost of research, development, and tooling necessary to launch new models in world markets. In addition to this general handicap, we had a special handicap within British Leyland which was highlighted by an article in the *Daily Mirror*, and by another in the *Financial Times*. The productivity of British labour forces in the engineering industry was in general less than half that of our overseas competitors, and this applied not only to car production, but also to steel manufacturing, ship-building and aircraft manufacturing, as well as many other service industries such as airlines, transport, gas and electricity. The British Leyland union troubles had become legendary, and the number of days being lost by strikes was absurd. Already in France, Renault had been nationalized; in Germany the Government had acquired a substantial shareholding in Volkswagen; Fiat in Italy was also becoming increasingly dependent upon government aid. With British Leyland's extra handicap, how could it manage on a private enterprise basis? I have already explained some of my ideas for changes in its policies and I am sure that in certain areas management can also be improved, but having said this, the fundamental problems of bad labour relations and pathetic productivity still remain.

I had for a long time thought that the Industrial Reorganization Corporation had done an excellent job in many ways, and that it should not have been disbanded when the Conservatives came back to power. I would have liked to have seen it given new objectives to consider. There are a few industries such as ship-building, aircraft manufacturing, machine tools, computers and car manufacture, which should be looked at on a *European* basis. Most countries in Europe have the same difficulties with these industries: they are all labour intensive, and therefore give rise to social problems; they all require massive financial outlay on research, development and tooling, and all of them tend to be cyclical. There must be a more rational answer to the problem of these industries looked at on a European basis, and I would have thought that the IRC would have been a ready-made nucleus for the British aspect of this. It would obviously take many years to sort out what needs to be done and perhaps more importantly how to go about it, but the job will have to be done in the end so why wait until it is *force majeure*?

With all these thoughts in mind I sat through the British Leyland meeting watching Donald Stokes being pilloried hour after hour. Towards the end I stood up in answer to a direct question from a shareholder and briefly addressed the meeting. I recommended shareholders to take the 10p offer, and said that I was going to accept in respect of my own shares. I stressed that the alternative course of liquidation, which some of them were recommending, would be useless as 'assets would disappear like snowflakes before the wind'. My intervention seemed to have a calming effect, but this may have been because some of the more militant shareholders had already let off steam, and were beginning to get tired. In the end the scheme went through and I must confess that I was quite glad to leave the British Leyland board, which in the previous two years or so had been a very depressing experience. Just as we were on the point of a breakthrough in profits, there would be another strike and so it went on. Furthermore, a non-executive role had not suited my style at all, as I had become used to being wholly executive and being able to carry through decisions to their conclusion.

It was in late May that Haw Par in Singapore announced a proposed merger with Pernas, the state-controlled Malaysian corporation. The merger would have been very advantageous for Haw Par, but it would have meant that effective control of the company would have passed to Malaysia. By this time, of course, Slater Walker no longer had a stake in Haw Par, but I was nevertheless interested to hear the news. I wondered to myself how Donald Ogilvy-Watson, the chief executive, had managed to persuade the authorities to let effective control of Haw Par go to Malaysia, with whom there was bitter rivalry, but it was all of only passing interest to me. It came to light later that Donald had not cleared the proposed merger in advance with the Singapore authorities, who did not like the idea at all and reacted vigorously in a number of ways. The Securities Industry Council announced that there had been a breach of the takeover code and the Stock Exchange of Singapore suspended the quotation of Haw Par shares. On 28 July the Finance Minister in Parliament announced that there had been 'serious wrong-doing' and that two inspectors had been appointed to investigate the affairs of Haw Par in four specific areas, one of which was an executive incentive scheme in a company named Spydar Securities. I knew very little about the other matters being investigated, but I had participated in the share incentive scheme along with five other executives. At that stage I had no worries about it, as I thought that it had all been set up with the best legal advice available locally, and I was aware that the group's auditors, who were also Haw Par's auditors, knew about it. However, the press soon picked up the sound of the tom-toms from Singapore.

I went on two weeks' holiday in August with my wife and our four children, and for one of the weeks my mother and my wife's mother and father came down to join us. We used to go to a very nice family hotel near Studland Bay, which had a small nine-hole golf course, plenty of facilities for children, and was fairly near the beach.

On this occasion my holiday was interrupted by several anxious telephone calls from the office as the Spydar affair gathered momentum. At the request of the Singapore authorities the Hong Kong police had started investigations into the books of Spydar in Hong Kong. As the *Far Eastern Economic Review* observed, 'Haw Par had infuriated the Singapore authorities'. The article referred only to Slater Walker's original controversial start in Singapore and the Pernas deal with Malaysia, as at that time the press were not aware of the Granite House sale. As they picked up the stories in the Singapore newspapers the British press referred to Spydar more frequently, and I began to realize that it could develop into a major problem for Slater Walker, as it was still owed $29m by Haw Par. I interrupted my holiday, and arranged a meeting across the bay at the Royal Bath Hotel in Bournemouth. Dick Tarling flew in from his holiday abroad and a leading counsel, our solicitors and our financial director came to the meeting.

Before I go further, I should explain the essence of the Spydar affair. In February 1972 Dick Tarling had suggested to me that we should institute an incentive scheme for the executives involved in our Far East operations. Participating members would have to enter into a restrictive covenant not to deal in the very active and increasingly buoyant Hong Kong and Singapore markets. Haw Par, with our blessing and help, was about to take an interest in two Hong Kong public companies—Kwan Loong and King Fung. A private company, subsequently named Spydar, would be formed and would purchase £100,000 worth of shares in Kwan Loong and £150,000 worth of shares in King Fung at Haw Par's acquisition prices. Dick Tarling suggested that I should participate in Spydar to give the other executives confidence in the company and encourage the belief that there would be an active future investment policy on an international basis if the Hong Kong market subsequently weakened. Dick thought that the new incentive scheme would have to be very attractive to dissuade the executives concerned from dealing personally in the Hong Kong market, as it was a particularly active one and they could have made considerable capital gains. We wanted them to concentrate the whole of their efforts on the company, knew that personal share dealing in our business could lead to conflicts of interest, and considered that the shareholding (through Spydar) in Kwan Loong, in particular, would provide a real management incentive, as it was to be the main vehicle for future expansion in Hong Kong.

My participation was to be £20,000 worth of shares in Spydar as was Dick Tarling's and Donald Ogilvy-Watson's; three other senior executives were to have £10,000 worth each; and the balance of £35,000 was to be allocated amongst junior executives at the recommendation of Donald Ogilvy-Watson. In addition the company was to have borrowings equal to its share capital of £125,000 so that the total amount it would invest would be £250,000. I was going to set up all of this during a visit to Hong Kong in early March 1972, but because of illness my arrival there was delayed by a fortnight. During this period the acquisitions of the shareholdings in Kwan Loong and King Fung were made and the share prices of those companies went up substantially as a result. On 15 March, shortly after I arrived in Hong Kong, we had a meeting at which I allocated the shares to Spydar at cost price in accordance with the prior agreement and in exchange for the restrictive covenants from the executives concerned. Minutes were taken of the meeting and the whole matter was left in the hands of one of our executives, a qualified solicitor, who was asked to liaise with Deacons, who were Haw Par's solicitors in Hong Kong, to tie up all the administrative details.

The Singapore authorities' point of view was that we should not have taken the Kwan Loong and King Fung shares into Spydar at Haw Par acquisition prices but instead at the much higher market prices at which the shares were standing by the time I arrived in Hong Kong. They also considered that the shareholders in Haw Par should have approved the incentive scheme. We argued that the Spydar share incentive scheme was preconceived and that there was considerable evidence to this effect. In addition, knowing that the shares in Kwan Loong and King Fung would automatically go to a premium *solely* because of our involvement, we would obviously allocate shares to our executives at cost price concurrently with the purchase by the company, as had always been our practice with incentive shares throughout the world. We had made no secret of the arrangement, as Haw Par solicitors had been consulted and the auditors in both Hong Kong and Singapore also knew about it. I understand that there was no disclosure requirement under Singapore law but, whatever requirement there may or may not have been, I naturally expected the executives concerned to have taken appropriate professional advice.

Our style of working had always been speedy and informal and therefore the evidence to support our argument tended to be fragmentary as opposed to meticulously documented; it was, however, of such substance that my advisers were confident that, whilst the share incentive scheme could have been set up much better, there was no question of any fraud having been involved. We talked over the position and as a result, although I had not been contacted by the inspectors appointed by the Singapore Government, I wrote to them giving full details of my own knowledge of the Spydar share incentive scheme. I naturally hoped that my explanations would be sufficient to allay the doubts that seemed to have arisen but, in view of the Singapore authorities' approach, I was not optimistic.

Our half-year results were announced on 20 August and showed a drastic fall in profits from £10.09m before tax to only £2.22m. In particular, investment dealing profits were almost non-existent as I had missed the first dramatic rise in the market, and commercial banking profits were at a low level, reflecting the large reduction in our loan book. The shares stood at 62p when the results were announced, and were still standing at about that level at the end of the month. They were no longer being evaluated on a profits basis, and any investment buying was in the hope of a recovery.

The fall in the Slater Walker share price had of course catastrophically affected my personal finances, and despite the excellent performance of Lubok I was still in an acutely difficult position. I had almost completed selling off my pictures, but my farmland was proving much more difficult to sell, and my overall interest charges were running at a high level. I was very worried about it all, but I still believed that I would be able to sell the whole of Slater Walker or, failing that, that the company would recover, and I had very high hopes for Lubok which gave me confidence that all would be well in the end.

We had continued to trim our overheads substantially, and planned to move to Oyez House which was being refurbished in preparation. In the meantime we had let Petershill House to Deloittes, who would be moving in when we were ready to leave. By this time the activity of the group had

Jak's new collection of cartoons from the Standard, I'm Off Right, Jak, is available from newsagents and bookstalls, at 45p. Or from the Evening Standard by post 55p.

"I think it's the Slater-Walker Christmas party!"

been reduced to such an extent that Tony Buckley and I agreed that it no longer made sense for him to remain with the company. He had some good institutional friends in the City who were prepared to back him in a 'shell' operation, and he had chosen Floreat Investment Trust as his vehicle for this purpose. Unfortunately, as a result of past loans to cover investments in companies such as Equity Enterprises, he had lost money on balance and owed Slater Walker the shortfall. He received no compensation when he left, but I did arrange for him to borrow approximately £500,000 against his Floreat shares, which were fully asset backed. As I saw it, the gain in the Floreat share price would help provide cover for the existing loan, and as a result he would be able to repay both loans. I believed that Tony would be successful and certainly the early performance of the Floreat shares was excellent, and at one stage the whole of both loans were fully covered again. Indeed, I was so confident about his prospects that I recommended Floreat shares to my mother, who bought them at a substantially higher level, and unfortunately hung on to them throughout. I have explained my thinking on this at some length, as the making of the second loan was criticized subsequently. It may have been an error of judgement on my part, but it certainly had a basically good intention behind it, and I thought it was in the best interests of Slater Walker at the time. In the event Tony did not make a success of Floreat and it worked out very badly for the company as a result.

By early September, events in the Far East had still not affected deposits, unit trust sales or insurance business. It is important to realize that banking, investment and insurance are fiduciary businesses, which all depend upon trust and confidence. If the Far East affair gathered further momentum the time would come when the business would suffer in all these areas, and I was therefore keeping a very keen weather eye on them.

By this time Pernas had withdrawn from the scene as they had realized that Singapore meant business and that the deal with Haw Par would not be allowed to proceed. The whole affair continued to gather momentum and by the end of September was being referred to every few days in the British press. As Ilsa Sharp said in a long article in the *Financial Times*, 'The failure of the Haw Par men to consult the Singapore Securities Industrial Council *prior* to announcing that coup across the Causeway (i.e. the Pernas deal with Malaysia) must also rank as a classic example of Westerners failing to pay even lip service to the Oriental concept of "face".' By mid-October our shares were under 50p and our banking people were beginning to notice for the first time slight difficulties in maintaining deposits at usual levels. There were two reasons for this—the first was that any sort of incident of the Spydar type would obviously have a generally adverse effect upon potential depositors, and the second was that most of the banking fraternity knew that Haw Par owed us US$29m, and if this was to be seriously disputed it would very adversely affect the banking subsidiary and as a result the group as a whole.

For the first time I began to realize that I should seriously consider resigning from the Slater Walker board. I had already had several talks with the Governor of the Bank of England, and until then I had never mentioned the idea of resigning to him and he had not raised the subject with me. I could see that if I resigned the growing unpleasantness of the Spydar situation would be removed from the company, and that it would clear the way for an independent board to negotiate a settlement with Singapore. I knew that there would be no hope of the Singapore authorities ever agreeing a settlement with me at the helm. The main difficulty was to find an effective substitute and the obvious man to come to mind was Jimmy Goldsmith. We had dinner together on Wednesday, 16 October, when I had a general discussion with him. As a large shareholder he had a vested interest, and as a good friend he was of course prepared to do all he could to help. Above all he had the personal ability, and would be able to persuade other men of influence and prestige to join the board with him. I told Jimmy that I would think it all over during the coming weekend and talk to him again on the Monday. If I decided to resign, he would try to form a new board and see the Governor to make final arrangements for a smooth transfer within a few days.

By Monday morning I had made my mind up to resign. I telephoned Jimmy to let him know the position and suggest that he should go into action. I then fixed an appointment at twelve o'clock with George Blunden of the Bank of England to tell him of my decision, as the Governor was not available at that time. George Blunden subsequently consulted the Governor who saw the merit of my argument and the rest of the week was spent making final plans.

It was a well kept secret, and when I finally resigned on Friday, 25 October it was quite a bombshell. As my statement put it:

Matters connected with the recent enquiry into the affairs of Haw Par in Singapore have received adverse publicity, which is damaging to Slater Walker Securities. In addition to this, a newly constituted board not connected with the original development of Haw Par will find it easier to resolve the outstanding problems with Haw Par and the authorities in Singapore. I find that my wish to retire from the City and the interests of Slater Walker Securities are now identical, and I have therefore resigned as Chairman and a Director of Slater Walker Securities and of its subsidiaries and associated companies. It is obviously a matter of great personal regret to me that I should leave in this way but I feel that it is in the interests of both employees and shareholders.

I am pleased to be handing over the chairmanship of Slater Walker Securities to Mr James Goldsmith, as a man of proven ability with a long record of success in the companies in which he is interested. I am sure that with the help of the board and executive team he will do an excellent job for shareholders.

I also resigned as chairman of Lubok Investments, chairman of a charity named Birthright and chairman of the Appeals Committee of the Royal College of Surgeons to make my withdrawal from the City complete, until the Spydar affair was sorted out and the Haw Par loan settled. The new board of Slater Walker Securities included Lord Rothschild and Ivor Kennington of Rothschilds; Charles Hambro and Peter Hill-Wood of Hambros, and Dominique Leca of Union d'Assurances de Paris, the largest insurance company in France. Hambros Bank and N.M. Rothschild became financial advisers to the company and Sir Ronald Leach, the well-known accountant, was appointed as a consultant.

By the time the announcement was ready to go out late on Friday afternoon the press had assembled outside the office and were also waiting for me on my return home. My resignation was the first item on the television news and headlines in all the papers for the next two days. We were plagued by the press at home during the weekend and the house was literally under siege. My four children quite enjoyed it all, in particular going to Sunday School hidden under a blanket, but we do not like exposing them to publicity and I have always tried to keep my family life as private as possible.

The press on the Saturday and Sunday were again full of the news which raged on into the following week. The degree of publicity was astounding: as the *Investors Chronicle* observed, 'Only the abdication of the Queen, one supposes, would command more column inches.' I suppose that it was such a big news item because Slater Walker had been the archetypal entrepreneurial company and I had dominated the financial news for several years beforehand. As the *Daily Telegraph* put it, 'Last night's changes at the top of Slater Walker Securities marked the end of one of the most remarkable stories in the City's long history—the rise of builder's son Mr Jim Slater and his creation of possibly the most remarkable investment machine ever seen.' It was, as Jimmy Goldsmith said to another newspaper, 'the end of an epoch'.

Jimmy's first move on becoming chairman was to arrange for Rothschilds and Hambros to make a detailed and in-depth study of Slater Walker Securities and its subsidiaries. Two leading firms of accountants, Price Waterhouse and Peat Marwick Mitchell, were also asked to prepare detailed reports on the overall position of the group. I had hoped that the change of board would help to restore the share price, but the reaction was quite the other way and the shares dropped within a matter of days to about 25p.

I continued to go into the office during the following month or so to give Jimmy whatever help I could and to clear up my personal effects. I knew that I had to get to grips with myself quickly to sort out my own very major financial problems, to deal with the Spydar allegations and to find and establish a new way of life.

PART THREE

SEVENTEEN

Double Insurance

F OR the first few weeks after my resignation I was in a state of shock and acted more by instinct than anything else. One of my priorities was to secure my financial position, otherwise, as my liabilities substantially exceeded my assets, I could be sued by one of my creditors and bankruptcy proceedings might follow. The most important thing was to buy time. It was therefore essential to develop plans for making money so that I could persuade my creditors that it was in their interest to wait for me to repay my debts in an orderly way.

My total shortfall was over £800,000 and I owed money to a joint stock bank, two insurance companies and a merchant bank. In spite of the problems I had experienced with property, I was still very bullish about the outlook for blocks of flats in the London area and in some provincial cities. The blocks could be bought very cheaply because they were in the main being sold by distress sellers such as the old Stern Group and First National. The banks did not like to lend against these properties as they were already up to their eyes in this kind of security and had many problems with their existing loan books arising from the fall in property values. On the other hand, individual flats in these blocks were still selling well; if they were vacant, they could be sold relatively easily to someone looking for a home or, if occupied, a large proportion of them could be sold to the sitting tenants. Colin Bray, who was looking after residential property at Slater Walker, wanted to set up on his own as this side of the company was being steadily run down. About a month after I resigned I agreed with Jimmy Goldsmith that Colin would join me, but still be available to Slater Walker on a consultancy basis if required.

My first property deal was to buy 464 maisonettes in Leeds. I formed a company named Bripalm and then approached a number of my friends to ask them to help finance it. My proposal was that they would be guaranteed a good rate of interest, have the security of the property through a debenture, and that any resultant profit would be shared in agreed proportions. I was very favourably surprised by the reaction to my proposals and, although there were a few nerve-racking moments before completion, I managed to form the syndicate and buy the property without undue difficulty. One of the major investors was an associated company of Lonrho, and their participation had resulted from a meeting I had with Tiny Rowland.

Once I had formed Bripalm and purchased one property I knew that I was on the right track. I had the method—now I needed the gearing. I put my shareholding in Bripalm into a company named Strongmead, which I had owned for some time and I decided to make this my new master company. When I had resigned from Slater Walker, Tiny Rowland had telephoned the same evening to say that he would do all he could to be of help. Over a lunch we agreed that, subject to his board's approval, Lonrho would participate in Strongmead on a fifty-fifty basis and provide several million pounds worth of finance on the condition that they approved each particular proposal on its individual merits. This gave me the gearing, which together with the method provided the formula with which to recoup my considerable financial losses: I had been worth eight million and now I was worth not far short of minus one million. The important thing in this sort of position is to think of a million as one not as a hundred ten thousands. I went to see my three main creditors with details of my plans to repay them; fortunately they took a friendly and pragmatic view of the situation, and agreed to give me time to build up Strongmead.

The next step was to acquire a small office and some staff. I took with me Peter Greaves and Peter Kellett, who had worked on my personal affairs while I was at Slater Walker: Peter Greaves had been my personal assistant and he became chairman of Strongmead; Peter Kellett had kept my personal financial records and accounts, and he became Strongmead's financial director. We soon built up a small nucleus of staff, and rented an office just off Wimbledon High Street. Peter Greaves had no time to buy any pictures for the office, so when we moved he had stuck Womble posters on the walls instead. The atmosphere reminded me very much of Hertford Street, but it had the great advantage of being only fifteen minutes away from my home.

After my resignation from Slater Walker I received a great number of sympathetic letters from relatives, friends, acquaintances, neighbours and associates, and also from complete strangers. I was offered the use of houses in the country and villas abroad, and there were many other very touching offers of practical help. Almost without exception I found people extremely pleasant after my fortunes changed, and this has reinforced my belief in the finer qualities of man. One of the advantages of running into major difficulties is that you do find out who your real friends are; far from being in any way disappointed, I found that mine were a source of strength beyond my best hopes.

During November and December 1975 I was still going into Slater Walker's offices to clear up my personal effects and to help Jimmy Goldsmith wherever possible. At this time the Hong Kong authorities had been requested by the Singapore Government to investigate Spydar and other corporate matters concerning Haw Par. The Hong Kong police came to London to take statements from those concerned in Spydar, and everyone fully cooperated with them. After their visit I wrote again to the Inspector in Singapore, as more evidence in support of our arguments had come to light. One of my greatest difficulties was gaining possession of any relevant evidence because local witnesses were scared stiff and nobody in Hong Kong and Singapore wanted to be involved. Fortunately I had an inside contact, who was able to let me have copies of the more important documents, so that I could make it absolutely clear that Haw Par's professional advisers in Hong Kong had been consulted about Spydar at an early stage.

One of Jimmy's priorities was to settle the Haw Par loan and to this end he made a visit to Singapore in December. Just before, at Jimmy's request, I had placed my Slater Walker shares at market price, which was 23p at the time, in order to clear the way for a settlement and to make it absolutely clear to the Singapore authorities that I was no longer associated with the company. Jimmy negotiated with the new Haw Par chairman, a Singapore Government appointee named Michael Fam, but he gained the distinct impression that Fam had very little real authority and only acted on orders from above. The loan totalled US$29m and Jimmy was prepared to offer a small discount to get it settled, but apparently the Singapore opening stance was that Haw Par had no intention of repaying the loan and would instead claim US$30m from Slater Walker. On his return Jimmy told me that he had found the Singapore approach to the problem totally unrealistic; some progress had been made by demolishing some of their wilder claims, but a large gulf still remained. I was very disappointed, because I had hoped that reason, as opposed to emotion, would prevail after my resignation from Slater Walker.

In February 1976, I suggested to Tiny Rowland that Lonrho should consider bidding for Lubok, as it was basically a cash company which also had some valuable tax losses. Negotiations took place between Jimmy and Tiny and their advisers, and a deal was struck which was quickly followed by a bid. I accepted in respect of my shareholding but a few months later had to sell my Lonrho shares in order to reduce my overdraft.

In spite of being in debt I did not find I had to change my life-style to any great extent. My creditors had realized that if I did not have a reasonable general setup and backcloth, I would be unable to make much progress in my efforts to repay them. I was living in the same house that I had bought when I was at Leyland, and until the time I left Slater Walker I had run the same car for ten years; we had never owned a villa abroad, a yacht, or any other indulgence of that nature. As I have said, we did not find that our friends suddenly disappeared, so in many ways life went on much as usual. My wife was a tower of strength at this difficult time and my mother also gave me tremendous moral support.

There was one apparent anomaly that seemed to worry some journalists. About four years earlier I had formed a charitable trust called the Slater Foundation. The purpose of this was quite simply to give money to charity. The £50,000 Fischer-Spassky chess prize had been out of my own funds, but other chess prizes to help Britain's younger players were given by the Slater Foundation. Other gifts of note were to Birthright, the Royal College of Surgeons, the London Symphony Orchestra and the National Gallery. More recently £5,000 was given to Tony Miles, the first young British chess player to become a grand-master since the Fischer-Spassky offer was made, and £65,000 was donated to the National Trust to help restore Claremont Gardens, which is near my home. The last two gifts in particular attracted some publicity, and there were questions as to how I could afford to give the money away. The answer is quite simply that the funds of the Slater Foundation are no longer my own, nor can I benefit from them in any way. The Slater Foundation has independent trustees of repute and, although I can make recommendations to them, I cannot in any way direct the activities of the trust, which is a completely separate entity.

During the early months of 1976 I was playing quite a lot of bridge at the Portland Club and thoroughly enjoying it. I also went up to Tulchan with my two boys and, on another occasion, with three friends, when I was the only member of the party not to catch anything.

In March I had a week's holiday in Barbados with some close friends, as Jimmy Goldsmith's guest. Helen could not manage to get away, but was happy for me to go provided I was back for my birthday on the 13th. During the previous few years I had invariably been away on business trips around that time and the children had been disappointed, as they enjoyed our birthdays as well as their own. With this very firmly in mind I joined Jimmy. I shared a small villa with Selim Zilkha, and we were later joined by Sidney Chaplin, Charles Chaplin's son. I spent a wonderful week playing a lot of tennis, swimming and sunbathing, and of course playing some backgammon.

John Aspinall and I agreed to travel back to London together late on the 11th. When the time came for our departure, the taxi we had ordered to take us to the airport did not turn up, so a friend of Jimmy's agreed to drive us there. Unfortunately he did not know the way. I was getting progressively more worried and to my annoyance John was finding the whole situation hysterically funny. Finally in our haste, we overshot the airport entrance, and when we backed the car up it went into a ditch. We got out and tried to move it. John is a very strong man and I am no weakling, but our efforts made absolutely no impression on the car. At that point I caught sight of a man on a bicycle and persuaded him to go up the road to the airport to get help quickly. About ten minutes later, when an interested crowd had gathered, a taxi drew up. The taxi driver was one of the largest men I have ever seen. John and I watched in amazement as, completely unaided, he easily lifted the car out of the ditch. We then jumped into his taxi and rushed to the airport—only to find that we had just missed the plane.

We returned to the villa and I then had the unenviable job of telephoning my wife to explain why I would now be arriving back on my birthday, instead of the day before. As I started the account of our misfortunes I felt instinctively from my wife's silence that there was a growing credibility gap. This became even greater when I reached the point where the giant Barbadian lifted the car out of the ditch single-handed. Just as I finished explaining this Sidney Chaplin, who was sitting nearby, called out in a loud voice, 'And then he said "Hey presto" and there was a turkey supper!' After that none of us could stop laughing and I decided that the full story would be best left until I got home.

During the first few months following my resignation there had been demands in some of the newspapers for a full-scale Department of Trade and Industry inquiry into Slater Walker. The *Sunday Times* published a crop of critical articles, which were circulated to a number of MPs, and this resulted in a few questions in the House of Commons. At one time it looked as if the Government might respond to this pressure. However, the company was already being investigated by the merchant banking advisers and in much more detail by two leading firms of accountants, and the Bank of England and DTI were being kept closely advised as the investigations progressed. In addition a full-scale DTI inquiry would have undermined confidence further, with disastrous side effects on the unit trust and insurance businesses, as well as costing both the Government and Slater Walker shareholders a great deal of money. In the event, on this occasion reason prevailed.

In a sense March, April and May were a kind of limbo period. I was waiting for the Singapore loan position to be settled and to see what other action, if any, was going to be taken by the Singapore authorities. I was also waiting for the result of the accountants' report on Slater Walker. By then they had started a more detailed special investigation into four quasi-group companies named Bion, Euroglen, Jaydean and Petershill Trust. During their general investigations the accountants had found that a considerable number of Slater Walker shares had been bought by these companies with money borrowed from Slater Walker's banking subsidiary. They concluded that there might have been a breach of Section 54 of the Companies Act, which makes it illegal for a company to lend money to finance the purchase of its own shares, unless the lending is made in the ordinary course of the company's business. The board had therefore asked the accountants to prepare an independent report to try to determine the position.

In the meantime there seemed to be good news from Singapore. Michael Fam was coming to London in June, accompanied by a member of the Attorney General's department, and it seemed for the first time that an overall settlement with Haw Par might be possible. This time the attitude of Michael Fam surprised Jimmy and Slater Walker's solicitors: the Singapore negotiating party really seemed to want to reach a settlement of all outstanding problems. A few months earlier they had issued writs against Slater Walker and the Spydar participants, but now they made it clear to Jimmy that they wanted the whole matter settled. He had a word with me and I, in turn, had a word with the other people involved, in some cases through their solicitors. There was no doubt that even though detailed legal advice had been taken locally, the Spydar scheme had been set up too casually, and there was a possibility that Haw Par's civil claim against the participants might succeed. In that event I would have had to repay the profits immediately, together with the legal costs and interest. Fam insisted that the Spydar matter had to be resolved before there could be an overall settlement, and therefore a genuine compromise was worked out. The Spydar participants would enter into interest-free promissory notes to repay Slater Walker the Spydar profits in five years time. The saving of legal costs and interest together with availability of credit, made this offer an attractive one, and by degrees everyone concerned came round to accepting it. It worked out as substantially less than half what might have had to be paid in the worst possible circumstances, and it was a sensible compromise.

It could be argued that I was naive to even consider settling the Spydar civil claim, but at that time Dick Tarling and I had an important insurance policy in our possession. We had both realized that if the Singapore authorities were to pursue matters further our most difficult task would be to persuade the courts in this country that their allegations were not made in good faith. The problem with any proceedings would be that the Singapore authorities would only have to prove a *prima facie* case against us. This meant that there would not be a trial in this country, but just a hearing to see whether or not there was 'a case to be heard'. The best layman's description of a *prima facie* case is that if you sneeze then *prima facie* you have a cold. Because of the casual way Spydar had been set up, there was a chance that the Singapore authorities would be able to demonstrate that there was a *prima facie* case. I was advised that in a full trial in any country with a fair judicial system there would be no doubt that I would be found not guilty, and I was also assured that no responsible prosecution would proceed on the facts as we knew them to be. However, knowing the approach of the Singapore authorities, I wanted double insurance.

We had accumulated some evidence, including a large number of press cuttings, that would help make our point that there was prejudice against Slater Walker in Singapore and that the proposed merger between Haw Par and Pernas had become a political issue. As the *Financial Times* reported on 29 September 1975, 'As it became clear that the deal was foundering in the face of Singapore's resistance, there were calls on the Malaysian Government to take retaliatory action. Razaleigh himself made it plain that failure to get the deal through would sour Malaysian-

Singapore relations. Delegates attending the annual conference in Kuala Lumpur in June of the United Malays National Organization (UMNO), Malaysia's predominant ruling party, attacked Singapore's intransigence in the matter, and demanded a ban on Malaysian food exports as well as the cutting off of water supplies to the island republic. The Singapore High Commission in Kuala Lumpur received several phone calls threatening bomb attacks on its office if the deal did not go through, and Mr Lee had to write a personal letter to Tun Razak to cool emotions by assuring him that the actions taken by Singapore on Haw Par were not aimed at foiling the Pernas initiative.'

We also had the February 1976 Amnesty International report which severely criticized Singapore, and press cuttings that made it clear that fair trials in Singapore were unlikely in political cases. However, as Singapore was a member of the Commonwealth and a large holder of sterling, we felt that there would still be a natural reluctance to believe our arguments.

We knew that Graham Starforth-Hill, one of the two inspectors appointed to investigate the affairs of Haw Par, had said in conversation to an associate of Dick Tarling that he was unhappy about the way the Attorney General had wanted the inquiry to be pursued. We needed absolute proof of this. Graham Starforth-Hill was coming to London in April to take evidence from Dick in connection with another matter concerning Slater Walker (Australia) and Dick had agreed to see him at Slaughter & May's offices. Ideally we would have wanted Starforth-Hill, who had resigned as an inspector, to give evidence on our behalf; as it was, we knew that he would not be prepared to do so because of the problem this would pose with the Singapore authorities, as well as giving rise to questions of professional confidence. However, Dick knew that Starforth-Hill, who had achieved great eminence in the legal profession in Singapore, was planning to leave that country within a few months and had no family there. Dick and I alone decided, with considerable reluctance, to take a tape recording of Dick's talks with him. We agreed that we would only use this evidence *in extremis*. Neither Dick Tarling nor I had ever recorded a conversation before, and it was not something that we decided to do lightly. In the circumstances, however, it seemed the only way that we could prove the truth of our arguments.

I was at Tulchan on a fishing trip when Dick made the recording, which covered two days' talks and about six hours' conversation in all. About five hours were irrelevant, but the other hour was exactly what we had been looking for. It was the silver thread that bound together the other fragmentary pieces of evidence we had collected. As soon as the recording was finished, transcripts were taken and everything was deposited in a safe place. We sincerely hoped that the time would never come when we would have to use this evidence, but nevertheless we slept more easily knowing of its existence.

Needless to say none of the Spydar participants would have considered reaching a settlement, which could have been construed as an admission of guilt, if they had thought that there was a strong probability of the Singapore authorities taking criminal action. I had heard on the grapevine a few months earlier that Singapore was considering starting extradition proceedings, but since then things seemed to have gone quiet. I thought it quite probable that there had been a change of heart following the blistering Amnesty International report issued in February. This report had demonstrated that Singapore was all but a police state, that the press was effectively Government controlled, and that there was an alarming number of prisoners who had been detained for years without trial. It went on to point out that in one case an important defence witness had been deported just before a trial, and in another case a lawyer had been suspended for acting for the defence. I had known of this for some time, but I was naturally delighted to see it made public by an independent organization. About three months after the report Singapore had resigned from Socialist International because a motion had been tabled calling for its expulsion on the grounds that 'its totalitarian regime has no affinity with social democratic principles'. I thought that these relatively recent blows to Singapore's prestige might well have deterred the authorities. In addition, armed with Dick's recording, I thought we could prove, if we had to, that the Singapore authorities were not acting in good faith. I was therefore much more open to the idea of settling the Spydar civil claim than I might otherwise have been.

It would obviously have been absurd for Slater Walker to take promissory notes from the Spydar participants if there was any question of criminal proceedings being taken against them. Equally obvious was the fact that the liberty of the individuals concerned was fundamental to their future capacity to repay Slater Walker. Fam went through the ritual of explaining to Jimmy Goldsmith that he could not speak for the Government, but as he was a Government appointee, accompanied by a member of the Attorney General's department, it was reasonable to assume that they communicated with each other. Slater Walker were naturally anxious to settle the outstanding litigation and in particular the loan, which had affected confidence so much, and it was therefore not long before a financial settlement was agreed. The wording of the press release was crucial and referred to the settlement as being 'the close of an episode'. It took a long time to agree on the final wording and it was particularly significant to us that it had to be cleared by the Attorney General's department and was, in fact, at one stage amended by them. In the circumstances it was not surprising that Jimmy and all concerned thought that the words 'the close of an episode' meant exactly what they said. A few months later everyone was to feel that they had been seriously misled by the Singapore authorities.

After I thought the Spydar affair had been settled, I began to relax a little. I went fishing in July and then in August I went to Studland for the annual family holiday. These summer holidays now seemed jinxed: the news of John Ford's death had overshadowed the one of 1974, and the beginning of the Spydar affair had interrupted our holiday in 1975. This time it was the turn of the DTI, with a Section 109 inquiry into whether there had been a breach of Section 54 of the Companies Act. At this point the investigating accountant's report was almost complete and the DTI had of course seen advance copies of it and been generally kept up to date with developments. Their conclusion was that there might have been a breach of Section 54; a Section 109 inquiry enabled them to obtain all the necessary books and records and take detailed statements from those concerned in an endeavour to clarify the position. Two senior officials were appointed to supervise the inquiry and I was asked to go up to London to attend before them together with my solicitor, George Staple of Clifford-Turner. I saw them on two separate occasions and detailed transcripts were taken, as any evidence I gave could be used against me in any future proceedings that might take place.

After answering their many detailed questions, I explained that our banking subsidiary had lent money to an associated company to buy Slater Walker shares in the ordinary course of its business. I went on to tell them that the shares had been accumulated for prospective deals with several major companies and that the purchase had been made in the best interests of the company. An example was the share exchange with Hutchison International, which resulted in Slater Walker making a multi-million pounds profit. I subsequently took leading counsel's opinion on the subject and he agreed with my interpretation. I heard no more for a few weeks while the matter was being actively considered by the DTI.

In July 1976 the investigating accountants' report on Slater Walker's overall position was published amidst a blaze of publicity. The report was critical of several aspects of the company's past activity and it is worth looking in detail at some of the points that were raised and subsequently taken up by the press.

The main item at issue was in connection with loans to directors and, in particular, the second loan to Tony Buckley, which I have already dealt with. The loans only fell for disclosure in the accounts that year, although they had always been disclosed in Canadian returns in order to maintain our quotation in Canada. We had never made any secret of the fact that our directors had bought associated company shares on borrowed money—in fact I frequently spoke publicly on exactly that subject, emphasizing that it helped to concentrate their minds. The other area of emotional reaction was on mortgages. There were several sizeable mortgages on directors' houses which provoked considerable criticism. I do not think anyone disputed the idea of the mortgages themselves, as this is a very common practice and a normal executive benefit, neither could it have been the non-disclosure because they only fell for disclosure that year. It must have been the amount of the mortgages that was the problem. This was based on a multiple of salary that was applied to all staff and I cannot see why a director should suffer in relation to the norm. To my mind one of the most important points was the rate of interest charged. This was 11 per cent per annum, which at the time the money was lent was a normal commercial rate for mortgages. No one drew attention to the fact that many joint stock banks had mortgage schemes and lent money to their staff at only $2\frac{1}{2}$ per cent per annum on a higher multiple of salary than that applied by Slater Walker. There are many other examples of similar schemes adopted by merchant banks, unit trust groups and other financial services companies. Loans like these are a much greater benefit to executives than the Slater Walker mortgage scheme.

There was also criticism of the insurance company for being too liquid. Anyone who had experienced the run on funds that we had, following the failure of Jessel's insurance company, would have erred on that side as well. I fully accept that I missed the sharp up-turn in the market at the beginning of the previous year, but having done that I thought it most prudent to remain liquid, especially as interest rates were so favourable and confidence was still at a low ebb.

The property portfolio, too, was criticized. Which portfolio would not have been suspect after the roaring bull market collapsed? Of course some of the properties were no longer worth book value on a forced realization, but equally that would apply to the portfolio of almost every property company in the country.

The investment side was given a good write-up and it was the banking subsidiary which came in for most criticism. It was said that we lent money to associates and that there were several very large loans. This really could not have been a surprise to anyone. The Bank of England knew, the press knew, and so did most intelligent shareholders. Of course the loan book looked rather sick after the ravages of the bear market, and as it was concentrated in a relatively few major areas (one of which was Haw Par), it was more vulnerable than most. I regret to say that a harsh look at the loan books of most major banks at that time would have shown some surprising results. There had of course been some public revelation of the problems of such companies as Keyser Ullman, First National, Grindlays Bank and William Brandt. Behind the scenes, however, most major banks were also having their worries; this was obvious from the number of failures of very sizeable public companies which themselves had large overdrafts from the joint stock banks.

It was also revealed that the Bank of England had supported Slater Walker to the tune of £40m. While I was chairman of the company we had not had a penny of support, even in the most difficult times, but when I resigned deposits evaporated. This was inevitable because of the crisis of confidence following the Spydar affair, and Jimmy had had to make sure before he took over as chairman that the Bank of England would support the company if the need arose. A further major problem was that the financial results showed large losses and a much depleted net asset value. Some of this was inevitable, but it was exaggerated by the fact that the new board were tending to regard their task as an orderly liquidation of assets. If, in very difficult markets, you look at any property or share portfolio you will find it impossible to realize earlier estimated values. A forced or speedy realization is always difficult, especially as the prospective buyer usually knows your difficulty.

It seemed that no positive steps could be taken to counterbalance adverse events. Over the previous five years I had regularly made an average of £10m per annum in share dealing profits. I had made plans to buy in Trust & Agency to save over £2m in tax, and also to bid for the balance of Estates House or sell our shareholding in it at a profit. In addition to this I would have invested heavily in the residential flat market. However, this kind of positive action could only have been taken by me in a climate of continued confidence, which would have been eroded as the Spydar affair developed. Following my resignation, Jimmy could not do any of these things either, because deposits had evaporated, funds were critically needed within the company, and he was dependent upon the Bank of England for support. Neither of us was therefore able to take the necessary steps to make money. The pity of it is that it would all have been tax free because of past losses being available for offset. The profits could then have been used to continue to buy in further long-term loan stock at a massive discount, thereby doubling the beneficial effect on the balance sheet. As it was, the net worth of the company continued to fall and there was nothing that anyone could do about it. Financial businesses are all about confidence, and when that is lost the penalties of being highly geared come into play.

· EIGHTEEN ·

Warrant for Arrest

ON 23 September 1976 the Department of Trade and Industry announced that they were issuing fifteen summonses against me in respect of alleged breaches of Section 54 of the Companies Act. These were summary offences to be tried at a hearing before the City Magistrates. The maximum fine was £100 for each offence, but nevertheless they ranked as a criminal charge, and the summonses stimulated a great deal of publicity. I consulted my solicitors and was asked by the police to attend at my solicitors' offices to receive the summonses. I was naturally disturbed by the DTI action, but not unduly worried, as it appeared to me to be a matter of interpretation of a relatively fine point of law. Leading counsel had advised that he agreed with my interpretation and at the very worst it would have been unfortunate, but not catastrophic, if I had lost the argument.

The following day, however, I was again headline news when it was reported authoritatively in several newspapers that the Singapore authorities had applied to extradite me, Dick Tarling and three other ex-Slater Walker executives on charges of fraud and conspiracy. The leak was reported in the *Guardian*, which is quite often first to report on confidential matters of this nature concerning Government departments. I first heard the news from my mother, who telephoned in a distressed state to say that she had read it in her newspaper. Apparently the extradition papers had been with the Home Office since June and they had been warned in late May that extradition proceedings were contemplated. This was a month before the final settlement with Haw Par and the agreed 'close of an episode'. Clearly the man from the Attorney General's department who had accompanied Fam had been busy elsewhere during his visit, as well as approving the press release on the final settlement.

Singapore, as a member of the Commonwealth, had made its application for extradition under the Fugitive Offenders Act 1967. This act applies to all Commonwealth countries on a reciprocal basis; it makes extradition between the UK and Commonwealth easier than with other countries, which enter into separate treaties under the Extradition Act. The basic idea might have been fine in 1967, but a lot has happened since then. For example the position of Uganda has become very different, and, if the application had come from that country, it would have been treated with extreme caution. In the case of Singapore, however, its Commonwealth membership coupled with its sterling balances made the criticisms of Amnesty International and Socialist International seem rather academic. I knew immediately that I had the biggest fight of my life on my hands and that I had to think out the problem carefully before taking any action.

An application for the return of a fugitive by a Commonwealth Government is first considered by the Home Secretary who has to issue 'an Authority to Proceed' before the matter can be taken any further. This is usually a formality over which there is little delay, and the papers are then sent to Bow Street for the magistrate to issue a warrant for arrest if he considers there is sufficient evidence on the face of the documents. The very fact that the Home Secretary had been considering the application for over three months seemed to imply that he was not altogether happy with the situation and that political considerations might be involved. I therefore decided that my first task was to try and get it over to the public that Singapore was not all that it seemed to be; second to try to stop the proceedings at the Home Office level; third to get bail if warrants were issued; fourth to finance and organize my defence; and fifth to arrange my business and personal affairs in such a way that I could devote most of my time during the following months to the legal preparations that would be necessary.

I did not have much time to persuade the public that in my view Singapore was not acting in the best interests of justice and that I would have no hope of a fair trial there. I saw several newspaper editors, as a result of which a few favourable articles appeared on the subject. I also agreed to go on the *Tonight* programme to be interviewed by Ludovic Kennedy. I had always been worried about giving a live performance but on this occasion I had much bigger worries. I needed the interview to be live because I wanted to talk about Singapore at length and I knew that there would be a risk of some of my observations being edited out of a recording. As we were walking off the set after the interview, Ludovic Kennedy turned to me and said, 'I thought that was fine, but there was rather too much on Singapore'. As far as I was concerned that had been the object of the exercise.

There was an important development on the following Saturday when William Rees-Mogg, the editor of *The Times*, came out with an editorial which made it clear that in his view the Singapore authorities had a way of getting the judicial results they required when the Singapore Government was interested in the outcome of a particular case. William Rees-Mogg has a unique reputation for integrity, and his article was a talking point for some weeks afterwards.

I also made the counter-attack more international by giving an interview to *Newsweek*, in which I again emphasized that in my view there

"Actually, we wanted the other Jim Slater!"

would be no hope of a fair trial in Singapore. Many international magazines would have thought twice about carrying such an article because Singapore buys a great deal of advertising space to promote their tourism and airlines. *Newsweek* itself had been critical of the regime on an earlier occasion and Singapore advertising with them had been suspended for some time afterwards as a result. I know most newspapers and magazines would not be affected by this kind of retaliation, but it must be a factor in some cases where budgets are tight. Certainly, as shown by their earlier action against *Newsweek*, the Singapore authorities seemed to think so.

I was receiving hundreds of letters from friends, neighbours, former associates and complete strangers, many of whom had also written to their MPs and the Home Secretary. A standardized reply was sent to all people who wrote to the Home Secretary and a slightly different version of it to those MPs who wrote to him. It explained that at first there was to be a hearing at Bow Street and after that I would have the right of appeal to the Divisional Court, in which I would be able to advance arguments that the application by the Singapore Government was not made in good faith and that it would be 'unjust and oppressive to return me'. If that failed there would still be the right of appeal to the Home Secretary.

Amongst the many letters and messages of support I received there was one that I particularly remember from Bill Black. He concluded with the words '*illegitimi nil carborundum*' which, he said, loosely translated means 'don't let the bastards get you down'. I also received an amusing letter from a young man the Slater Foundation had backed a few years earlier to go on an expedition to South America to explore some hitherto relatively unknown regions. He had returned from the expedition and fallen on troubled times and, after wishing me all the best, he wrote:

It's a crazy world. I am now overqualified and unemployable. In the past two months, having invested all I could in camera and sound recording equipment and film, I have travelled some 800 miles down the Tana River in an inflatable boat, shot rapids, capsized, lost equipment, been trapped in mud, not been eaten by countless crocodiles, traversed pools containing more than eighty hippo, been charged by elephant, stung and bitten by innumerable tsetse flies, mosquitos and all manner of biting flies, infested with ticks, burnt, rained on, scratched, gone without sleep and generally made very uncomfortable, suffered the many river ailments, may well have picked up bilharzia, which is endemic on the river—all this to try to make a film and thus a living. And back home the assistant bank manager, archtick that he is, has been sitting in comfort and complete serenity, gorging himself on the colossal interest I pay on my overdraft.

Clearly I was not alone in having a few problems.

My second task was to try to persuade the Home Office not to let the matter go any further. Together with my legal advisers I prepared and sent a seven-page letter to the Home Secretary, explaining the background and that we had reason to believe that if the proceedings commenced they would ultimately give rise to far greater problems and embarrassment in our relationship with Singapore than could possibly be occasioned by cutting them off at that early stage. My solicitors and those of Dick Tarling were invited to see Home Office officials and went through the arguments with them. It would, however, have been an almost unprecedented move for the Home Secretary to have intervened, and a day or so later we heard that the die was cast and that the papers had been forwarded to the Bow Street Magistrate.

The papers were with the magistrate for over a fortnight, which was again an unusually long time for proceedings of this nature. During this time I read in the *Sunday Times*, and the following week in the *Economist*, that there were three main allegations against me and a total of nine charges. The first allegation concerned Spydar and covered six of the charges, the second allegation concerned Melbourne Unit Trust and the third an offer document for shares in M & G. I learned that the *Economist* obtained their very detailed information from a Singapore source. It was of course a wholly novel situation for a 'fugitive' to learn weeks in advance that criminal charges were pending against him, and to read in newspapers and magazines details of those charges before either he or his solicitors were formally advised of them. Since my conscience was clear and I had no desire to run, I could only watch the situation build up with an almost fascinated horror.

On 25 October Dick Tarling and I were finally arrested after the magistrate had issued the necessary warrants. In the meantime Singapore had dropped the Melbourne and M & G allegations against me and only the six charges concerning Spydar remained. The formal arrest was by appointment at Bow Street and when I arrived at 9.30 there was a mass of photographers and reporters waiting outside. Dick Tarling arrived with his solicitor shortly afterwards and we were both formally charged. The policeman on duty read through Dick's charges in detail, refreshing himself now and then with a drink of water, and this took about three-quarters of an hour. I then told him that I would take my charges as read and handed him a brief statement. After my fingerprints were recorded, which was a singularly messy business, a photograph was also taken and I handed in my passport. Dick and I then appeared before the Chief

Metropolitan Magistrate and obtained bail, which was not in any way opposed by the Singapore Government. Two local friends of mine stood bail for me and by 11.30 I was on my way back to the office in Wimbledon feeling rather the worse for wear.

Now I had the task of financing and organizing my defence. I was fortunate to have the services of Clifford-Turner as my solicitors, and a senior litigation partner, George Staple, agreed to concentrate almost full-time on the case during the critical months ahead. George, who had been working on my affairs for the previous year, knew the Spydar position intimately and was a tower of strength. A leading QC, David Hirst, had been advising me from an early stage, and as the Spydar affair developed he had suggested that we also brought in John Mathew who specialized in criminal law and had a great deal of experience in fugitive cases. It was agreed between us that John would act for me in the Magistrates Court, and John in turn suggested that Dai Tudor-Price should act as his junior, as they worked well together. That, then, was the team: John Mathew and Dai Tudor-Price, backed up by George Staple, and with David Hirst advising in the wings. The estimated costs were very substantial and I was fortunate that four of my friends clubbed together to finance them for me. I told them that in the unlikely event of my losing they would have a promissory note from me which they would be able to sell at a very substantial discount.

My last task was to ensure that my business and personal affairs were put on a basis which enabled me to concentrate my main energies in preparing for the coming battle. I had a word with Tiny Rowland, who fully understood the problem, and I explained that property was going to have to take a back place for a few months. Fortunately my new business ran like clockwork anyway, and there was very little difficulty in arranging my affairs in this way.

I knew that I was going to be able to think about little other than the case until it was over. On the day before my arrest I decided to write this book, which was to prove valuable therapy as it took my mind completely off the extradition proceedings during my free time. I found, probably as a result of extra adrenalin, that I had a strong driving force and I powered through the book at great speed.

One of the first steps we took was to apply to the City Magistrates to have the Section 54 case delayed until after Spydar, which by then had been fixed for hearing at the Horseferry Road court on 5 January 1977; it was agreed that the Section 54 case should be heard on 3 February.

We then had many conferences at John Mathew's chambers. All of us, except Dai Tudor-Price, had worked on Spydar for a year and knew the facts intimately. We decided that I should put in a detailed written statement and attach to it other evidence which we considered helpful to my cause and which, though in the possession of the Singapore authorities, had been completely ignored by them. The wording of my statement was very carefully considered and took a long time to draft in its final form. Clearly the Singapore authorities had already concluded that the allegations and charges concerning Melbourne Unit Trust and M & G should not have been brought against me and our task was to persuade the magistrate that the Spydar charges were also ill-founded.

My contact with expert lawyers made me realize that they can always see two sides to every argument, and for that reason you do seem at times to go round in circles. For example, Dick Tarling had sent a telex about Spydar including the words, 'Take no action on Tokengate concept we discussed, pending full discussions in Hong Kong'. We argued that, as we had had to spell out to Ogilvy-Watson that no action should be taken, the agreement must already have been at an advanced stage ready for action to be taken. The counter-argument, however, was that 'Take no action . . .' meant what it said and that any agreement there had been was dead after that. Another time I said triumphantly to John Mathew, 'I have just remembered that three months after Spydar I gave the £50,000 chess prize, and I have checked up and in that year I also gave four times as much as that to charity. Surely that shows I was not interested in the money as such and makes the whole concept of fraud a ridiculous one?' To which John replied in a world-weary way, 'Unfortunately, Jim, that's what they all say!' Apparently all alleged criminals are very generous. I would have idea after idea, only to be told, 'Jim, that's a good jury point, but not a good magistrate's point' or something similar.

Looking back, it was very much a team effort and many of the better points were an amalgam of all of our ideas. As the weeks went by and 5 January approached our confidence in our arguments became very strong, but there was always a niggling doubt, which was of course exaggerated by the horrific consequences if the magistrate found against me. During these critical few months I was given great moral support by my wife and mother, and also by all my friends. Another source of strength was the support I received from my legal advisers. I was seeing a great deal of them and our relationship became a very close and effective one.

It was during this time that I won my greatest personal battle, the one against myself. The threat of being extradited to Singapore to face the hostility and bias, not to mention Changi jail, was obviously difficult to live with. I was also getting interesting titbits of information which helped keep my fears alive. For example, a leading American businessman who had just passed through Singapore wrote to a friend of mine, 'In Singapore they are all looking forward to feasting on poor Jim Slater's blood!' This did not help my morale but it helped me to face the worst. I decided that in the event of a trial in Singapore I would handle my own defence to save costs, make the point that in my view the trial was a farce anyway, and take the opportunity of telling the Singapore authorities and the world press a few home truths in words that my counsel might have found difficult. I then asked myself if I could face Changi jail and the answer was a positive 'yes'. After the fuss I was going to create in Divisional Court and then in Singapore I knew that the last thing that the Singapore authorities would want would be for me to suffer harsh treatment in jail. As a leading international editor told me, Lee Kuan Yew's great moment would come when, and if, he got me to Singapore, and after that I would only be an embarrassment to him.

Once I had faced the worst I was in a strange way cauterized and felt almost immune from fear. I had begun to lose weight and to lose my sense of humour—both returned. Now I had to reassure my family. Fortunately the children had little or no idea of what was really going on. They thought that I was fighting a legal case against a Chinaman and they were flatteringly confident that I would win. My wife and I were very close at this difficult time. She was a great comfort and source of strength to me and held the house and family together while I concentrated on the legal fight. I was able to tell her that I was very confident of winning but that if it came to the worst, I knew I could face it, and friends would ensure that she and the children were financially secure. My mother was my main worry. She was seventy-four and had not been in good health. Fortunately she has great moral courage and faith, and she was convinced that I would win. Once she knew that I could face the worst, she was able to do so as well, and I found that she continued to cheer me up each week when I went to see her instead of it being the other way round.

A friend wrote to me enclosing a copy of Rudyard Kipling's wonderful poem 'If', which took on a new meaning for me. I was particularly moved by the lines:

> If you can meet with Triumph and Disaster
> And treat those two imposters just the same;

There was no doubt in my mind that I had had the 'Triumph' and now my share of 'Disaster' was in danger of assuming equal, if not greater, proportions. Looking back on it all, it was obvious that both were 'imposters' and the real things that mattered were relationships with family and friends, and my own convictions and beliefs. I remember that I was very impressed when I saw Bukovsky on television after his release from a Russian prison in which he had been subjected to torture and brainwashing. After all that he had been through he had in his eyes a look of inner strength and conviction which reinforced my belief that the real battleground was within myself. I know that from that moment I confronted and overcame my fear I have been conscious of an inner strength which has changed, and will continue to change, my approach to life.

· NINETEEN ·

In Court

WE spent Christmas at home as usual and New Year's Eve at a friend's house near by. As we welcomed in the New Year, I reflected that 1977 could hardly be worse than 1976, but then I realized that there were permutations that made even that possible.

The hearing took place on 5 January at Horseferry Road, before Mr Kenneth Barraclough, the Chief Metropolitan Magistrate. It started at 10.30 but I had to arrive half an hour earlier to surrender to my bail and attend to other legal formalities. As I arrived at the court I was met by a large contingent of pressmen to whom I could say nothing except 'good morning' because the whole matter was *sub judice*. On the first day the press gallery in the court room was full, but after a few days it began to thin out. I sat with my solicitor, George Staple, next to me and John Mathew and Dai Tudor-Price just in front of us. Dick Tarling was on my left with his solicitor next to him and his two counsels in front of them. On the extreme left of the court was the prosecution led by Mr Ronald Waterhouse QC, supported by two counsels and a bevy of solicitors. The magistrate sat in front of us at a higher level and immediately in front of him sat the magistrate's clerk. This was to be our 'class room' for the next two and a half weeks and all of us were going to get very used to the scenery.

The whole of the evidence relied upon by the prosecution had been served upon us shortly after I had been charged. The evidence was contained in the sworn statements of the witnesses, with a mass of related accompanying documents. In fugitive cases the witnesses are rarely called, because they are usually resident in the requisitioning country, and the prosecution are allowed to rely on their statements, which the defence are unable to challenge. The procedure is that counsel for the prosecution presents his case to the magistrate based upon the statements and documents, and witnesses are only called if they are available in this country. When the prosecution have completed their submissions, the defence can then call any witnesses they wish and submit that no *prima facie* case has been made out.

I thought at first that court hours were very easy but soon found the days rather tiring. We used to meet in a small room at Horseferry Road for a half-hour talk before the hearing started at 10.30. The hearing went on until one o'clock, when we went to Dick Tarling's flat where he would lay on an excellent snack lunch. We were back in court by two o'clock and finished by four. After that we frequently had conferences at John Mathew's chambers which lasted until seven or eight in the evening. By the end of the week I felt exhausted and was beginning to wonder how lawyers kept it up year in year out.

The prosecution wanted to take all the charges on Spydar, Melbourne Unit Trust and M & G together, instead of taking Spydar on its own first. It took Ronald Waterhouse six working days to open his case, followed by two further days for two witnesses he called. Day after day headline-catching phrases like 'secret profits', 'syphoning' and 'what's wrong in London is wrong in Singapore' were churned out by him. He seemed to have difficulty in using words like 'confidential' and 'transaction'—preferring more emotive words like 'secret' and 'manoeuvre'. I found it very depressing and, after hearing it all day and then reading about it at night and the following morning, I began to think that perhaps I might have got the odds wrong.

We did not intend to call a single witness and worked instead from the prosecution's own evidence, supplemented by the additional information supplied with my statement. The difficulty of not being able to challenge the affidavits of all the prosecution witnesses was demonstrated by one of the witnesses who was called. He was Mr Booker, who had been Haw Par's solicitor in Singapore and had been alternate director to Dick Tarling. The prosecution gave us a copy of the statement he would have sworn in which he said: 'Nor was any mention that such arrangements were proposed or under consideration made to me in March 1972 when I was introduced to Slater by Watson'. We would not have been able to challenge this except for the happy accident that Mr Booker had come to Scotland for Christmas, and when the time came for him to swear his affidavit he was in the United Kingdom. For this reason he had to come to court to make a formal deposition. When it came to his evidence, it only required two brief questions from John Mathew to establish that I had only met Mr Booker for a few minutes at a cocktail party when I was surrounded by many other people. It would obviously not have been the right setting in which to ask Mr Booker for his advice about Spydar, and after John's intervention the prosecution did not try to capitalize on that point any further. I should emphasize that in Magistrates Court we were only concerned with whether or not there was a *prima facie* case and there was therefore no question at that stage of trying to demonstrate that the prosecution were acting in bad faith. There were however a number of points like the Booker evidence, which gave a certain flavour to the proceedings and must have helped my case.

The final prosecution witness was a professional accountant who was put forward as a technical expert on matters concerning Melbourne Unit Trust and M & G. In a sense, therefore, it was a day off for me. I felt in a way strangely detached from the proceedings. I had won my battle against fear, earlier, and my sense of humour had reasserted itself. I recall on one occasion I passed a note on a point that occurred to me to Dai Tudor-Price, addressing him as LF (short for learned friend), and signing myself as F (short for fugitive). In his reply he wrote 'A or P' in front of my F and explained that the AF stood for 'alleged' fugitive and the PF for 'purported' fugitive. I replied with another note, saying that after what had happened to me during the last few years I thought that BF might be a more appropriate description. Dick Tarling had also not lost his sense of humour. During one of our lunches he was talking to his counsel about possible questions for the prosecution's expert witness on the accounts, and suggested that the counsel should start by asking him to add up eight and five. Dick went on to say that if the witness answered thirteen, we would be no worse off, but if he answered anything else Dick's counsel would have gained an immediate psychological advantage.

Towards the end of the prosecution's case I came home one night and told my wife that she must prepare herself for the possibility of the case going to the Divisional Court. I had just caught my first cold for about a year and I was feeling twenty-five degrees below par. I told her that my advisers had also become rather depressed by having to just sit and listen while the prosecution droned on and on. It was Helen's finest hour. She asked me to sit down and listen, and then asked me some key questions. 'Was the magistrate listening?' Answer: 'Yes'. 'Did the prosecution raise any fresh point that was a surprise to us?' Answer: 'No'. 'Did the prosecution appear to gain support from the magistrate?' Answer: 'No';

and so it went on. The final question was 'What has changed then?'
Answer: 'Nothing'. Helen's last words were not a question but an order—
'You go in tomorrow and tell your advisers all this and tell them to
concentrate on thinking positively and having the right vibes.' Answer:
'Yes, Helen'. The next morning at our ten o'clock meeting I passed on
Helen's orders and everyone agreed that she had a point. Our vibes did
change for the better and on the following Monday John Mathew got up
to answer the prosecution's case. I am not given to eulogies but to say that
he demolished it would be an understatement. To give just one illustration
of his approach, at one point he said something along these lines:

'The prosecution have made four submissions about the 15th March
minutes in Hong Kong: first, that it is a crucial document; second, that it
is the first and only written evidence of the alleged allocation of the shares
to the participants; third, that it is more "a note of action to be taken"
than minutes of a meeting; fourth, that it is a very unusual document to
find in a conspiracy case, because it sets out the terms of the conspiracy.

'I am happy to say that, for once, I totally agree with each of their
submissions: One, the minutes were crucial, and it was for this reason that
the inspectors were provided with a copy by Mr Slater in the early stages
of their inquiry. Two, it is only the documentary evidence available of the
allocation, and dishonest persons would undoubtedly have prepared a
back-dated document which was more helpful to them. Three, it is more
of "a note for action", simply because it was implementing a prior oral
agreement. Four, it is a very unusual document to have in a conspiracy
case because dishonest people do not keep records of their misdeeds and
then gratuitously produce them. Yet in the same breath the prosecution
allege that this was an agreement born in secrecy. The simple explanation
is that there was no conspiracy and these minutes simply record a prior
agreement, as my client has said right from the beginning of the original
inquiry into the affairs of Haw Par.'

And so it went on. John Mathew did not call any witnesses, he simply
examined the prosecution's threadbare case and tore it apart shred by shred.
It was interesting to see the gradual change of expression on the faces of
certain of the prosecution aides. I was reminded of a cartoon series about
a young child called 'Nipper'; when Nipper's father was happy this was
illustrated by a one-line curving smile and when he was unhappy the line
was simply inverted. After John Mathew had been on his feet for two days
there were many inverted smiles on the prosecution side of the court.

After John Mathew sat down, Dick Tarling's counsel spoke for about two days and then Ronald Waterhouse replied for the final day. In all we were in court for thirteen working days, after which the magistrate adjourned until the following Wednesday morning to consider his decision. In spite of my confidence, it was a very long weekend and a long Monday and Tuesday before we all assembled before him again. Mr Barraclough was five minutes late, which added to the tension, and when he opened with the comment 'I want it to be clearly understood that this is not a court of trial', I had an uneasy feeling that perhaps we had overestimated the strength of our arguments.

The magistrate continued: 'There are six charges against Mr Slater. In the first four he is charged with conspiracy to commit a criminal breach of his trust as a director of Haw Par Brothers International Ltd, and in the other two charges, he is charged, as a director, of furnishing false and misleading statements to shareholders. There is no evidence that Mr Slater was a director of that company. Indeed, it is agreed that he never was, but it is said by the prosecution that he "purported to act" as such. There is no evidence that he held himself out as being a director. It is then said that he aided and abetted others upon these charges. But he has not been charged as an aider and abetter, only as a principal—and the evidence, in any event, falls short of that which would establish a *prima facie* case of conspiracy to steal and cheat. The result is that on none of these charges should Mr Slater be committed for trial, and he is discharged.'

The magistrate did, however, commit Dick Tarling on all except two of the Spydar charges.

After I had shaken hands with my legal advisers and thanked them, I stepped out of the court feeling rather dazed. There was a large crowd of photographers and reporters waiting for me, including television and radio. The first question was about Dick Tarling and I replied that the decision to commit him spoiled what would otherwise have been a very joyous occasion for me. I could not say more as the matter was *sub judice*, but I did say that I would be doing all I could to help him. Someone then asked if I would be celebrating that evening and I replied that I probably would, as I thought some friends might arrange a celebration. At that moment a woman reporter from a leading daily newspaper asked me with a thin smile if Mr Tarling would be joining us. Bearing in mind that a committal order in custody had just been made against Dick and that extradition would have grave personal implications for him and his family, I thought this question was in the worst possible taste. I was horrified, and said to her that I thought the question was a sick one.

There was a pause before she replied that she did not think so. I have mentioned this incident to illustrate that the press, like most institutions, has its good and bad elements, and that dealing with reporters is not all milk and honey.

The day after the hearing I received an enormous number of letters and scores of greetings telegrams, and this continued for more than a week. Complete strangers kept coming up to me in the street to say how pleased they were about the result. It was all very heart-warming and I basked in it for a day or so before settling down to the next task, which was to prepare for the Section 54 hearing a few days later on 3 February.

While we had all been concentrating on Spydar, Roger Hopkins of Clifford-Turner had been preparing my defence against the alleged breaches of Section 54. His researches showed that according to the Jenkins Committee reports, and those of other similar bodies, the original purpose of Section 54 was to prevent the position of shareholders and creditors being prejudiced when control of a company was passing with the use of money borrowed from the company itself—in other words using a company's own money to buy control of it. Indeed there had never before been a prosecution brought where control of the company was not passing. It is quite a different concept when only a relatively small percentage of shares are involved, and it is interesting to note that in America, with its highly sophisticated financial approach and regulatory bodies such as the SEC, companies are allowed to buy in their own shares.

Roger's research was helpful in assessing the spirit of the law, but then we came to the substance of it. As I have already explained, in Britain it is not a breach of Section 54 for a company to lend money for the purpose of buying its own shares if that loan is made in the ordinary course of its business. The detailed figures that Roger had prepared made it clear that the loans were 'ordinary' to Slater Walker both as to size and purpose. We had a conference at John Mathew's chambers and agreed on our approach. Again we decided to call no witnesses of our own but simply to question the prosecution's only witness and through those questions introduce into the evidence Roger's additional financial schedules. The hearing was at the Guildhall Court before Sir Hugh Wontner and two other magistrates, one a solicitor and the other an accountant, and it only lasted a day. John Mathew did an excellent job and the magistrates found in my favour.

A few weeks afterwards we heard from the DTI that they intended to appeal by way of case stated to the Divisional Court. Apparently they were anxious to clarify the law relating to Section 54 as there might be new legislation on the subject. My solicitors liaised with theirs and with the Magistrates' Clerk, and the magistrates then stated the case for Divisional Court. The DTI then applied to the Divisional Court, as a result of which the case stated was modified. The Divisional Court should hear the DTI's appeal towards the end of 1977.

Shortly after the DTI appeal, the *Sunday Times* published an article indicating that the Singapore authorities were contemplating *certiorari* proceedings. The prosecution has no right to appeal against a magistrate's decision under the Fugitive Offenders Act and *certiorari* has never before been resorted to in Fugitive Offenders' cases. *Certiorari* is an ancient means by which the proceedings of inferior tribunals can be brought before the High Court for review; it can be invoked when it is thought that jurisdiction has been exceeded or when there is a clear error of law on the face of the record.

The Singapore authorities argued that the magistrate had reached his decision about me because I was not a director of Haw Par and, if this were the basis for his decision, it was bad in law. The Singapore authorities were very critical of the quality of evidence of press comment in all the court proceedings, but nevertheless, to support their request to the Divisional Court for leave to apply for *certiorari*, they included a press cutting purporting to give details of the magistrate's words when he cleared me of all the charges. The wording was materially different from the record of the magistrate's clerk. After referring to whether or not I was a director, in the press cutting the magistrate was quoted as saying, 'The evidence, in my view, falls short of that which would be necessary to establish a *prima facie* case of conspiracy, and to steal and cheat.' In fact the magistrate had said, 'and the evidence, in any event, falls short of that which would establish a *prima facie* case of conspiracy to steal and cheat'. The words 'in any event' clearly meant 'regardless', 'nevertheless', 'irrespective' of the foregoing; whereas the words 'in my view' could be said to have implied 'bearing in mind', or 'in the light of' the foregoing. My solicitors pointed out this important error to the solicitors acting for the Singapore Government, who at our request then gave the Divisional Court the proper wording shown by the court record. When the time came for the hearing the three judges ruled unanimously that the request for leave to apply for *certiorari* should not be granted.

The request for leave in Divisional Court was heard just before Dick Tarling's appeal on 25 April. Dick had been busy preparing his appeal against all the charges and of course getting ready his arguments on bad faith. To some extent the general climate of the western world's relationship with Singapore was more helpful to Dick's case, as Arun Senkuttevan, a *Financial Times* journalist, had been arrested to stand trial in Singapore and, with another journalist, had made a subsequent television confession. The sight of men a few weeks after arrest refuting life-long convictions in these television confessions to the nation must be a very chilling one, and fortunately this time the world's press reported upon the unreality of it all. There were leading articles which were very critical of Singapore's regime in the *Guardian*, *The Times*, *Financial Times* and *Economist*, and also in the *New York Times*.

When it came to Dick's appeal, he was in Divisional Court for a total of fifteen working days. The big set-back was that the tapes were ruled inadmissible, as was a great deal of other evidence. For example, Dick was not able to rely upon my statements on Spydar used in Magistrates Court and, when Jimmy Goldsmith's affidavit on the settlement came to be read, the accompanying press release and a letter Jimmy had written to me at the time were also disallowed. The rules of evidence in fugitive cases are very strict indeed and in many ways seem to me to be unfair, as it is obviously extremely difficult for an individual to prove that a government is not acting in good faith. Most potential first-hand witnesses are either resident in the country in question or for other reasons would not wish to oppose the government publicly.

When the Divisional Court hearing ended on 17 May 1977 they reserved their judgement. It was not until 29 July that the Court was reconvened before Lord Justice Shaw and Mr Justice Nield. The sixty-day waiting period put a tremendous strain upon Dick and his family, and it was with great disappointment that he finally heard that, although he was discharged from custody on nine charges, his application failed in respect of six.

Lord Justice Shaw, in his judgement, also gave detailed reasons for rejecting the Singapore Government's application for leave to apply for orders of *certiorari* and of *mandamus* in respect of the Chief Metropolitan Magistrate's decision in my case. In essence he said that their Lordships considered that no error of law was disclosed on a proper reading of either the *Financial Times'* or Court Clerk's version of the Magistrate's decision. Although their Lordships made their decision before embarking on Dick's application, in the event, their conclusion on my *certiorari* hearing became academic as they also discharged Dick on all the Spydar charges which were identical to my own. They said that although much argument had been directed by the Singapore Government to the issue of dishonesty and, on the surface, a series of factors provided formidable support for those allegations, indications of it were 'refuted and expunged by equally cogent factors'. As if to ram home their decision, they also found that there was no appropriation under the Theft Act and that the Singapore Government had no jurisdiction in the case of Spydar, as there was no evidence of any act in Singapore in furtherance of the alleged conspiracy.

Their Lordships did, however, find that there was evidence which warranted Dick's trial on five of the Melbourne Unit Trust charges, which did not involve a fraudulent intention. They said: 'His complicity (if any) appears to us to derive from errors of judgement and the exercise of an intermittent and remote control more than from any dishonest intention.' They said the evidence also warranted Dick's trial on the M & G charge which concerned the terms of a takeover letter.

Applications by both Dick and the Singapore Government for leave to appeal to the House of Lords were refused, but the operation of the Court's order was stayed until 10 October with liberty to petition the House. The subject matter of the Melbourne Unit Trust and M & G charges therefore remains *sub judice* and for that reason I have only referred to them both in very brief terms.

The Court had also 'anxiously considered' the question of prejudice in Singapore because 'some of the matters raised on behalf of the Applicant may not be without substance'. However, in their view, it had not been established that the case fell within the provisions of the Act relating to prosecution or prejudice concerned with race or nationality. So much, therefore, for our 'double insurance' and the false comfort we had both drawn from the revelations contained in the tape-recording.

My own task now is to do what I can to help Dick in his efforts to defend himself, and to pick up the pieces in my own life. I have the major undertaking of rebuilding my financial position to repay my creditors fully. The Spydar affair has been a very negative phase in my life. The repayment of debts also has a negative flavour, but on the other hand it has a more positive aspect and is a major challenge which I shall welcome.

TWENTY

Final Assessment

WHEN I look back today at the Slater Walker saga, I can see that there are a number of important lessons to be learned. If I were starting again with foreknowledge I would tackle many problems differently. Before I attempt to summarize its strengths and weaknesses, however, I think it might be useful to put Slater Walker and its activities into historical and political perspective.

In many ways Slater Walker was a product of its own time, in sympathy at the beginning with the feeling that many British companies badly needed reorganizing, that boards of directors were frequently too cosy, self-perpetuating and inefficient, and that the shareholder was given a raw deal. It was also generally thought that we needed a new breed of manager, younger and more meritocratically based than before, and that above all we needed a change. The Labour Government of the day reflected this mood to some extent by forming the Industrial Reorganization Corporation. After this phase, it was felt that we should have a more dynamic approach to overseas development, particularly in Europe. Slater Walker again was in the forefront of this movement in commercial terms. The last Conservative Government's easy money policy was the final major single influence on the company, and we took advantage of it to the full while the climate was favourable, but of course suffered when the climate changed. I am not advancing these arguments in any sense as an excuse, but simply to explain that we were for many years not only following the trend but exaggerating it to the point of excess.

Slater Walker rapidly became a very large company; and it was always very noticeable. In a sense our early success became a legacy and as a result we always had a high profile. When I resigned most of the press had leading editorials on the subject and attempted to draw up their own balance sheets of the good and bad points, the achievements, the mistakes, and the lessons to be learned. I agree with many of their comments and will now try to make my own assessment of the position.

At the beginning, some of the smaller industrial acquisitions were a mistake, as they took up a disproportionate amount of time and effort. Subsequently they should have been sold off and we should have built up a few major industrial divisions on a long-term basis. When we sold all of our industrial interests we lost our social justification and this in itself made long-term survival difficult, unless we could quickly find a new role and identity.

To try and start substantial banking and insurance companies almost from scratch was not a wise decision. If we had bought or merged with a well-established bank, which was already part of the social and commercial fabric and had the right professional team, it might have been accepted but the move to an embryo investment bank was regarded as parasitical. For this reason, after 1968, we were in a sense always fighting uphill. We almost made it on our own, and in 1971 to 1972 it looked as if we would, but we failed to merge at the right time and then the extreme bear market, compounded by the Spydar affair, caught us in a vulnerable position. In general terms pure banking is not very remunerative if you are right because of the exceptionally high gearing and it is very costly if you are wrong. In extreme bear markets new banking organizations are more likely to be wrong than right for all the reasons I have already mentioned.

Our move into property was rather late, but if I had gone liquid a year earlier it could still have been successful. I underestimated the problem of liquidating a sizeable property portfolio and was too worried about staff morale at the critical moment.

In the early years we achieved too much too soon, as a result of which I had to recruit executives too quickly. I had to build an almost instant management structure and inevitably there were a number of bad choices. I think the overall calibre of management would have been better if we had grown a little more slowly and, in certain instances, we would have attracted a better type of manager. The speed and informality of our management style had great advantages, but it also had disadvantages, as became particularly apparent when it came to the Spydar affair. A more structured company would have formalized the incentive scheme (if indeed it had one at all) in a much more careful and deliberate way administratively. At the time we were busy conquering the world and were not too worried about red tape.

Many of the men joining us were only attracted by the opportunity of making a substantial personal gain through our option scheme and share stakes. In some instances this worked extremely well, but in others the executives were not of the right moral fibre or ability, and when markets turned their limitations became only too obvious. With the extreme bear market the problems of having lent money to our executives became in some cases very acute, and I soon realized that only a few of them really had a principal's mentality. The others had to be comforted and helped out of trouble wherever possible and were only suitable candidates for option schemes.

As I have already explained the satellite concept had several flaws. We should have restricted ourselves to a few carefully selected concerns, with hand-picked well-supervised teams concentrating in a few different industries. As with our own executives, the choice of some of the satellite managers was poor and satellites only really succeeded where the chief executive had the necessary ability and a principal's mentality in both good times and bad.

Against this, we gave hope to a large number of young executives that they might not have to wait for dead men's shoes to be promoted. We helped to get over the concept that young men could succeed in executive positions, and some of ours did in fact go on to do exceptionally well. Slater Walker of Canada, now Talcorp, and Slater Walker of South Africa, now Unisec, are both companies which we built almost from nothing, with young men in the key executive positions.

We undoubtedly improved the lot of shareholders in many companies with large assets and indifferent management. We made sleeping boards of directors more active than they had been in the past and helped to wake up dormant company management. This happened not only in the companies we approached ourselves, but more generally, as the fear of an approach spread to many board rooms. Whilst there is an obvious need for dedication to making products and providing services in industry, we stimulated a keener desire to make money at the same time. We also contributed to the rationalization of a number of industries.

To an extent we stirred up some of the more slumbering elements in the City, as many of our ideas were highly innovative. In the takeover field we introduced a number of new techniques, which in some instances helped to shape the present takeover code. When we were on the other side, competitive merchant bankers knew that we were around. On the other hand, we tried to be rather too clever in some instances by adopting the minimum disclosure required by the law rather than a higher level to make the nature of our activities completely clear. For example, in the case of disclosing shareholdings held by the company and investment clients, we should have adopted the fullest disclosure procedures right from inception. In fact we gained very little from cleverness of this sort and lost a lot more in terms of image.

At the conclusion of its editorial when I resigned in October 1975 the *Investors Chronicle* said, 'Yet if the balance sheet produces a minus for the Slater phenomenon the City must record in a separate account that for ten years James Slater was the shrewdest judge of financial markets in the square mile.' The *Sunday Telegraph* editorial made the comment that it was my misfortune that I 'could never translate short-term successes into long-term strength', and I agree that I was too inclined to take a short-term view of everything. I did have hair-trigger reactions in market terms and tended to act almost instantly. In retrospect, a number of moves that were right and expedient in the short term were wrong in the long term. As a result of this tendency of mine we were constantly changing tack and failed to establish a real identity in later years. Also, I failed to pull off the big deals. The merger with Pearsons, the oil deal with Occidental Petroleum, the mergers with Warburgs and Hill Samuel—any of these deals would have changed the Slater Walker story completely. The backgammon player who always loses the big games has no real excuse, and I have none either.

The general feeling of the press was that the Slater Walker example had been pernicious as well as creative. They considered that the worst excesses of some of the satellite companies had caused a series of ill-conceived mergers, and that industrial tension had been caused in many cases as a result of assets being sold off or companies being radically changed following a takeover.

The heading of *The Times* editorial in October 1975 was 'The City still needs risk-takers'. It started off by saying that there was no doubt that my career 'shook the City, in both the positive and negative senses of that word'. It went on to point out that I 'forced others to modernize their ways', but I had also 'probably frightened an almost equal number into behaving imprudently in order by short-term performance to remain out of reach of a Slater Walker takeover'. It also drew attention to the poor quality of some of the managers of satellite companies and said that they were 'largely responsible for the fact that financial manipulation without regard for industrial results or political and social opinion had its current reputation'. The editorial concluded on the note that it was important that the wrong lessons were not learned; it expressed concern that my fall, combined with the general effects of the prolonged recession and bear market, would lead to an even more prolonged period when it would be difficult for men of 'ambition and a disregard for the established ways of doing things' to make headway.

I think it would be a great pity if, because of the outcome of the Slater Walker saga, youth, ambition, risk-taking and innovative thinking were to be in any way discredited. These qualities are still exactly what is needed in British industry. In my case, the early success of Slater Walker, and the satellite system in particular, created a monster that was beyond my personal control. I also went into areas like banking and insurance which, because of their fiduciary nature, are not suited to risk-taking on a massive scale, and then came a bear market of incredible intensity coupled with the Spydar affair. Like most good qualities youth, ambition, risk-taking and innovation also have an adverse side, especially if they are allowed to run unchecked. Real opportunity must be given to the best of our young managers, and their ambition and innovative ideas must be encouraged. They should also be fully prepared to take calculated risks when necessary, but all of this should be tempered with an element of caution, check and counter-balance which was lacking in my case during the critical years. Slater Walker in South Africa and Canada, where we had excellent outside board representation of high calibre, managed to achieve the best of both worlds. There we had youth at the helm in the key executive positions, my innovative thinking in the early stages, and the readiness to take calculated risks counter-balanced by the cautionary influence of strong board representation. I do not know if this is the answer, but it is certainly a formula that is far more likely to succeed than a return to the financial conservatism which made British industry stagnant for so many years and which helped to create all the asset situations in the first place.

I have many regrets, not least of which is not succeeding with Slater Walker and as a result letting down supporters and people who had invested with confidence and hope in the company. On the other hand, the last few years have in many ways been the most rewarding—I have strengthened many personal relationships with both family and friends, and I have found within myself a strength I did not know I possessed. I do not feel at all bitter about what has happened and I keenly look forward to the future. The last twelve years have taught me some invaluable lessons which I intend to invest in my new endeavours.

Appendix

THE price earnings ratio of a company indicates the number of times you need to multiply the net earnings (i.e. the post-tax profits) of that company to find out how much the whole company is worth in the stock market. For example, if a company was earning £200,000 a year before tax, assuming corporation tax was 50 per cent, this would result in net earnings of £100,000 per annum. The *average* price earnings ratio in the UK market in February 1977 was approximately 7.5, and this meant that an average company making £100,000 after tax would have been valued then in the stock market at £750,000. If the company was above average in the view of the investors, particularly in regard to its past and estimated future growth rate, its share price and therefore its price earnings ratio would be higher. Conversely, if it had an inferior growth record and poor prospects its price earnings ratio would be lower than the average.

Assuming that a company earning £100,000 per annum after tax was highly regarded by investors, it might have a price earnings ratio as high as 10, and this would mean that the whole company would be worth £1,000,000 in the stock market. If that company had 500,000 shares in issue, each share would then be quoted in the stock market at £2. If, on the other hand, the company was poorly regarded by investors, the price earnings ratio might be as low as 5, in which case the total worth of the company would be only £500,000, and the individual shares would therefore be quoted in the market at only £1 each.

Of course the future earnings growth of an industrial company is not the only measure of the value of that company. It is undoubtedly the most important single criterion, but such factors as surplus assets and surplus cash are also taken into account by the stock market. It would, however, be quite possible for a company to be valued by the stock market at

£500,000, even though its total underlying asset value was as much as £1m. The market's view would be that the company was in a chosen line of business, and all it could earn on those assets was £100,000 after tax, with poor future prospects. For that reason it would be only worth a multiple of five times those earnings, regardless of the value of its assets. It is, after all, the earnings out of which dividends are paid to shareholders, and in the final analysis these are what interest them most.

If a company is fortunate enough to have a very high market rating, its shares will stand at a high price in relation to its underlying assets. Still taking the example of a company making after-tax profits of £100,000 per annum with net assets of £1m, if its price earnings ratio was 20 the company would be worth double its asset value at £2m, and each share would sell in the market for £4. It would obviously pay a company with such a high rating to take over, in exchange for some of its shares, a less fortunate company that had a very low rating.

In 1967 to 1969 particularly, Slater Walker's shares enjoyed a very high price earnings ratio of about 30, which compared with the market average of about 18 during the same period. At times in 1968 the Slater Walker price earnings ratio was even higher, and the share price was three-and-a-half times the attributable asset value. To be able to exchange Slater Walker shares in volume for the assets of other companies was obviously highly beneficial to Slater Walker shareholders. It was also beneficial to them to exchange Slater Walker shares at those levels simply for *cash*. The idea of exchanging shares for cash may seem a strange one. The attraction of doing this can best be illustrated on a very small scale by imagining a middle-aged man, who had a small but thriving business, which was dependent to a considerable extent upon his personal ability and expertise. Let us assume that his business had underlying net assets of £100,000 and was earning £20,000 per annum, which after tax was, say, £10,000 per annum. Even though future earnings were likely to increase quite substantially, I would argue that this man would be well advised to accept a cash offer of, say, thirty times the net earnings of £10,000. A cash sum of £300,000, even in 1968, could have been invested to yield very substantially more than the earnings of the man's business, and, more importantly, the uncertainty factor would have been eliminated. Any number of things could have happened to spoil the future earnings prospect—the man might die or become seriously ill; there might be a bad fire; the company might experience unexpectedly severe competition or economic conditions might change dramatically. I have ignored capital gains tax to make the analogy accurate, as a company exchanging its shares for shares in another company, whose main asset was cash, would not have to pay any taxation. It paid the businessman to exchange the shares in his business for cash, just as it paid Slater Walker to exchange its shares for cash in 1968. The key point was of course that the multiplier (price earnings ratio) of 30 was far too high to apply to the net earnings of the man's business, as indeed the multiplier of 30 was far too high to apply to any company's earnings then.

This rationalization with hindsight is relatively easy: the advantage was to be able to see it at the time. Everyone sees *now* that the market was far too high in 1968, and this is clearly shown by the fact that the average price earnings ratio had come down from the high of over 22 in April 1972 to 7.5 in February 1977. In other words, at one point the *average* share was three times too high, and as Slater Walker was thought to be well above the average its shares had an absurdly high rating.

The basic point to remember is that usually it pays a company to exchange its shares for cash or other solid assets when the price earnings ratio of that company is far higher than the market average. Astronomic price earnings ratios rarely last for long, as they thrive on excessive hope, and for that reason the most has to be made of them while they persist.

Acknowledgements

The author and publishers are grateful for permission to reproduce the following copyright material:

Cartoon by ffolkes on page 109 from the *Spectator*; cartoon by Arv on page 127 from the *Investors Chronicle*; cartoon on page 175 by Heath from the *Sunday Times*; calendar on page 169 and cartoon by Arv on page 183 from the *Investors Review*; cartoons by Jak on pages 217 and 240 from the *Evening Standard*.

Photographs from the following: A.E.C., page 2 (above and below); British Leyland, page 3 (below); *The Times*, page 4 (above right and left); Desmond O'Neill Features, page 5; Camera Press, page 6 (above left); *Evening Standard*, page 6 (above right); *Financial Times*, page 6 (below); Keystone, page 7 (below); and Henri Cartier-Bresson, page 8 (below).

Index

National Provident Institution, 153
National Trust, 49, 228
National Union of Vehicle Builders, 21
National Westminster Bank, 194, 199, 205
Needs, Ted, 24, 88
New York Times, 254
New Zealand, 32, 134
Newman's Holdings, 90, 95, 102
Newnes, George, 5
Newsweek, 240–1
Nicholas, Sir Alfred, 88–9
Nichols, Jim, 153
Norcros, 193
North Sea oil, 137–8, 190

Observer, 128, 136, 153, 205, 207
Occidental Petroleum, 137, 259
Ogilvy, Angus, 63, 210
Ogilvy-Watson, Donald, 145, 213, 215, 244
OPEC, 189–90
Oriental Carpets, 114–15
Owen, Bernard, 73, 78
Oyez House, 138, 173

P & O, 58, 62, 90, 113, 133
Pacific Harbour, 134
Panchaud, Gerald, 201–2
Panmure Gordon, 130, 143
Park Royal Vehicles Ltd, 20–6, 27, 37, 53, 88
Parkinson, C. Northcote, 38
Pearce-Bunting, J., 148
Pearson (S.) & Son, 122–4, 259
Peat Marwick Mitchell, 220
Pendock, Simon, 59, 61, 64, 65, 75, 86, 133–4, 153
Peoples Department Stores, 149
Permali, 210
Pernas, 213, 214, 218, 231–2
Petershill Trust, 230
Petrosian, 164
Philip, Prince, 26
Phillips Brocklehurst, 118
Pike, Geoffrey, 128
Pioneer, 150, 193
Piper oil-field, 137
Plane, Jack, 30–1, 33, 42, 43
Plane (J.H.) (Africa) Ltd, 30, 31, 42–3
Plastalon Holdings, 101

Plumley, Ronald, 131
Poole, Lord, 122–4
Portland Club, 209, 228
Portugal, 32
Potter, Stephen, 99, 211
Powell, Enoch, 208
Powell, Sir Richard, 150
Preston Manor, 7
Preston Park, 7
Priam Investments, 122, 126, 140
Price Waterhouse, 220
Productofoam Holdings Ltd, 125; Slater buys control of, 55–7, 105; Slater Walker shareholding in, 60, 71; risk of share suspension, 61; Slater sells personal interest in, 63; Cork Manufacturing takeover, 67, 68, 72; buys into Coral Plastics, 76; and Greengate & Irwell, 84, 89; Slater Walker wholly controls, 89; unsuitability as investment for Slater Walker, 90
Prudential, 60, 62

Quinton, Bryan, 59, 64, 65, 123

Ralli Brothers (Bankers) Ltd, 100, 112–13, 119
Ralli Holdings Ltd, 106, 112, 114, 115
Ralli International, 119, 122; formation of, 115; buys Millars Timber & Trading, 115–16; growth, 140, 142, 146, 168; Slater Walker reduce shareholding in, 143; Bowater merger, 170–1, 181
Range Rovers, 108
Rank, 119, 146
Rayne, Sir Max, 111, 132
Razaleigh, 231–2
Recanati, Harry, 112–13
Redundancy Act, 79
Rees-Mogg, William, 240
Renault, 212
Rennies, 29
Renu Plating Company, 15–17, 18–19, 23, 36
Rhodesia, 32
Richardson, Gordon, 62
Risley, 17
Ritchie, Martin, 170
Robinson, William, 116, 121
Rockware, 182, 187